"Great book! Whittaker delivers ideas that are
orable. He really knows how to inspire enginee
testing."

—*Patrick Copeland, Director of Test Engineering, Google*

"James has perfected a fantastic manual testing methodology. The touring concept not only works, but it works so well that we've started sharing the tour concepts in the internal testing courses taught to all of our testers. If you want to bring your manual testing processes into the 21st century then read this book."

—*Alan Page, Director, Test Excellence, Microsoft*

"I began working with James at IBM in 1990. Even then, he was inspiring testers and developers to think outside the box. With this book he's taken his passion for software quality to a whole new level. Read it and watch yourself become a better tester. James is the real deal and this book should be read by every tester and software developer on the planet who cares about software quality or just wants to have more fun doing what they do."

—*Kaushal K. Agrawal, Sr. Director of Engineering, Cisco Systems*

"James Whitaker is a true visionary in the world of testing. uTest and our global community of QA professionals regularly look to James for inspiration, interpretation of trends, and overarching testing wisdom. Now he's finally written it down for everyone else and our industry will be smarter because of it."

—*Doron Reuveni, CEO and Co-Founder, uTest*

"Only someone like James Whittaker would think of combining the idea of tourism with software testing in such a novel way—and only James could pull it off. The tours approach provides a memorable and extremely effective mental model that combines right degree of structure and organization with plenty of room for exploration and creativity. Bugs beware!"

—*Alberto Savoia, Google*

"James is one of the best speakers around on software testing and reading his book is much like hearing him speak. If you want to increase your knowledge of testing and make yourself a better tester, this is the book for you."

—*Stewart Noakes, Chairman and Co-Founder, TCL Group Ltd.*

"I've been doing exploratory testing for some time now and James' tours have given what I do a name, a focus and more importantly some actual guidance. This book is going to make the job of teaching and performing exploratory testing a whole lot easier."

—*Rob Lambert, Senior Test Consultant, iMeta Technologies Ltd*

"I'm pretty pumped up about this work—it's sane, it's new, and I, a normal human, can understand and use it without first studying the combined works of various pompous, dead philosophers. I didn't have to resort to a dictionary once in the chapters I read. I genuinely feel this work is at the forefront of some long-awaited and sorely-needed evolution for our field."

—*Linda Wilkinson, QA Manager, NetJets, Inc.*

Exploratory Software Testing

Exploratory Software Testing

James A. Whittaker

Addison-Wesley

Upper Saddle River, NJ • Boston • Indianapolis • San Francisco
New York • Toronto • Montreal • London • Munich • Paris • Madrid
Capetown • Sydney • Tokyo • Singapore • Mexico City

The publisher offers excellent discounts on this book when ordered in quantity for bulk purchases or special sales, which may include electronic versions and/or custom covers and content particular to your business, training goals, marketing focus, and branding interests. For more information, please contact:

U.S. Corporate and Government Sales
(800) 382-3419
corpsales@pearsontechgroup.com

For sales outside the United States please contact:

International Sales
international@pearson.com

Visit us on the Web: informit.com/aw

Library of Congress Cataloging-in-Publication Data:

Whittaker, James A., 1965-
Exploratory software testing : tips, tricks, tours, and techniques to guide manual testers / James A. Whittaker. — 1st ed.
p. cm.
ISBN 978-0-321-63641-6 (pbk. : alk. paper) 1. Computer software—Testing. I. Title.
QA76.76.T48W465 2009
005.1'4—dc22
2009023290

Pearson Education, Inc
Rights and Contracts Department
501 Boylston Street, Suite 900
Boston, MA 02116
Fax (617) 671 3447

ISBN-13: 978-0-321-63641-6
ISBN-10: 0-321-63641-4

Text printed in the United States on recycled paper at Courier in Westford, Massachusetts.

Second printing July 2011

Editor-in-Chief
Karen Gettman

Acquisitions Editor
Chris Guzikowski

Development Editor
Mark Renfrow

Managing Editor
Kristy Hart

Senior Project Editor
Lori Lyons

Copy Editor
Keith Cline

Indexer
Tim Wright

Proofreader
Apostrophe Editing Services

Publishing Coordinator
Raina Chrobak

Cover Designer
Alan Clements

Senior Compositor
Gloria Schurick

This book was written in large part while I was an architect at Microsoft. It is dedicated to all the talented testers who crossed my path while I was there. Thanks, you changed the way I thought, worked, and envisioned the discipline of software testing. Keep up the good work!

0010101011011000100100101010110110001001001001010101

Table of Contents

Foreword

I first met James Whittaker several years ago while he was a professor at Florida Institute of Technology. He was visiting the Microsoft campus in Redmond and spoke to a small group of testers about—what else—testing. It was clear from that first meeting that James has a good sense of humor and a deep knowledge of testing. Years in front of the classroom had obviously given him a chance to develop an ability to connect with those willing and eager to learn.

James joined Microsoft in 2006, and over the past three years, I've had the opportunity to spend plenty of time with James and get to know him better. I'm happy to report that both the humor and the ability to connect with testers are still key parts of his approach to teaching and communication. It seems like every time I talked to him there was another tester or test team that he had connected with and inspired. Although we never worked on the same team at Microsoft, we have had more than a few opportunities to work together on cross-company initiatives as well as share ownership of a lecture session for new Microsoft employees. (Of course, by "share," I mean that James created the presentation and I stole his jokes.) Where we really had a chance to connect over numerous hours during the course of his tenure at Microsoft was Microsoft's soccer pitch. We probably spent a hundred hours over the past three years kicking a ball back and forth while discussing our ideas about improving software testing and development.

One important thing to know about James is that when he has an idea, he wants to test it and prove it. (Would you expect any less in a great tester?) What makes this attribute work so well for him is that he isn't afraid to fail and admit an idea won't work. Perhaps my testing nature makes me more cynical than average, but I'm somewhat happy to say that I've shot down more than a few of James' "great ideas" over the past few years. It lends some truth to something James tells his mentees: "Behind most good ideas is a graveyard of those that weren't good enough." A successful innovator has to be able to shed his ego.

In my role at Microsoft, I have the opportunity to observe and be a part of countless new and creative ideas—but I see many potentially fantastic inventions fail because the inventor doesn't take the creative idea and develop it until it's practical. As James and I continued to meet and discuss testing ideas, I was able to watch him take several of his ideas and methodically develop them into practical, usable creations that spread around Microsoft into the hands of real testers. His idea for a Tester's Heads Up Display was one of these ideas that was vetted on our soccer pitch, refined in practice, and resulted in a practical way for testers to consume and use real-time test data while they worked. Microsoft gave James an award for that one, and Visual Studio is keen to ship the concept in a future version of their testing product.

I was also there when James latched on the touring metaphor to guide software testing. He might not have been the first person to talk about tours, but he was the first person I know of to fully work out the metaphor and then coach a few dozen test teams in using it successfully on real (and very complicated) software. He grew his collection from a few tours to dozens—constantly developing and redefining the concepts until they were just right. Some of the tours James came up with didn't work. Lucky for you, James wasn't afraid to throw those out, so you don't have to read about them here. What ended up in this book is a collection of software testing tours that flat out just work. They've been tested, then refined, and then tested again. James' ability to use storytelling to describe a concept shines in these explanations. For such a great testing book, I found that sometimes I *forgot* this was a testing book. I don't know exactly what it is about the metaphor and the act of testing that make tours work so well, but I can't say enough about how well the tours work in real-world practice. The concept is essential enough that Microsoft is adding training on "testing tours" to the technical training course offered to all new testers who join Microsoft.

If you're even a little bit interested in improving your skills or those of your team, this book will have something for you. It's a great read and something you will find yourself referring to repeatedly for years to come.

Alan Page
Director of Test Excellence, Microsoft

0010101011011000100100100101010110110001001001001010101

Preface

"Customers buy features and tolerate bugs."
—Scott Wadsworth

Anyone who has ever used a computer understands that software fails. From the very first program to the most recent modern application, software has never been perfect.

Nor is it ever likely to be. Not only is software development insanely complex and the humans who perform it characteristically error prone, the constant flux in hardware, operating systems, runtime environments, drivers, platforms, databases, and so forth converges to make the task of software development one of humankind's most amazing accomplishments.

But amazing isn't enough, as Chapter 1, "The Case for Software Quality," points out, the world needs it to be high quality, too.

Clearly, quality is not an exclusive concern of software testers. Software needs to be built the right way, with reliability, security, performance, and so forth part of the design of the system rather than a late-cycle afterthought. However, testers are on the front lines when it comes to understanding the nature of software bugs. There is little hope of a broad-based solution to software quality without testers being at the forefront of the insights, techniques, and mitigations that will make such a possibility into a reality.

There are many ways to talk about software quality and many interested audiences. This book is written for software testers and is about a specific class of bugs that I believe are more important than any other: bugs that evade all means of detection and end up in a released product.

Any company that produces software ships bugs. Why did those bugs get written? Why weren't they found in code reviews, unit testing, static analysis, or other developer-oriented activity? Why didn't the test automation find them? What was it about those bugs that allowed them to avoid manual testing?

What is the best way to find bugs that ship?

It is this last question that this book addresses. In Chapter 2, "The Case for Manual Testing," I make the point that because users find these bugs while using the software, testing must also use the software to find them. For automation, unit testing, and so forth, these bugs are simply inaccessible. Automate all you want, these bugs will defy you and resurface to plague your users.

The problem is that much of the modern practice of manual testing is aimless, ad hoc, and repetitive. Downright boring, some might add. This book seeks to add guidance, technique, and organization to the process of manual testing.

In Chapter 3, "Exploratory Testing in the Small," guidance is given to testers for the small, tactical decisions they must make with nearly every test case. They must decide which input values to apply to a specific input field or which data to provide in a file that an application consumes. Many such small decisions must be made while testing, and without guidance such decisions often go unanalyzed and are suboptimal. Is the integer 4 better than the integer 400 when you have to enter a number into a text box? Do I apply a string of length 32 or 256? There are indeed reasons to select one over the other, depending on the context of the software that will process that input. Given that testers make hundreds of such small decisions every day, good guidance is crucial.

In Chapter 4, "Exploratory Testing in the Large," guidance is given for broader, strategic concerns of test plan development and test design. These techniques are based on a concept of tours, generalized testing advice that guides testers through the paths of an application like a tour guide leads a tourist through the landmarks of a big city. Exploration does not have to be random or ad hoc, and this book documents what many Microsoft and Google testers now use on a daily basis. Tours such as the *landmark tour* and the *intellectual's tour* are part of the standard vocabulary of our manual testers. Certainly, test techniques have been called "tours" before, but the treatment of the entire tourist metaphor for software testing and the large-scale application of the metaphor to test real shipping applications makes its first appearance in this book.

Testing in the large also means guidance to create entire test strategies. For example, how do we create a set of test cases that give good feature coverage? How do we decide whether to include multiple feature usage in a single test case? How do we create an entire suite of test cases that makes the software work as hard as possible and thus find as many important bugs as possible? These are overarching issues of test case design and test suite quality that have to be addressed.

In Chapter 5, "Hybrid Exploratory Testing Techniques," the concept of tours is taken a step further by combining exploratory testing with traditional script or scenario-based testing. We discuss ways to modified end-to-end scenarios, test scripts, or user stories to inject variation and increase the bug-finding potential of traditionally static testing techniques.

In Chapter 6, "Exploratory Testing in Practice," five guest writers from various product groups at Microsoft provide their experience reports from the touring techniques. These authors and their teams applied the tours to real software in real shipping situations and document how they used the tours, modified the tours, and even created their own. This is the first-hand account of real testers who ship important, mission-critical software.

Finally, I end the book with two chapters aimed at wrapping up the information from earlier chapters. In Chapter 7, "Touring and Testing's Primary Pain Points," I describe what I see as the hardest problems in testing and how purposeful exploratory testing fits into the broader solutions.

In Chapter 8, "The Future of Software Testing," I look further ahead and talk about how technologies such as virtualization, visualization, and even video games will change the face of testing over the next few years. The appendixes include my take on having a successful testing career and assemble some of my more popular past writings (with new annotations added), some of which are no longer available in any other form.

I hope you enjoy reading this book as much as I enjoyed writing it.

Acknowledgments

I want to thank all Microsoft testers for their never-ceasing effort to improve the quality of Microsoft software. I also want to acknowledge Microsoft managers for allowing the many collaborators on this material to try something new. The fact that it worked clearly illustrates the wisdom of test managers at the company!

I also want to thank the following Microsofties who read, critiqued, reviewed, contributed to, or otherwise helped me think through the touring tests:

David Gorena Elizondo, Mark Mydland, Ahmed Stewart, Geoff Staneff, Joe Alan Muharsky, Naysawn Naderi, Anutthara Bharadwaj, Ryan Vogrinec, Hiromi Nakura, Nicole Haugen, Alan Page, Vessie Djambazova, Shawn Brown, Kyle Larson, Habib Heydarian, Bola Agbonile, Michael Fortin, Ratnaditya Jonnalagadda, Dan Massey, Koby Leung, Jeremy Croy, Scott Wadsworth, Craig Burley, Michael Bilodeau, Brent Jensen, Jim Shobe, Vince Orgovan, Tracy Monteith, Amit Chatterjee, Tim Lamey, Jimbo Pfeiffer, Brendan Murphy, Scott Stearns, Jeff MacDermot, Chris Shaffer, Greg B. Jones, Sam Guckenheimer, and Yves Neyrand. Other non-Microsofties were helpful as well, and thanks go to Gitte Ottosen, Rob Lambert, Beth Galt, Janet Gregory, Michael Kelly, Charles Knutson, and Brian Korver. Finally, my new Google colleagues Alberto Savoia and Patrick Copeland deserve thanks not only for their encouragement, but also for their future contributions to exploratory testing at Google.

About the Author

James Whittaker has spent his career in software testing and has left his mark on many aspects of the discipline. He was a pioneer in the field of model-based testing, where his Ph.D. dissertation from the University of Tennessee stands as a standard reference on the subject. His work in fault injection produced the highly acclaimed runtime fault injection tool Holodeck, and he was an early thought leader in security and penetration testing. He is also well regarded as a teacher and presenter, and has won numerous best paper and best presentation awards at international conferences. While a professor at Florida Tech, his teaching of software testing attracted dozens of sponsors from both industry and world governments, and his students were highly sought after for their depth of technical knowledge in testing.

Dr. Whittaker is the author of *How to Break Software* and its series follow-ups *How to Break Software Security* (with Hugh Thompson) and *How to Break Web Software* (with Mike Andrews). After ten years as a professor, he joined Microsoft in 2006 and left in 2009 to join Google as the Director of Test Engineering for the Kirkland and Seattle offices. He lives in Woodinville, Washington, and is working toward a day when software just works.

CHAPTER 1
The Case for Software Quality

0110010110110001 0100

"Any sufficiently advanced technology is indistinguishable from magic."

—*Arthur C. Clarke*

The Magic of Software

The above quote from the famous British futurist and author of the 1968 classic *2001: A Space Odyssey* is cited in many fields but is probably more relevant to the magic of software than any other single invention. Consider

- That in 1953, Francis Crick and James Watson described the structure of deoxyribonucleic acid (DNA) as a double-helix structure and thus began a scientific pursuit of the Promethean power of genetics. But unraveling the sheer volume and complexity of the genetic information contained in DNA was a computational problem far ahead of its time. It was the magic of software decades later that was the deciding factor in unlocking the genetic code and the full promise of DNA research. During the years 1990 to 2003, scientists working on the Human Genome Project[1] mapped the *entire genetic blueprint of a human being*. It is hard to imagine, impossible in my mind, that such an effort could have succeeded without the computing power and tireless effort of sophisticated software code. Science invented software, but now it is software that is helping to unlock the promise of science.

  The result of this marriage between science and software will ultimately extend human lifespan, cure diseases currently out of science's reach, and create new medical applications that will easily pass Clarke's test for magic in this humble technological era. The coming advances of medical science will owe their existence to the magic of software.

---

[1] See www.ornl.gov/sci/techresources/Human_Genome/home.shtml.

- That the existence of planets orbiting distant stars (so called *extrasolar planets* or *exoplanets*) has been theorized at least since Isaac Newton hypothesized the possibility in 1713.[2] Various astronomers have used exoplanets to explain rotational anomalies in various stars, including Peter van de Kamp in 1969, who explained wobbles in the motion of Barnard's star by the presence of a planet 1.6 times the mass of Jupiter. However, all of this was speculation until 2003, when the first actual exoplanet was confirmed. The difference wasn't new science but the use of software to advance and aid existing science. It was only after the software-assisted invention of ultrasensitive instruments and the use of software to analyze the data they return that such accuracy became possible. By 2006, only 3 years later, more than 200 exoplanets had been discovered, and more than 300 exoplanets have been confirmed as of this writing.[3]

  It's hard to imagine that the instruments necessary to perform such a search would be possible without software, which played a role not only in the design and use of the instruments themselves but also in the analysis of the data they produce. And now, thanks again to software, the universe is as close as your home computer, vastly increasing the number of eyes looking for exoplanets. If an earthlike exoplanet is ever found, you may rest assured that the magic of software will be central to its discovery and confirmation.

- That the ability for the autistic to communicate has long been a subject of argument, with many experts arguing against parents and caregivers who claim to understand their charges. Is the meaning of what seem to be random and uncontrollable body movements simply in a language that the nonautistic cannot translate? Could the power of software bridge this gap?

  For example, a YouTube video[4] was produced by a "severely" autistic girl using specialized software and input/output devices that allowed her to translate her body language into English. I think Arthur C. Clarke himself would have been pleased at this most astounding and humanizing bit of technological magic.

I could cite many more such cases, and even a cursory look at the world around us would bear witness to many more. The rapid societal, technological, and cultural changes of the past 50 years dwarf any such change in any other period of human existence. Certainly war, radio, television, and the automobile have had their effect on our society, but now all those also fall under the domain of software, for war is waged with software-driven technology, and all of our most sophisticated inventions have been made more so by software. The more software a device contains, the more it is indistinguishable from magic.

---

[2] In *Philosophiae Naturalis Principia Mathematica.*

[3] A good history appears at http://en.wikipedia.org/wiki/Extrasolar_planet#cite_note-13.

[4] www.youtube.com/watch?v=JnylM1hI2jc or search for "the language of autism."

And it will be software that drives even more such innovation over the next 50 years. The wonders we and our children will see will seem magical even by today's sophisticated standards.

Software has the power to connect, simplify, heal, and entertain; and humankind is in great need of this power. We face global problems whose nonsolution could result in near extinction of our species. Climate change, overpopulation, killer diseases, worldwide financial meltdowns, alternative energy, near-Earth asteroids...there are many problems that simply *require* software as part or all of their solution. The scientific theories to address these problems will be modeled, and their solutions proven with software. What-if scenarios will be studied, tweaked, and perfected with software. Devices that are part of the solution will contain massive numbers of lines of code. It is through software that the only worthwhile future for this planet lies.

And yet we must ask this question: *Do we trust software to perform these globally important tasks?* Software bugs have been responsible for many disasters, from stranded ships[5] to exploding rockets[6] to the loss of life[7] and fortune.[8] Software is designed by imperfect humans, and our creations and inventions echo this unnerving tendency to fail. Bridges collapse, airplanes crash, cars break down, and nothing we build manages to successfully navigate around human error.

But if there were an Olympic event for failure, a World Cup for products that cause angst and grief, software would surely rout the competition. Among all the products ever made, software is peerless in its ability to fail. Ask yourself right now how often you've been inconvenienced by software failure. Has someone else gone out of his or her way to relate a miserable software-related experience? Do you know anyone who has used computers who doesn't have a horror story related to software? As a member of the IT industry, how often do your non-IT friends ask you to fix their computer?

It is the paradox of our lifetime that the one thing humankind is relying on to make its future is the very thing we'd least like to place a bet on for being there when we need it! Software is essential to our future, and yet software fails at an alarming rate in the present.

---

[5] "Software leaves navy smart ship dead in the water," *Government Computing News*, available at www.gcn.com/print/17_17/33727-1.html?topic=news#.

[6] "Ariane 5 flight 501 failure, report by the inquiry board," available at http://sunnyday.mit.edu/accidents/Ariane5accidentreport.html.

[7] "Patriot Missile's Tragic Failure Might Have Been Averted — Computer Glitch Probably Allowed Scud To Avoid Intercept, Army Says," available at http://community.seattletimes.nwsource.com/archive/?date=19910815&slug=1300071.

[8] "Software costs 59.5 billion a year, study says," available at www.infoworld.com/articles/hn/xml/02/06/28/020628hnnistbugs.html?s=rss&t=news&slot=2.

Here are a few examples of failure that you may recognize. If you've managed to avoid them all, congratulations, but I expect that any reader of this book could build a similar bug parade.[9]

The Failure of Software

One sure fire way to light the fire under software testers in a presentation is to demo bugs. Books aren't the best medium for such demos, but I suspect those reading this book will be able to imagine the bug reports they would write if the following failures appeared on their screen.

Figure 1.1 is one I call "Daddy, are we there yet?" This bug was absurd enough that it's doubtful it caused anyone to actually take this route. A more likely outcome is that the user took driving direction from another mapping tool. Loss of customers is a major side effect of buggy software, particularly in the cloud where so many alternatives exist. Credit to thedailywtf.com, who first published it.

FIGURE 1.1 Daddy, are we there yet? This bug has been fixed.

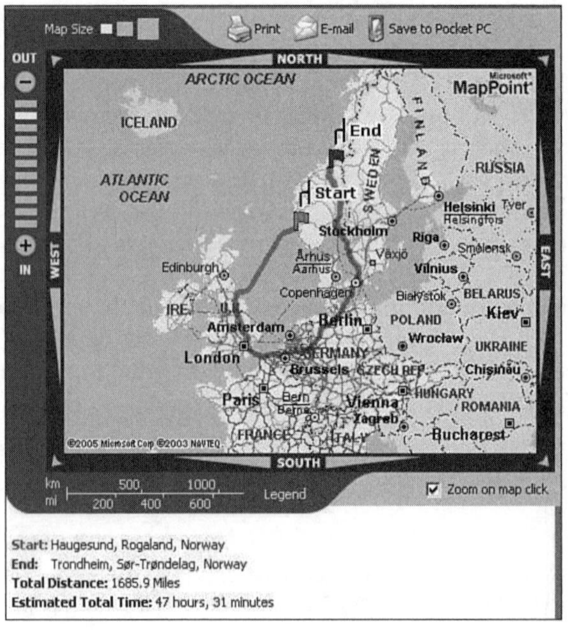

[9] A reviewer questioned my choice of failures, citing examples of lost billions, stranded ships, and medical disasters as more motivational. I've chosen the less-alarmist approach and decided to favor bugs that most testers would be most likely to come up against in their day-to-day testing job. Besides, I think these are really funny, and I find laughter highly motivational.

Even if you aren't Norwegian, you have to admit this is a pretty inconvenient route. Unless, of course, you fancy a very long pub crawl through England followed by a long route around Amsterdam (in case the wife is in the car?).

GPS indeed.

But it isn't just inconvenience that bothers users. Figure 1.2 represents data loss, one of the most insidious types of failures. Luckily, this bug was found and fixed before it managed to bite a real user.

FIGURE 1.2 A loss of data and a problem with the menus.

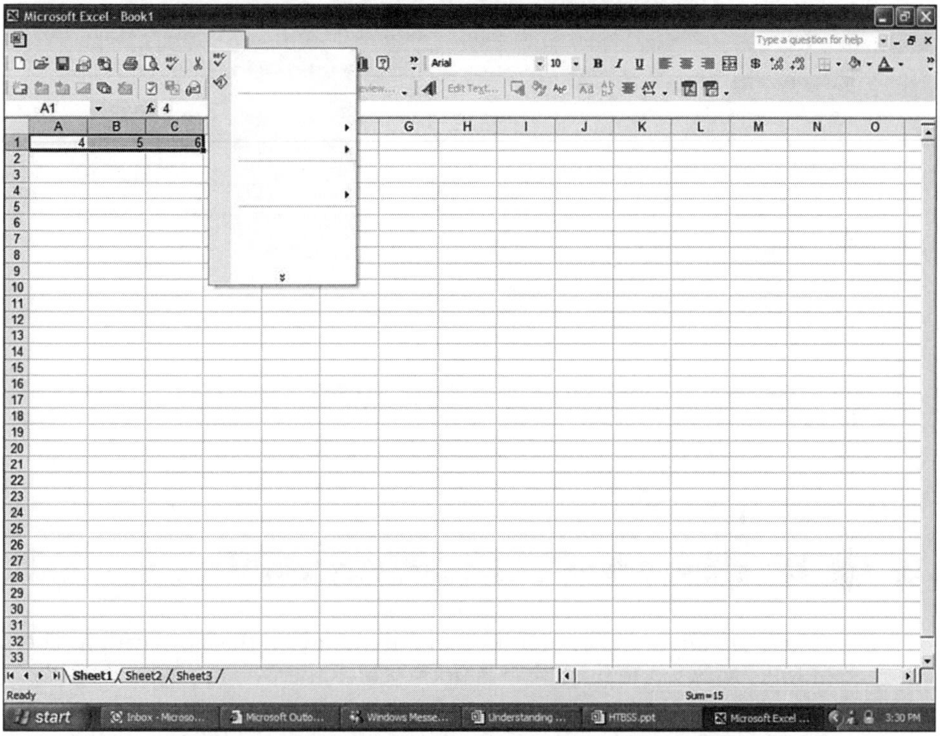

Excel manages to corrupt the open file, causing the data to disappear. An interesting side effect is that the memory corruption is so bad that the application itself struggles, manifested by the menus disappearing along with the data. Clearly, the user's angst at the blank spreadsheet (sans the three lone integers in the first row; were they left simply to remind the user of what she lost?) is eclipsed only by her shock at the total absence of any menus or menu items. She may look to the menus for hope to recover her lost data, but she will be sorely disappointed.

Advantage...software.

Sometimes failures tip the scales *toward* users, and it is the producers/purveyors of software who suffer. Consider Figure 1.3 from a web app that provides wireless Internet access to hotel guests. Look carefully at the URL and find the CGI parameter "fee." By exposing this to the user, it is changeable by the user. It's doubtful that the honor system was what the developer had in mind for collecting payment.

FIGURE 1.3 The exposed CGI parameter unintentionally makes payment optional.

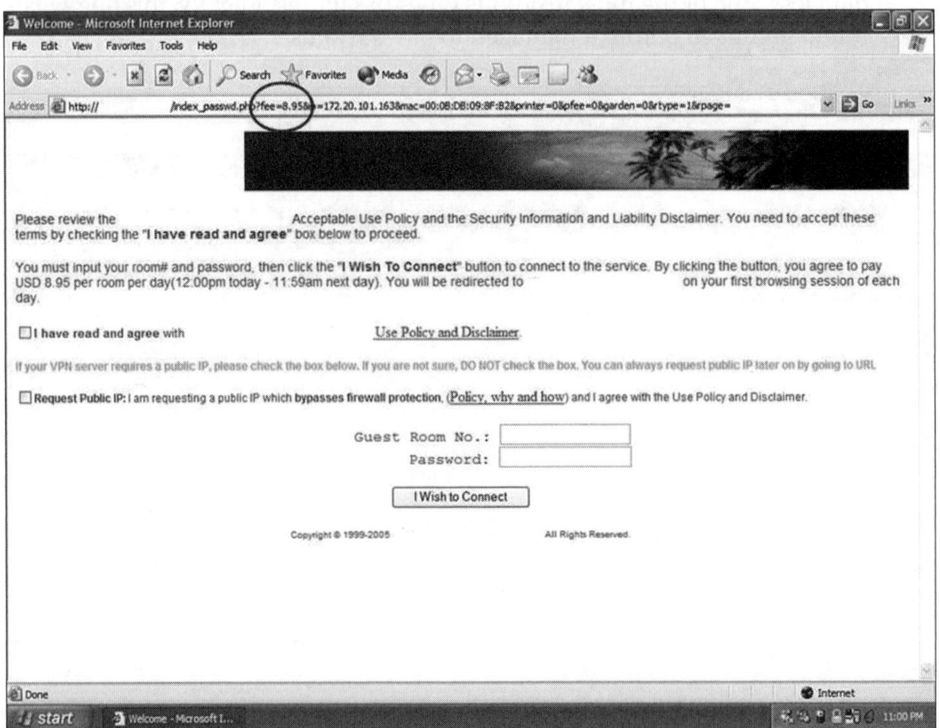

There are any number of folks making money on this application. The good folks who wrote the libraries upon which the web app is built sold them to the good folks who wrote the web app who sold it to the hotel who then (via said web app) sell the ability to connect to the Internet to their guests. But all this ends up being for nothing for the poor hotel.

Notice the URL and the CGI parameter "fee" (conveniently circled), which has a value of 8.95. Not a bad deal for Internet access, eh? But by displaying the value in the URL, they may as well have called the parameter "free" rather than "fee" because simply changing it to 0.00 and hitting enter will accomplish the bargain of the year. Not enough? Well, change it to a negative number and you'll lend truth to William Shatner's (the vociferous spokesman for priceline.com) claim that you really can get a good deal on a hotel.

Other bugs are out to hurt users in ways that simply destroy their productivity. There's nothing like ruining the day of a few thousand users the way the glitch in Figure 1.4 did. This is an example of "missed a spot": a well-tested feature where one scenario was overlooked, only to have it inconvenience a few thousand users. Luckily in this case, they were employees (the author included) of the software vendor itself.

FIGURE 1.4 A million plus emails creates a huge problem for the thousands of people who have to take the time to delete them.

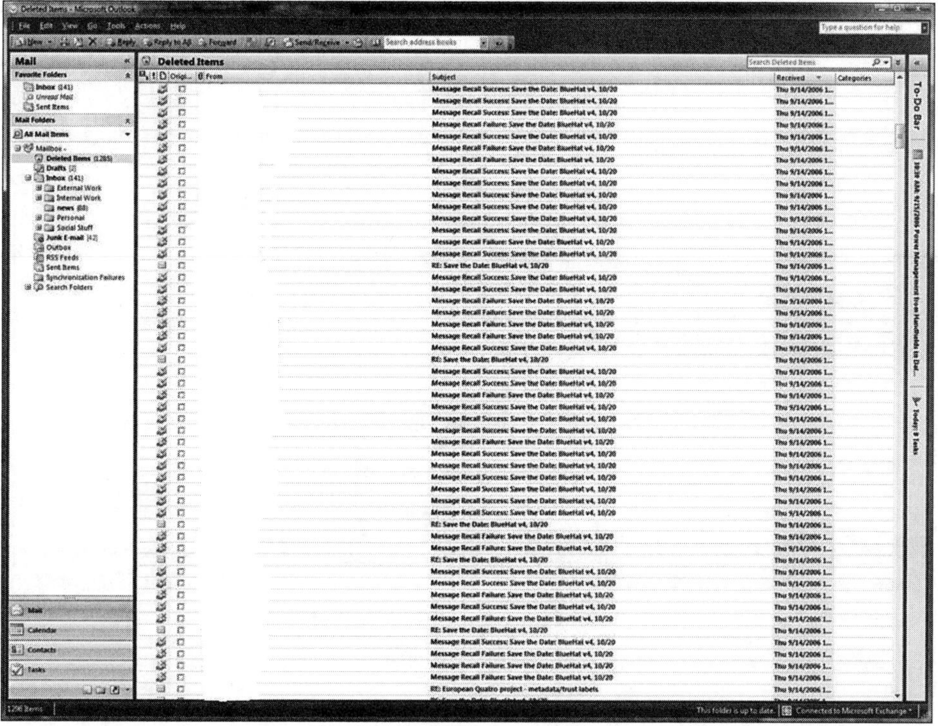

This bug is actually intended functionality gone horribly wrong. Outlook has a useful feature that allows a sender to recall a message that was sent in error. The problem is that this particular message was sent *from a distribution list email address* that contains a few thousand people. The sender, using the distribution list, made a mistake in the email and dutifully recalled it. However, the many thousand message recalls then came back *to the distribution list,* which, by design, Outlook sent to every email address in the distribution list. The result: thousands of people getting thousands of emails. A considerable productivity sink when you account for how long it takes to press the Delete key a few thousand times.[10]

---

[10] This is a real bug experienced firsthand by the author courtesy of a then-1,275 member mailing list (bluehat…an internal security conference held at Microsoft). This means 1,275 people got 1,275 emails each. Worse, someone wrote a script to clean said email inboxes and distributed the script, only to recall it because instead of fixing the problem, it actually made it worse.

And then there are the small inconveniences, the things that make you go hmm, as shown in Figure 1.5. This is a montage of various error messages often displayed to show just how confused the software is or as the last gasp of the software before it dies completely. I am not the only tester I know who collects these as reminders of why testing is so important.

FIGURE 1.5 A montage of software failures. Many testers collect such snapshots as they make great wallpaper.

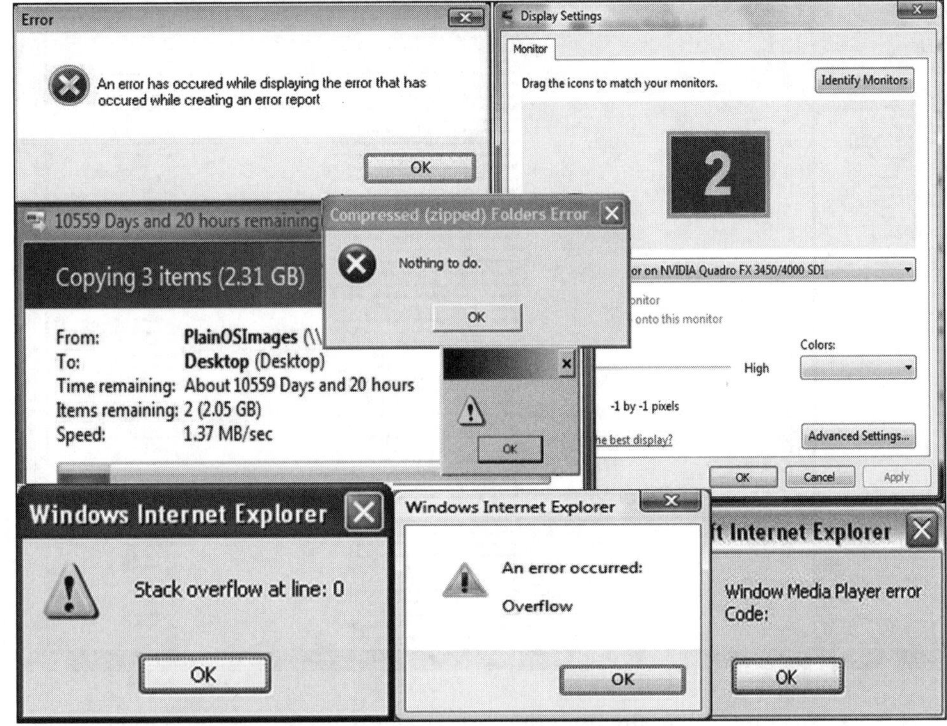

Is it any wonder that software developers and drug dealers share the same moniker, *user,* for their customers?[11] We don't call them something sweet like sponsor, customer, client, or patient, the way other industries do. We use the same term as those folks who knowingly sell something bad and rely on addiction to bring the suckers back! Hey user, how about another hit, uh, I mean upgrade!

Bugs are a taint on the magic of software. As we weave software's magic to solve increasingly difficult and important problems, we must study these mistakes and misfirings so that we better understand how to

[11] I am not the first person to point out that drug dealers and software developers use the term user for their clientele. However, I couldn't track down the original source. I do know one thing: The moment we start calling them johns, I will leave this profession and never return. Sharing a term with drug dealers is one thing, but with pimps it is quite another.

minimize and mitigate the taint of bugs. This book is about a tester's view on accomplishing just that: Understanding how bugs manifest and ways to go about finding them so that the promise of software's magic can be fulfilled.

Conclusion

Science created the magic of software, and now the magic of software is creating new science. We're going to need this magic to solve many of the world's most pressing problems, from overpopulation to global warming to curing disease and extending human life. Given this crucial role for software, it is imperative that software quality be as high as possible. The failures of the past are simply no longer acceptable.

In the next chapter, we discuss the various defect-prevention and detection strategies to help us understand how manual testing fits into the overall strategy for achieving high-quality software. Later chapters discuss the details of what strategic, thoughtful manual testing entails.

Exercises

1. Name some ways in which software has changed the world. Think about the previous generation or even the way things were 20 years ago.
   a. How is technology changing the way children are raised?
   b. How is technology changing the way teenagers interact with their peers?
   c. How has technology changed business? Government?
   d. Can you name five negatives about technology and software?
2. Spend a few moments with your favorite search engine and experiment with search terms similar to "software failure." See whether you can find examples of the following:
   a. The software of a famous vendor failed catastrophically.
   b. A software failure caused loss of human life.
   c. It was argued that software threatened the American democracy.
   d. The financial costs attributed to software failure exceed $1 billion.
   e. A software failure affected more than 10,000 people, 100,000 people, and more.

3. How will software play a role in helping solve some of the hardest of the world's problems? If you consider global warming or a cure for cancer, how important is a tool like software to people who research solutions to these problems?
4. Look again at the example bug using Microsoft Outlook's message-recall feature. There were 1,275 people on the bluehat mailing list at the time this screenshot was taken. How many emails did that generate? Try to form a theory of how Microsoft managed to miss this bug.

CHAPTER 2
The Case for Manual Testing

"There are two ways to write error-free programs; only the third one works."

—*Alan J. Perlis*

The Origin of Software Bugs

The origin of software bugs begins with the very origin of software development itself. It's clearly not the case that we started out with perfect software and invented ways to screw it up.[1] Indeed, the term *bug* has been in common use within software development from the inception of the discipline[2] and is a nomenclature that is used today in every office, garage, dorm room, data center, laboratory, bedroom, cafe, and every other place where software is developed. The first software had bugs, the latest software has bugs, and so have all the bits and bytes in between. Software is not, and likely never will be, bug free.

It's interesting to note that Hopper's moth (see the second footnote) was not a bug actually created by a programmer. Instead, it was an operational hazard that the developers didn't consider in their design. As we shall see in later chapters, a developer's failure to understand, predict, and test potential operational environments continues to be a main source of software failure. Unfortunately, the answer is more complex than closing the windows to keep out the moths. But let's not get ahead of ourselves. We'll talk about programmer-created bugs and bugs that creep in through the operational environment throughout this book.

---

[1] My late mentor Harlan Mills had an interesting take on this: "The only way for errors to occur in a program is by being put there by the author. No other mechanisms are known. Programs can't acquire bugs by sitting around with other buggy programs."

[2] According to Wikipedia, the creation of the term *bug* has been erroneously attributed to one of the earliest and most famous of software developers, Grace Hopper, who, while reacting to a moth that had managed to imbed itself into a relay, called it a bug. Read http://en.wikipedia.org/wiki/Software_bug for earlier uses of the term in hardware, mechanics, and even by Thomas Edison himself.

Preventing and Detecting Bugs

In light of inevitable failure, it seems appropriate to discuss the various ways to keep bugs out of the software ecosystem so as to minimize failures and produce the best software possible. In fact, there are two major categories of such techniques: bug prevention and bug detection.

Preventing Bugs

Bug-prevention techniques are generally developer-oriented and consist of things such as writing better specs, performing code reviews, running static analysis tools, and performing unit testing (which is often automated). All of these prevention techniques suffer from some fundamental problems that limit their efficacy, as discussed in the following subsections.

The "Developer Makes the Worst Tester" Problem

The idea that developers can find bugs in their own code is suspect. If they are good at finding bugs, shouldn't they have known not to write the bugs in the first place? Developers have blind spots because they approach development from a perspective of *building* the application. This is why most organizations that care about good software hire a second set of eyes to test it. There's simply nothing like a fresh perspective free from development bias to detect defects. And there is no replacement for the tester attitude of *how can I break this* to complement the developer attitude of *how can I build this.*

This is not to say that developers should do no testing at all. Test-driven development or TDD is clearly a task meant as a development exercise, and I am a big believer in unit testing done by the original developer. There are any number of formatting, data-validity, and exception conditions that need to be caught while the software is still in development. For the reasons stated previously, however, a second set of eyes is needed for more subtle problems that otherwise might wait for a user to stumble across.

The "Software at Rest" Problem

Any technique such as code reviews or static analysis that doesn't require the software to actually run, necessarily analyzes the software *at rest.* In general, this means techniques based on analyzing the source code, object code, or the contents of the compiled binary files or assemblies. Unfortunately, many bugs don't surface until the software is running in a real operational environment. This is true of most of the bugs shown previously in Chapter 1, "The Case for Quality Software": Unless you run the software and provide it with real input, those bugs will remain hidden.

The "No Data" Problem

Software needs input *and* data to execute its myriad code paths. Which code paths actually get executed depends on the inputs applied, the software's internal state (the values stored in internal data structures and variables), and external influences such as databases and data files. It's often the accumulation of data over time that causes software to fail. This simple fact limits the scope of developer testing, which tends to be short in duration.

Perhaps tools and techniques will one day emerge that enable developers to write code without introducing bugs.[3] Certainly it is the case that for narrow classes of bugs such as buffer overflows[4] developer techniques can and have driven them to near extinction. If this trend continues, the need for a great deal of testing will be negated. But we are a very long way, decades in my mind, from realizing that dream. Until then, we need a second set of eyes, running the software in an environment similar to real usage and using data that is as rich as real user data.

Who provides this second set of eyes? Software testers provide this service, using techniques to detect bugs and then skillfully reporting them so that they get fixed. This is a dynamic process of executing the software in varying environments, with realistic data and with as much input variation as can be managed in the short cycles in which testing occurs. Such is the domain of the software tester.

Detecting Bugs

Testers generally use two forms of dynamic analysis: automated testing (writing test code to test an application) and manual testing (using shipping user interfaces to apply inputs manually).

Automated testing carries both stigma and respect.

The stigma comes from the fact that tests are code, and writing tests means that the tester is necessarily also a developer. Can a developer really be a good tester? Many can, many cannot, but the fact that bugs in test automation are a regular occurrence means that they will spend significant time writing code, debugging it, and rewriting it. Once testing becomes a development project, one must wonder how much time testers are spending thinking about testing the software as opposed to maintaining the test automation. It's not hard to imagine a bias toward the latter.

The respect comes from the fact that automation is cool. One can write a single program that will execute an unlimited number of tests and find tons of bugs. Automated tests can be run and then rerun when the application code has been churned or whenever a regression test is required. Wonderful! Outstanding! How we must worship this automation! If testers

[3] In my mind, I picture the ultimate developer bug-finding tool to work on their code as they type. It will work in a way similar to spell checkers for documents. The moment a developer types a bug into the code editor, the errant fragment will be underlined or, perhaps, corrected automatically. The whole point is that we place the *detection* of the bug as close as possible to the *creation* of the bug so that the bug doesn't get into the software at all. The less time a bug lives, the better off we'll all be. But until such technology is perfected, we'll have to keep on testing. We're in this for the long haul!

[4] Buffer overflows are found by injecting more data into an input field than the underlying code can handle. Their cause and specific ways to find them are explained in *How to Break Software Security* (Addison-Wesley, 2004) on page 41.

are judged based on the number of tests they run, automation will win every time. If they are based on the *quality* of tests they run, it's a different matter altogether.

The kicker is that we've been automating for years, decades even, and we still produce software that readily falls down when it gets on the desktop of a real user. Why? Because automation suffers from many of the same problems that other forms of developer testing suffers from: It's run in a laboratory environment, not a real user environment, and we seldom risk automation working with real customer databases because automation is generally not very reliable. (It is *software* after all.) Imagine automation that adds and deletes records of a database—what customers in their right mind would allow that automation anywhere near their real databases? And there is one Achilles heel of automated testing that no one has ever solved: the oracle problem.

The oracle problem is a nice name for one of the biggest challenges in testing: *How do we know that the software did* what *it was supposed to do when we ran a given test case?* Did it produce the right output? Did it do so without unwanted side effects? How can we be sure? Is there an oracle we can consult that will tell us—given a user environment, data configuration, and input sequence—that the software performed exactly as it was designed to do? Given the reality of imperfect (or nonexistent) specs, this just is not a reality for modern software testers.

Without an oracle, test automation can find only the most egregious of failures: crashes, hangs (maybe), and exceptions. And the fact that automation is itself software often means that the crash is in the test case and not in the software! Subtle/complex failures are missed. One need look no further than the previous chapter to see that many such crucial failures readily slip into released code. Automation is important, but it is not enough, and an overreliance on it can endanger the success of a product in the field.

So where does that leave the tester? If a tester cannot rely on developer bug prevention or automation, where should she place her hope? The only answer can be in manual testing.

Manual Testing

Manual testing is human-present testing. A human tester uses her brain, her fingers, and her wit to create the scenarios that will cause software either to fail or to fulfill its mission. Human-present testing allows the best chance to create realistic user scenarios, using real user data in real user environments and still allowing for the possibility of recognizing both obvious and subtle bugs.

Manual testing is the best choice for finding bugs related to the underlying business logic of an application. Business logic is the code that implements user requirements; in other words, it is the code that customers buy the software for. Business logic is complex and requires a human in the loop to verify that it is correct, a task that automation is too often ill-suited to accomplish.

Perhaps it will be the case that developer-oriented techniques will evolve to the point that a tester is unnecessary. Indeed, this would be a desirable future for software producers and software users alike, but for the foreseeable future, tester-based detection is our best hope at finding the bugs that matter. There is simply too much variation, too many scenarios, and too many possible failures for automation to track it all. It requires a "brain in the loop." This is the case for this decade, the next decade, and perhaps a few more after that.

I wish it was just that easy, but historically the industry has not been good at manual testing. It's too slow, too ad hoc, not repeatable, not reproducible, not transferable, and there isn't enough good advice out there for testers to get good at it. This has created a poor reputation for manual testing as the ugly stepchild of development. It's unfortunate that this is the case, but such is the hand we are dealt.

It's time we put the best technology available into the process of manual testing. This is the subject of exploratory testing that this book addresses. I want the industry to get past the idea of ad hoc manual testing and work toward a process for exploratory testing that is more purposeful and prescriptive. It should be a process where manual testing requires careful preparation yet leaves room for intelligent decision making during testing. Manual testing is too important to treat it with any less respect.

We may look to a future in which software just works, but if we achieve that vision, it will be the hard work of the manual testers of this time that makes it possible.

Scripted Manual Testing

Many manual testers are guided by scripts, written in advance, that guide input selection and dictate how the software's results are to be checked for correctness. Sometimes scripts are specific: Enter this value, press this button, check for that result, and so forth. Such scripts are often documented in spreadsheet tables and require maintenance as features get updated through either new development or bug fixes. The scripts serve a secondary purpose of documenting the actual testing that was performed.

Often, scripted manual testing is too rigid for some applications, or test processes and testers take a less-formal approach. Instead of documenting every input, a script may be written as a general scenario that gives some flexibility to the testers while they are running the test. At Microsoft, the folks who manually test Xbox games often do this. So an input would be "interact with the mage," without specifying exactly the type of interaction they must perform. Thus it is possible that scripted testing can be as rigid or as flexible as necessary, but for the flexibility to work, testers are going to need very specific advice for how to handle choice and uncertainty, and this is more the domain of exploratory testing.

In this book, we are only interested in the flexible type of scripted testing.

Exploratory Testing

When the scripts are removed entirely (or as we shall see in later chapters, their rigidness relaxed), the process is called *exploratory testing*. Testers may interact with the application in whatever way they want and use the information the application provides to react, change course, and generally explore the application's functionality without restraint. It may seem ad hoc to some, but in the hands of a skilled and experienced exploratory tester, this technique can prove powerful. Advocates argue that exploratory testing allows the full power of the human brain to be brought to bear on finding bugs and verifying functionality without preconceived restrictions.

Testers using exploratory methods are also not without a documentation trail. Test results, test cases, and test documentation are generated as tests are being performed instead of being documented ahead of time in a test plan. Screen capture and keystroke recording tools are ideal for recording the result of exploratory testing. Just because it's manual testing doesn't mean we can't employ automation tools as aids to the process. Indeed, even those who "handcraft" furniture do so with the assistance of power tools. Handcrafting test cases should be no different. Manual testers who use debug builds, debuggers, proxies, and other types of analysis tools are still doing manual testing; they are just being practical about it.

Exploratory testing is especially suited to modern web application development using agile methods.[5] Development cycles are short, leaving little time for formal script writing and maintenance. Features often evolve quickly, so minimizing dependent artifacts (like pre-prepared test cases) is a desirable attribute. If the test case has a good chance of becoming irrelevant, why write it in the first place? Are you not setting yourself up for spending more time maintaining test cases than actually *doing* testing?

The drawback to exploratory testing is that testers risk wasting a great deal of time wandering around an application looking for things to test and trying to find bugs. The lack of preparation, structure, and guidance can lead to many unproductive hours and retesting the same functionality over and over, particularly when multiple testers or test teams are involved. Without documentation, how do testers ensure they are getting good coverage?

This is where guidance comes into play. Exploratory testing without good guidance is like wandering around a city looking for cool tourist attractions. It helps to have a guide and to understand something about your destination (in our case, software) that can help your exploration to be more methodical. Looking for beaches in London is a waste of time. Looking for medieval architecture in Florida is equally so. Surely *what* you are testing is just as important to your strategy as how you test it.

---

[5] The number of proponents of exploratory testing is large enough now that its case no longer needs to be argued, particularly among the agile development community. However, I argue it here anyway to help those testers who still have to convince their management.

There are two types of guidance for exploratory testers to help in the decision-making process: *exploratory testing in the small,* which aids in local decision making while running tests; and *exploratory testing in the large,* which helps testers design overall test plans and strategies. Both are summarized here and covered in detail in Chapter 3, "Exploratory Testing in the Small," and Chapter 4, "Exploratory Testing in the Large." Finally, a third class of exploratory testing that combines elements of exploration with scripted manual testing is discussed in Chapter 5, "Hybrid Exploratory Testing Techniques."

Exploratory Testing in the Small

Much of what a manual tester does is about variation. Testers must choose which inputs to apply, what pages or screens to visit, which menu items to select, and the exact values to type into each input field they see. There are literally hundreds of such decisions to make with every test case we run.

Exploratory testing can help a tester make these decisions. And when a tester uses exploratory testing strategy to answer these sorts of questions, I call this *exploratory testing in the small* because the scope of the decision is small. A tester is looking at a certain web page or dialog box or method and needs focused advice about what to do for that specific situation. This is necessarily a localized decision-making process that testers will perform dozens of times in a single test case and hundreds of times over the course of a day of testing.

The problem is that many testers don't know what to do in the variety of "small" situations that they encounter. Which value do you enter into a text box that accepts integers? Is the value 4 better (meaning more likely to find a bug or force a specific output) than the value 400? Is there anything special about 0 or about negative numbers? What illegal values might you try? If you know something about the application—for example, that it is written in C++ or that it is connected to a database—does that change the values you might try? What, indeed, is the sum total of exploratory testing wisdom that we can use to help us make the right small decisions as we test?

Chapter 3 is devoted to passing along some of this wisdom. I'll be the first to admit, that most of it is not mine. I've been lucky enough to work around some of the best software testers to grace this planet. From IBM to Ericsson to Microsoft, Adobe, Google, Cisco, and many more names far less recognizable, I've gathered what I think is a large portion of this advice and I reproduce it here. Much of this information was embodied in *How to Break Software,* and so readers of that book can consider this an update to the body of knowledge that was published there. But as the attitude of that book was about finding bugs, the purpose of this book is much broader. Here we are interested in more than finding bugs. We want to force software to exhibit its capabilities and gain coverage of the application's features, interfaces, and code and find ways to put it through its paces to determine its readiness for release.

Exploratory Testing in the Large

There is more to testing, however, than making all the small decisions correctly. In fact, it is possible to nail all the small decisions and still not have an overall set of tests that confirm (or reject) release readiness. The sum total of all the test cases is definitely more than the individual parts. Test cases are interrelated, and each test case should add to the others and make the entire set of test cases better in some substantive, measurable (or at least arguable) way.

This points to the need for a strategy that guides test case design and exploration. Which features should a single test case visit? Are there certain features or functions that must be tested together? Which feature should be used first, and how do we decide which subsequent features to test? If there are multiple testers on a project, how can we make sure their strategies complement each other and they don't end up testing the same things? How does an exploratory tester make these larger scope decisions about overall test cases and testing strategy?

I call this *exploratory testing in the large* because the scope of the decisions to be made encompasses the software as a whole instead of a single screen or dialog. The decisions made should guide how an application is explored more than how a specific feature is tested.

In Chapter 4, I use a tourism metaphor to guide exploratory testing in the large. Think about it this way: As a tourist visiting a new city, you will use *in-the-large* advice to choose which restaurant to visit, but you will use *in-the-small* advice to choose what meal and drink to order. In-the-large advice will help plan your entire day and advise you on how to plan your entire stay, the landmarks you visit, the shows you see, and the restaurants at which you dine. In-the-small advice will help you navigate each of these events and plan the subtle details that a larger plan will always leave out. By perfecting the combination of the two, you've entered the world of an expert exploratory software tester.

Combining Exploration and Scripting

It isn't necessary to view exploratory testing as a strict alternative to script-based manual testing. In fact, the two can co-exist quite nicely. Having formal scripts can provide a structure to frame exploration, and exploratory methods can add an element of variation to scripts that can amplify their effectiveness. The expression *opposites attract* is relevant in the sense that because formal scripts and exploratory methods are at opposite extremes of the manual testing spectrum, they actually have a lot to offer each other. If used correctly, each can overcome the other's weaknesses, and a tester can end up in the happy midpoint of a very effective combination of techniques.

The best way that I have found to combine the two techniques is to start with formal scripts and use exploratory techniques to inject variation into them. This way, a single script may end up being translated into any number of actual exploratory test cases.

Traditional script-based testing usually involves a starting point of user stories or documented end-to-end scenarios that we expect our eventual users to perform. These scenarios can come from user research, data from prior versions of the application, and so forth, and are used as scripts to test the software. The added element of exploratory testing to traditional scenario testing widens the scope of the script to inject variation, investigation, and optional user paths.

An exploratory tester who uses a scenario as a guide will often pursue interesting alternative inputs or pursue some potential side effect that is not included in the script. However, the ultimate goal is to complete the scenario so that these testing detours always end up back on the main user path documented in the script. The detours from the script can be chosen based on structured ways of modifying specific steps in the script or by exploratory excursions off the script and then back again. Chapter 5 is dedicated entirely to script-based exploratory testing because it is one of the key tools in the manual tester's arsenal of techniques.

The techniques in Chapters 3 through 5 have been applied in a number of case studies and trials throughout Microsoft, and the results are presented in Chapter 6, "Exploratory Testing in Practice," as experience reports written by the testers and test leads involved in these projects. Chapter 6 examines how the exploratory testing techniques were applied to several different classes of software from operating system components to mobile applications to more traditional desktop and web software. Also, special tours written specifically for a particular project are described by their authors.

The remainder of the book highlights essays on, respectively, building a testing career and the future of testing, followed by past and current essays and papers while I was a professor at Florida Tech and an architect at Microsoft. Since I have now left Microsoft, this book may be the only place that the latter material can be found.

Conclusion

The world of manual exploratory testing is one of the most challenging and satisfying jobs in the IT industry. When done properly, exploratory testing is a strategic challenge and a match of wits between the manual tester and an application to discover hidden bugs, usability issues, security concerns, and so forth. For far too long, such exploration has been done without good guidance and has been the realm of experts who have learned their craft over many years and decades. This book contains much of that experience and wisdom in the hopes that many new experts emerge quickly, allowing higher-quality testing and thus higher-quality applications to enter the technology ecosystem.

We need the human mind to be present when software is tested. The information in this book is aimed at focusing the human mind so that testing is as thorough and complete as possible.

Exercises

1. Why can't we just build software to test software? Why isn't automation the answer to the software-testing problem?
2. What type of code is automation good at testing? What type of code requires manual testing? Try to form a theory to explain why.
3. What types of bugs is automation good at detecting? What types of bugs is automation bad at detecting? Give examples.

CHAPTER 3
Exploratory Testing in the Small

"Any sufficiently advanced bug is indistinguishable from a feature."

—*Rich Kulawiec*

So You Want to Test Software?

The above quote is one of my favorites and captures much of the complexity of software testing in a single sentence. If we can't tell features from bugs, how can we possibly do a good job of testing? If the product's specification and documentation aren't good enough to tell bugs from features, isn't testing impossible? If the symptoms of failure are so subtle as to evade both automated and manual attempts to expose them, isn't testing useless?

Imagine the following job description and ask yourself whether you would apply for it:

> Software tester wanted. Position requires comparing an insanely complicated, poorly documented product to a nonexistent or woefully incomplete specification. Help from original developers will be minimal and given grudgingly. Product will be used in environments that vary widely with multiple users, multiple platforms, multiple languages, and other requirements yet unknown but just as important. We're not quite sure how to define them, but security and performance are paramount, and post release failures are unacceptable and could cause us to go out of business.

Okay, so it's tongue-in-cheek, but it is close enough to the mark that I bet anyone who has been in the industry long enough can appreciate the accuracy of this job description. For those of you lucky enough for this to seem like a foreign concept, you have my congratulations.

Testing such a complex product as software against incomplete expectations for nebulous quality concerns seems like an impossible ambition. Indeed, the lack of good information makes testing a lot harder than it has to be, and all testers suffer from this. However, we've been testing software for several decades, and notwithstanding the bugs shown in Chapter 1, "The Case for Software Quality," that software has managed to change the world. Clearly, there is a lot we know about testing.

So what is it that software testers actually do when they approach this impossible task? Well, the first step is to appreciate the enormity and complexity of testing. Approaching it lightly and assuming that it will be easy is a really great way to fail. Admitting that no matter what you do will be inadequate is the right beginning attitude. Testing is infinite; we're never really done, so we must take care to prioritize tasks and do the most important things first. Because testing really is infinite, we'll never be finished. The goal is to get to the point that when the software is released, everything we have *not done* is less important than everything we *have done*. If we achieve this, we help minimize the risk of releasing too early.

Testing is about making choices. It's about understanding the complexities involved in running tests and analyzing the information available to help us choose between the many possible variables inherent in the testing process. This chapter is about those choices *in the small*. It covers the little choices that exploratory testers make as they explore an application's functionality, from how to decide which inputs to enter into a text box and how to interpret error messages, to understanding the relationship between prior inputs and those you might choose to enter later. In subsequent chapters, we discuss larger issues of exploration, but we first need to acquire the tools necessary to make the small decisions wisely.

The one nice thing about exploratory testing in the small is that there isn't a lot of information necessary to perform these tasks. In-the-small testing is really about encapsulating testing experience and expertise with knowledge of how software is composed and how it executes in its operational environment so that we can make good choices during testing. These are very tactical techniques meant to solve small problems that every tester faces many times every day. They are not intended as a complete testing regime or even particularly useful for overall test case design. Those *in-the-large* issues are presented in the next two chapters.

The information presented in this chapter breaks choices into five specific properties of software that an exploratory tester must reason about as she tests: inputs, state, code paths, user data, and execution environment. Even taken individually, each of these presents a testing problem too large to solve with finite resources. Taken as a whole, the process of testing is mind bogglingly enormous. Thankfully, there is a great deal of guidance about how to approach this problem, and this chapter presents a collection of specific tactics that describe this guidance and how to use it to make in-the-small testing decisions.

Testing Is About Varying Things

Testers are tasked with answering questions such as the following:

- Will the software work as designed?
- Will the software perform the functions for which the user bought it?
- Will the software perform these functions fast enough, secure enough, robust enough, and so on?

Testers achieve these tasks by putting the software in some specific operational environment and then applying input that in some way mimics expected usage. This is where the trouble starts and the whole problem of infinity hits well-meaning testers square in the face. There are too many inputs to apply them all. There are too many environments to replicate them all. In fact, the number of variables of which there are "too many" is disturbing. This is why testing is about *varying things.* We must identify all the things that can be varied during a test and make sure we make smart decisions when we choose specific variations and exclude (out of necessity) other variations.

This reduces testing to a task of selecting a subset of inputs (and environments, etc.), applying those, and then trying to infer that this is somehow *good enough.* Eventually, the software has to ship, and testing can no longer impact the shipping code. We have a finite time to perform what is ultimately an infinite task. Clearly, our only hope lies in how we select those things that we can vary. We select the right ones, and we help ensure a good product. We select the wrong ones, and users are likely to experience failures and hate our software. A tester's task is crucial *and* impossible at the same time!

One can easily see that completely ad hoc testing is clearly not the best way to go about testing. Testers who learn about inputs, software environments, and the other things that can be varied during a test pass will be better equipped to explore their application with purpose and intent. This knowledge will help them test better and smarter and maximize their chances of uncovering serious design and implementation flaws.

User Input

Imagine testing a huge application like Microsoft Office or a feature-rich website like Amazon. There are so many possible inputs and input combinations we could potentially apply that testing them all simply isn't an option.

It turns out that it is even harder than it seems. Wherever a tester turns, infinite possibilities hit them head on. The first of these infinite sets are inputs.

What You Need to Know About User Input

What is an input? A general definition might be something like this:

> An *input* is a stimulus generated from an environment that causes the application under test to respond in some manner.

This is very informal but good enough for our purposes. The key point is that an input originates from outside the application and causes some code in the application to execute. Things such as a user clicking a button is an input, but typing text into a text box is not until that text is actually passed to the application and it gets the opportunity to process it.[1] Inputs must cause the software to execute and respond in some manner (including the null response).

Inputs generally fall into two categories: *atomic* input and *abstract* input. Things such as button clicks, strings, and the integer value 4 are atomic inputs; they are irreducible, single events. Some atomic inputs are related, and it is helpful to treat them as abstract input for the purposes of test selection. The integer 4 and the integer 2048 are both specific values (that is, atomic input). However, a tester could have chosen 5 or 256 to enter instead. It makes better sense to talk about such inputs in abstract terms so that they can be reasoned about as a whole. We can, for example, talk about an abstract input *length* for which we could enter any of the atomic values from 1 to 32768.

Variable input requires abstraction because of the large number of possible values that variable input can assume. Positive integers, negative integers, and character strings (of any significant length) are all *practically infinite* in that during a given testing cycle, we cannot apply them all. Without such exhaustive testing, we cannot ensure the software will process them all correctly.[2]

Any specific application accepts an arbitrarily large number of atomic inputs. Applying them all is unlikely, so from an input point of view, testing is about selecting a subset of possible inputs, applying them, and hoping that the subset will cause all the failures to surface and that we can assume

---

1 This is assuming that the text box is separate from the application under test and can be legitimately viewed as a preprocessor of inputs. Of course, you may specifically want to test the functionality of the text box, in which case everything you type into it is an atomic input. It all depends on how you view the scope of the application.

2 Treating two or more atomic inputs the same is known as *equivalence classing* those inputs. The idea is that there is no reason to submit the atomic input 4 and then separately submit 2, because they are in the same equivalence class. If you test one, you don't need to test the other. I once heard a consultant claim that equivalence classes for testing was a myth (or maybe it was illusion, I don't recall). His claim was that you can't tell whether 2 and 4 are the same or different until you apply them both. From a completely black box point of view, this is technically true. But common sense would have to be completely abandoned to actually plan your tests around such a narrow view of the world. Why not check the source code and find out for sure? If the inputs cause the same code path to be generated, and both fit into their target data structures, they can be treated as equivalent for testing purposes. Don't allow stubbornness to force you into testing the same paths over and over without any real hope of finding a bug or exploring new territory.

the software is good enough when the other, previously untested inputs are submitted by actual users. To do this well, software testers must hone their skills in *selecting one input as a better test than another input.* In this and subsequent chapters, we talk about strategies to accomplish this.

But it gets harder than that. If all we had to worry about was the selection of a set of atomic inputs, testing would be much easier than it actually is. Two additional problems complicate input selection far more.

The first is the fact that inputs can often team up on software to cause it to fail. In fact, the *combination* of two or more inputs can often cause an application to fail even when the software has no problem with those inputs individually. You may perform a search for CDs just fine. You may independently perform a search for videos just fine. But when you search for both CDs *and* videos, the software goes pear shaped. Testers must be able to identify which *inputs interact with one another and ensure they appear together in a single test case* to have confidence that these behaviors are properly tested.

Finally, inputs can also cause problems depending on the *order* in which they are applied. Inputs *a* and *b* can be sequenced *ab, ba, aa,* or *bb.* We could also apply three or more consecutive inputs, which creates even more sequences (*aaa, aab, aba, ...*). And when more than two inputs are involved, there are even more sequence choices. If we leave out any specific sequence, it may very well be the one that causes a failure. We can order a book and check out, or we can order two books and check out, or we may choose to check out and then add to our order and check out a second time. There are too many options to contemplate (much less test) them all. Testers must be able to *enumerate likely input sequences and ensure they get tested* to have confidence that the software is ready for real users. Again, this is a topic we turn to in this and subsequent chapters.

How to Test User Input

The cursor sits in a text box, happily blinking away waiting for an input to be entered. Every tester faces this situation many times during the course of a day's testing. What do you do? What strategy do you employ to decide on one input over another? What are all the considerations? It never ceases to amaze me that there is no one place a new tester can go to learn these strategies. It also amazes me that I can ask 10 testers what they would do and get 12 different answers. It's time these considerations get documented, and this is my attempt to do so.

The place to begin is first to realize that your software is not special. There is a temptation for testers to imagine that the software they test is somehow different from every set of bits ever assembled into a contiguous binary. This simply is not the case. All software, from operating systems, APIs, device drivers, memory-resident programs, embedded applications, and system libraries, to web applications, desktop applications, form-based UIs, and games, all perform four basic tasks: They accept input, produce output, store data, and perform computation. They may exist in vastly different operational environments. Inputs may be constructed and transmitted to them in very different ways. Timing may be more of an issue in some types of applications than others, but all software is fundamentally the same, and it is this core similarity that I address in this book. Readers must take this general information and apply it to their own application using the specific rules that govern how their application accepts input and interacts with its environment. Personally, I have tested weapons systems for the U.S. government, real-time security monitors, and antivirus engines, cellular phone switches, operating systems from top to bottom, web applications, desktop applications, large server apps, console and desktop game software, and many other apps that time has expunged from my memory. I am presenting the core considerations that apply to them all, and will leave the actual application of the techniques in the capable hands of my readers.

Legal or Illegal Input?

One of the first distinctions to be made is positive versus negative testing. Are you trying to make sure the application works correctly, or are you specifically trying to make it fail? There are good reasons to do a lot of both types of testing, and for some application domains, negative testing is particularly important, so it helps to have a strategy to think through which good or bad values to test.

The first way that testers can slice this problem is based on what the *developers* think constitutes an illegal input. Developers have to create this partition very precisely, and they usually do so by writing error-handling code for what they see as illegal inputs. The decisions they make on how and when to create error handlers needs to be tested.

It is good to keep in mind that most developers don't like writing error code. Writing error messages is rarely cited as the reason people are attracted to computer science. Developers want to write functional code, the code that serves as the reason people want to use the software in the first place. Often, error-handling code is overlooked or quickly (and carelessly) written. Developers simply want to get back to writing "real" functional code as quickly as possible, and testers must not overlook this area of applications because developer's attitude toward it often ensures it is ripe with bugs.

Imagine developers writing functional code to receive an input. They may immediately see the need to check the input for validity and legality, and therefore they must either (a) stop writing the functional code and take care of the error handler, or (b) insert a quick comment (for example, "insert error code here") and decide to come back to it later. In the former case, their brains have to context-switch from writing functional code to writing the error routine and then back again. This is a distracting process and creates an increased potential for getting it wrong. In the latter case, it isn't unheard of to never get back to writing the error code at all, as developers are busy people. More than once I have seen such "to do" comments left in published and released software!

Developers have three basic mechanisms to define error handlers: input filters, input checks, and exceptions. Here's how they work from a tester's point of view.

Input Filters

Input filters are mechanisms to prevent illegal input from reaching the application's mainline functional code. In other words, an input filter is written to keep bad input out of an application so that there is no need for the developer to worry about illegal values. If an input reaches the application, it is assumed to be a good input, and no further checks need to be made because input can be processed without worry. When performance is an issue, this is often the technique developers employ.

Input filters don't produce error messages (that's how they are distinguished from input checks, which are described next); instead, they quietly filter out illegal input and pass legal input to the application in question. For example, a GUI panel that accepts integer inputs may completely ignore any character or alphabetic input and only display the numeric input that is typed into its fields (see Figure 3.1).

FIGURE 3.1 This dialog box from PowerPoint allows the user to type numeric input only, thus filtering out invalid characters.

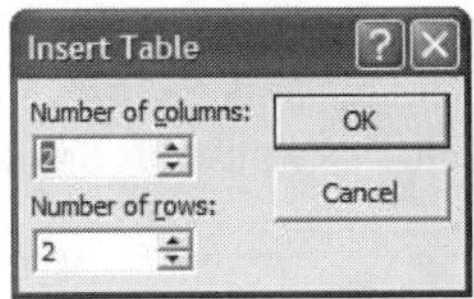

Also, the so-called list box or drop-down box is a type of input filter, in that it allows only valid inputs to be selected (see Figure 3.2). There is a clear advantage to developers because they can now write code without any further checks on input to complicate matters.

FIGURE 3.2 Another way to filter inputs is to allow users to choose from a predefined list of valid values.

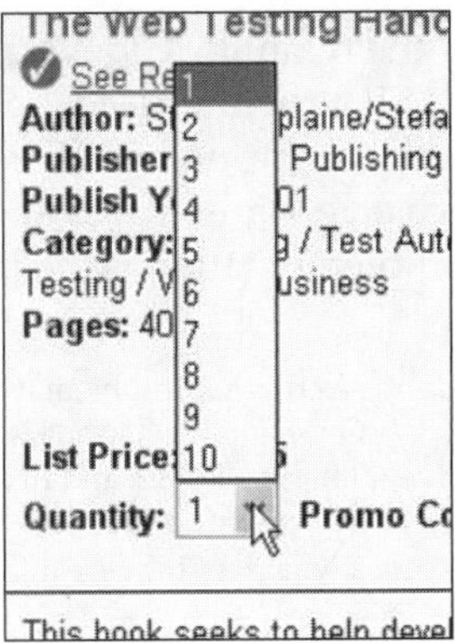

From a testing point of view, we need to check a couple of things regarding input filters:

- First, *did the developers get it right?* If the developers partitioned the space of legal versus illegal input incorrectly, serious bugs can be the result. Imagine mistakenly putting an illegal input in the legal category. This would allow an illegal value into the software's only line of defense (assuming that no further checks are made). If a tester suspects that this is the case, she must write a bug report so that the code gets fixed.[3] The opposite is also serious: Putting a legal input into the illegal category will cause denial of service and serious user frustration, because what they are trying to do is perfectly legitimate and the software prevents them from doing it.
- Second, *can the filter be bypassed?* If there is any other way to get input into the system, or to modify the inputs after they are in the system, the filter is useless, and developers will need to implement further error checking. This is a great bug to find before release because serious security side effects can be the result. Figure 3.3 shows a modified quantity value (achieved by editing the HTML source of this particular web page), which if it is not further checked will result in the user being charged a negative value and thus rip off the seller who uses this software for their online store.

FIGURE 3.3 Bypassing input constraints can be dangerous, as this negative number in the Quantity field shows. This technique is demonstrated in Chapter 3 of *How to Break Web Software.*

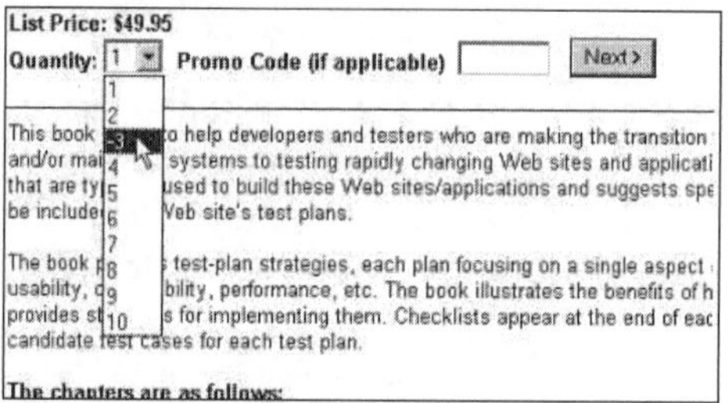

Input Checks

Input checks are part of the mainline code of an application and are implemented as IF/THEN/ELSE structures (or CASE, SELECT structures or lookup tables). They accept an input, and IF it is valid, THEN allow it to be processed, ELSE produce an error message and stop processing. The telltale sign of an input-check implementation is the presence of an error message

---

3 In cases where developers don't see this as a problem, you might have to do a little more testing to convince them otherwise. Once an illegal input is in the system, apply inputs that make the software use that illegal input as often and in as many ways as possible to force any potential bugs to surface. This way you can strengthen your bug report with some more detailed information that exposes what bad things can happen when illegal inputs get processed.

that is generally descriptive and accurately reflects the nature of the invalidity of the input in question.

The error message here is key to the exploratory tester, and my advice is that each error message should be read carefully for mistakes and for clues to the mind of the developer. Error messages often describe fairly exact reasons why the input was invalid and how to fix it. This will give us new ideas for additional test input to drive other types of error messages to occur and, perhaps, cases that should result in error but do not.

The key difference between an input check and an exception (which is covered next) is that the input check is located immediately after the input is read from an external source. The code for reading the input has as its successor an IF statement that checks the input for validity. Therefore, the error message itself can be very precise: "Negative numbers are not allowed" is such a precise message; it tells the user exactly what was wrong with the input in question. When error messages are more general, it is an indication that an exception handler is being used. The topic of exceptions is tackled next.

Exception Handlers

Exception handlers are like error checks, but instead of checks on individual inputs, exception handlers are checks on anything that fails in an entire routine. Error handlers are located at the end of a program or in a separate file completely and handle any specified errors that are raised while the software is executing. This means that input violations are handled, but so is any other failure that can occur, including memory violations and so forth. By their very nature, exceptions handle a variety of failure scenarios, not just illegal inputs.

This means that when an error message is produced as a result of an exception being raised, it will be much more general than the specific wording possible for error checks. Because the exception could be raised by any line of code in the failing routine for any number of reasons, it's difficult for them to be anything more than "an error has occurred" because the handler code can't distinguish the exact nature of the problem.

Whenever a tester encounters such an open-ended, general error message, the best advice is to continue to test the same function. Reapply the input that caused the exception or vary it slightly in ways that may also cause a failure. Run other test cases through the same function. Tripping the exception over and over is likely to cause the program to fail completely.

Illegal inputs should be either ignored or result in some error message (either in a popup dialog or written to an error log file or some reserved area of the UI). Legal inputs should be processed according to the specification and produce the appropriate response. Any deviation from this and you've found a legitimate bug.

Normal or Special Input?

There are normal inputs, and then there are special inputs. A normal input has no special formatting or meaning and is readily digestible by the software under test. Normal inputs are those that the developers plan for and usually the ones that real users favor. Special inputs can come about through some extraordinary circumstance or by complete coincidence or accident. For example, a user may mean to type Shift-c into a text field but accidentally type Ctrl-c instead. Shift-c is an example of a normal input, the capital C character. But Ctrl-c has a completely different meaning assigned by, for example, the Windows operating system, to be *copy* or even *cancel.* Pressing Ctrl-c or some other special character in an input field can sometimes cause unexpected or even undesirable behavior.

All Ctrl characters, Alt, and Esc sequences are examples of special characters, and it is a good idea to test a sampling of these characters in your application and report undesirable behavior as bugs. Testers can also install special fonts that end users are likely to use and test different languages this way. Some fonts, such as Unicode and other multibyte character sets, can cause software to fail if it has been improperly localized to certain languages. A good place to start is to look at your product's documentation and find out what languages it supports; then install the language packs and font libraries that will enable you to test those special inputs.

Another source of special characters comes from the platform on which your application is running. Every operating system, programming language, browser, runtime environment, and so forth has a set of reserved words that it treats as special cases. Windows, for example, has a set of reserved device names such as LPT1, COM1, AUX. When these are typed into fields where a filename is expected, applications often hang or crash outright. Depending on the container in which your application runs, the special characters you type in input fields may be interpreted by the container or by your application. The only way to find out for sure is to research the associated special characters and apply them as test input.

Default or User-Supplied Input?

Leaving text fields blank is an easy way to test. But as easy as it is for the tester, the same cannot be said of the software under test. Indeed, just because the tester didn't do anything doesn't mean the software doesn't have some hard work to do.

Empty data-entry fields or passing null parameters to some API requires that the software execute its default case. Often, these default cases are overlooked or poorly thought out. They are also routinely overlooked in unit testing, so the last defense is the manual tester.

Developers have to deal with nonexistent input because they cannot trust that all users will enter non-null values all the time. Users can skip fields either because they don't see them or don't realize they require a value. If there are a lot of data-entry fields (like those on web forms that ask the user for billing address, shipping address, and other personal information), the error message may also change depending on which field was left blank. This, too, is important to test.

But there is more to explore beyond just leaving fields blank. Whenever a form has prepopulated values, these are what I call *developer-assigned defaults*. For example, you may see the value ALL in a print form field for the number of pages to print. These represent what developers think are the most likely values a reasonable user will enter. We need to test these assumptions, and we need to ensure that no mistakes were made when the developers selected those values as defaults.

The first thing to try when you see developer-assigned defaults is to delete the default value and leave the field blank. (This is often a scenario developers don't think of. Because they took the time to assign a default, they don't imagine a scenario where they have to deal with a missing value.) Then start experimenting with other values around the default. If it's a numeric field, try adding one, try subtracting one. If it is a string, try changing a few values at the front of the string, try changing some at the tail of the string, try adding characters, try deleting characters. Try different strings of the same length and so on and so forth.

Input fields with default values prepopulated are often coded differently than fields that are presented with no default value at all. It pays to spend some extra time testing them.

Using Outputs to Guide Input Selection

This section has so far been about how to select inputs, and up to now all the techniques have been based on choosing inputs according to their desirable (or even undesirable) properties. In other words, some properties (type, size, length, value, and so forth) make them good as test input. Another way to select an input is to consider the output that it might (or should) generate when it is applied.

In many ways, this is akin to the behavior of a teenager trying to get permission of his parents to attend a party. The teen knows that there is one of two answers (outputs), yes or no, and he asks permission in such a way as to ensure his parents will favor the former output. Clearly, "Can I go to a wild and unsupervised rave?" is inferior to "May I join a few friends at Joey's?" How one frames the question has a lot to do with determining the answer.

This concept applies to software testing, as well. The idea is to understand what response you want the software to provide, and then apply the inputs that you think will cause that specific output.

The first way many testers accomplish this is to list all the major outputs for any given feature and make sure they craft test input that produces those outputs. Organizing the input/output pairs into a matrix is a common way of making sure that all the interesting situations are covered.

At the highest level of abstraction, a tester can focus on generating *illegal* outputs or *legal* outputs, but most of the former will overlap the technique described earlier concerning the generation of error messages. Some such overlap is unavoidable, but you should try to focus on varying legal outputs as much as possible to ensure that new functionality and scenarios are covered.

This is a very proactive way of thinking about outputs; testers determine in advance what output they want the application to generate, and then explore scenarios that generate the desired response. A second way of thinking about outputs is more reactive but can be very powerful: Observe outputs, and then choose inputs that force the output to be recalculated or otherwise modified.

When the software generates some response for the first time, it is often the default case: Many internal variables and data structures get initialized from scratch the first time an output is generated. However, the second (or subsequent) time a response is generated, many variables will have preexisting values based from the prior usage. This means that we are testing a completely new path. The first time through we tested the ability to generate an output from an uninitialized state; the second time through we test the ability to generate the output from a *previously initialized state*. These are different tests, and it is not uncommon for one to pass where the other one fails.

A derivative of the reactive output test is to find outputs that persist. Persistent outputs are often calculated and then displayed on the screen or stored in a file that the software will read at some later time. If these values can be changed, it is important to change them and their properties (size, type, and so forth) to test regeneration of the values on top of a prior value. Run tests to change each property you can identify.

The complexity of input selection is only the first of the technical challenges of software testing. As inputs are continually applied to software, internal data structures get updated, and the software accumulates state information in the form of values of internal variables. Next we turn to this problem of state and how it complicates software testing.

State

The fact that any, some, or all inputs can be "remembered" (that is, stored in internal data structures) means that we can't just get by with selecting an input without taking into account all the inputs that came before it. If we apply input *a*, and it changes the state of the application under test, then applying input *a* again cannot be said to be the same test. The application's state has changed, and the outcome of applying input *a* could be very different. State impacts whether an application fails every bit as much as input does. Apply an input in one state and everything is fine; apply that same input in another state and all bets are off.

What You Need to Know About Software State

One way to think about software state is that we have to take the context created by the accumulation of all prior inputs into account when we select future inputs. Inputs cause internal variables to change values, and it is the combination of all these possible values that comprises the *state space* of the software. This leads us to an informal definition of *state* as follows:

> A *state* of software is a coordinate in the state space that contains exactly one value for every internal data structure.

The state space is the cross-product of every internal variable. This is an astronomically large number of different internal states that govern whether the software produces the right or wrong response to an input.

The math is not encouraging. In theory, we must apply every atomic input (which we've established is a very large number) for every state of the application (which is an even larger number). This isn't even possible for small applications, much less medium to large ones. If we enumerated this as a state machine where inputs cause a transition from one state to the next, we'd require a forest of paper to draw it.

For the hypothetical shopping example, we'd have to ensure that we can perform the "checkout" input for every possible combination of shopping cart entries. Clearly, we can treat many cart combinations as functionally equivalent,[4] and we can focus on boundary cases such as an empty cart, without having to test every single instance of a shopping cart. We discuss such strategies for doing so in later chapters.

How to Test Software State

Software state comes about through the application's interaction with its environment and its history of receiving inputs. As inputs are applied and stored internally, the software's state changes. It's these changes we want to test. Is the software updating its state properly? Does the state of the application cause some inputs to exhibit faulty behavior? Is the software getting into states it should never be in? The following are the major considerations for testing input and state interactions.

The input domain for software is infinite, as discussed in the previous section. We cited input variables, input combinations, and input sequences for this particular difficulty. However, the added dimension of state also has the effect of complicating a tester's life even further. Software state comes about because of its ability to "remember" prior inputs and accumulate software state. State can be thought of as encapsulating the input history in that it is the way that software remembers what users did in previous occasions in which they used the software.

Because software state comes about through the successive application of input, testing it requires multiple test cases and successively executing, terminating, and re-executing the software. Software states are visible to testers if we take the time to notice how our input affects the system. If we enter some inputs and later see the values we entered, those inputs are stored internally and have become part of the state of the application. If the

---

[4] We're back to the concept of equivalence classes again. If they really are an illusion, software testers are in some very serious trouble.

software uses the inputs in some calculation and that calculation can be repeated, the inputs must be stored internally, too.

Software state is another way of describing the sum total of prior inputs and outputs that the software "remembers." State is either *temporary,* in that it is remembered only during a single execution of the app and forgotten when the application is terminated, or *persistent,* in that it is stored in a database or file and accessible to the application in subsequent executions. This is often referred to as the *scope* of data, and testing that the scope is correctly implemented is an important test.[5]

Much of the data that is stored either temporarily or persistently cannot be seen directly and must be inferred based on its influence on software behavior. If the same input causes two completely different behaviors, the state of the application must have been different in the two cases. For example, imagine the software that controls a telephone switch. The input "answer the phone" (the act of picking up the receiver on a land line or pressing the answer button on a cell phone) can produce completely different behaviors depending on the state of the software:

- If the phone isn't registered to a network, there is no response or an error response.
- If the phone is not ringing, a dial tone is generated (in the case of a land line) or a redial list is presented (in the case of a cell phone).
- If the phone is ringing, a voice connection to the caller is made.

Here the state is the status of the network (registered or unregistered) and the status of the phone (ringing or idle). These values combined with the input we apply (answering the phone) determine what response or output is generated. Testers should attempt to enumerate and test as many combinations as are reasonable given their time and budget restraints and based on expectations of risk to the end user.

The relationship between input and state is crucial and a difficult aspect of testing, both in the small and in the large. Because the former is the subject of this chapter, consider the following advice:

- **Use state information to help find related inputs.**

  It is common practice to test input combinations. If two or more inputs are related in some manner, they should be tested together. If we are testing a website that accepts coupon codes that shouldn't be combined with sale prices, we need to apply inputs that create a shopping cart with sale items and also enter a coupon code for that order. If we only test the coupon code on shopping carts without sale items, this behavior goes untested, and the owners of the site may end up losing money. We must observe the effects on the state (the shopping cart items and their price) as we test to notice this behavior and determine whether

[5] Getting the scope of data wrong has security implications. Imagine entering an input that represents a credit card number, which is supposed to be scoped only for single use. We must re-execute the application to test that the number is not incorrectly scoped as a persistent piece of state.

developers got it right. Once we determine that we have a group of related inputs and state data (in this example, sale items, coupon codes, and the shopping cart), we can methodically work through combinations of them to ensure we cover the important interactions and behaviors.

- **Use state information to identify interesting input sequences.**

  When an input updates state information, successive applications of that same input cause a series of updates to state. If the state is accumulating in some way, we have to worry about overflow. Can too many values be stored? Can a numeric value grow too large? Can a shopping cart become too full? Can a list of items grow too large? Try to spot accumulating state in the application you are testing, and repeatedly apply any and all inputs that impact that accumulation.

Code Paths

As inputs are applied and state is accumulated in the application under test, the application itself is executing line after line of code as its programming dictates. A sequence of code statements makes a path through the software. Informally, a *code path* is a sequence of code statements beginning with invocation of the software and ending with a specific statement often representing termination of the software.

There is a substantial amount of possible variation in code paths. Each simple branching structure (for example, the IF/THEN/ELSE statement) causes two possible branches, requiring that testers create tests to execute the THEN clause and separately the ELSE clause. Multibranch structures (for example, CASE or SELECT statements) create three or more possible branches. Because branching structures can be nested one inside the other and sequenced so that one can follow another, the actual number of paths can be very large for complex code.

Testers must be aware of such branching opportunities and understand which inputs cause the software to go down one branch as opposed to another. It isn't easy to do, particularly without access to the source code or to tools that map inputs to code coverage. And the paths that are missed may very well be those with bugs.

Branches are only one type of structure that increase the number of code paths. Loops make them truly infinite. Unbounded loops execute until the loop condition evaluates to false. Often, this loop condition itself is based on user input. For example, users determine when to stop adding items to their shopping cart before they proceed to checkout: They've left the shopping loop and continue on to the checkout code.

There are a number of specific strategies for gaining coverage of code paths that are explored throughout this book.

User Data

Whenever software is expected to interact with large data stores, such as a database or complex set of user files, testers have the unenviable task of trying to replicate those data stores in the test lab. The problem is simple enough to state: Create data stores with specific data as similar as possible to the type of data we expect our users to have. However, actually achieving this is devilishly difficult.

In the first place, real user databases evolve over months and years as data is added and modified, and they can grow very large. Testers are restricted by a testing phase that may only last a few days or weeks, and so populating it with data must happen on much shorter time scales.

In the second place, real user data often contains relationships and structure that testers have no knowledge of and no simple way of inferring. It is often this complexity that causes the software that worked fine in the test lab to break when it has to deal with real user data.

In the third place, there is the problem of access to storage space. Large data stores often require expensive data centers that are simply not accessible to testers because of the sheer cost involved. Whatever testers do has to be done in a short period of time and on much smaller byte-scales than what will happen in the field after release.

An astute tester may observe that a simple solution for all this complexity would be to use an actual user database, perhaps by arranging a mutually beneficial relationship with a specific beta customer and testing the application while it is connected to their real data source. However, testers must use real data with great care. Imagine an application that adds and *removes* records from a database. Tests (particularly automated ones) that remove records would be problematic for the owners of the database. Testers must now do extra work to restore the database to its original form or work on some expendable copy of it.

Finally, another complication (as though we hadn't enough complications already) surfaces to cause us angst when we deal with real customer data: *privacy*.

Customer databases often contain information that is sensitive in some way or even contains PII (personally identifiable information). In an age of online fraud and identity theft, this is a serious matter that you do not want to expose to your test team. Any use of real customer data must provide for careful handling of PII.

This makes both *having* and *lacking* real customer data problematic!

Environment

Even if it were possible to test every code path with every user input, state combination, and user data, software could still fail the moment it is installed in an environment it has never seen before. This is because the environment itself is an input source, and therefore testers need to ensure they test as many potential user environments as practical before release.

What's in an environment? Well, it's different depending on what type of an application you are testing. In general, it is the operating system and how it is configured; it is the various applications that coexist on that operating system that might interact with the application under test; it is any other driver, program, file, or setting that may directly or indirectly affect the application and how it reacts to input. It's also the network that the application is connected to, and it's available bandwidth, performance, and so forth. Anything that can affect the behavior of the application under test is part of the environment we must consider during testing.

Unlike user data, which is passive in its effect on software (data sits and waits for the software under test to manipulate it), the environment is actively interacting with our software programmatically. It provides input to our software and consumes its output. The environment consists of not only resources like the Windows Registry but also applications that are installed that interact with shared components. The sheer number of such variations is beyond our reach to re-create. Where are we going to get all the machines to re-create all those customer environments on? And if we had the hardware, how would we select the right subset of environments to include in our testing? We can't test them all, but any tester who has been around has experienced a test case that runs fine on one machine and causes a failure on another. The environment is crucial, and it is devilishly difficult to test.[6]

Conclusion

Software testing is complicated by an overload of variation possibilities from inputs and code paths to state, stored data, and the operational environment. Indeed, whether one chooses to address this variation in advance of any testing by writing test plans or by an exploratory approach that allows planning and testing to be interleaved, it is an impossible task. No matter how you ultimately *do* testing, it's simply too complex to do it completely.

However, exploratory techniques have the advantage that they encourage testers to plan as they test and to use information gathered during testing to affect the actual way testing is performed. This is a key advantage over plan-first methods. Imagine trying to predict the winner of the Super

---

[6] Environment variation and testing is not covered in this book. However, Chapters 4 and 5 as well as Appendixes A and B of *How to Break Software* treat this topic at length.

Bowl or Premier League before the season begins. This is difficult to do before you see how the teams are playing, how they are handling the competition, and whether key players can avoid injury. The information that comes in as the season unfolds holds the key to predicting the outcome with any amount of accuracy. The same is true of software testing, and exploratory testing embraces this by attempting to plan, test, and replan in small ongoing increments guided by full knowledge of all past and current information about how the software is performing and the clues it yields during testing.

Testing is complex, but effective use of exploratory techniques can help tame that complexity and contribute to the production of high-quality software.

Exercises

1. Suppose an application takes a single integer as input. What is the range of possible atomic inputs when the integer is a 2-byte signed integer? What if it is a 2-byte unsigned integer? What about a 4-byte integer?
2. As in question 1, suppose an application takes a single integer as input. Can you get by with just entering the integer 148 and assuming that if the software works when 148 is entered it will work when any integer is entered? If you answer yes, explain why. If you answer no, specify at least two conditions that will cause the software to behave differently if given 148 or another valid integer.
3. For question 2, what other values might you enter besides integers? Why would you want to do this?
4. Describe a case in which the *combination* of inputs can cause software to fail. In other words, each input taken on its own does not expose a failure, but when the inputs are combined, the software fails.
5. Imagine a web application that requests shipping information from a customer, including name, address, and several other fields. Most often, the information is entered in bulk, and then the information is checked only after the user clicks a Next or Submit button. Is this an example of an input check or an exception handler? Justify your answer.
6. Describe a case in which the *order* of inputs can cause software to fail. In other words, if you apply the sequence of inputs in one order and the software works, changing the order in which the inputs are applied might cause the software to fail.
7. Suppose you have a situation where software fails after it has been left running continuously for a long period of time. Would you ascribe this failure to input, state, code paths, environment, or data? Explain your reasoning.

CHAPTER 4
Exploratory Testing in the Large

"A good traveler has no fixed plans and is not intent on arriving."

—*Lao Tzu*

Exploring Software

The techniques presented in the preceding chapter help software testers make the numerous small decisions on-the-fly while they are running test cases. Those techniques are good for choosing among atomic inputs and arranging atomic inputs in combination or in sequence. This chapter is about the larger decisions testers must make concerning feature interaction, data flows, and choosing paths through the UI that result in making the application do real work. Instead of decisions regarding atomic inputs that serve some immediate purpose on a single input panel, we'll reason about inputs to guide us toward some larger goal. An exploratory tester will establish such goals in advance of actual testing and let the goal guide her during testing sessions. We accomplish this with a tourism metaphor that treats exploration of software using the tools of a conventional tourist: organized tours, guidebooks, maps, and local information. This helps us set goals that can then guide our decision making during testing.

In *How to Break Software* and its series companions,[1] I used a military metaphor to describe software testing. Given that those books were aimed exclusively at breaking software, it was a metaphor that helped get the attack-minded test strategies of those books into the heads of readers. I've received overwhelmingly positive feedback from my readers that they found the metaphor helpful (and fun!), and so I am encouraged to use the same approach, with a different metaphor, for this book whose purpose is much broader.

---

[1] Whittaker, *How to Break Software* (Addison-Wesley, 2003); Whittaker and Thompson, *How to Break Software Security* (Addison-Wesley, 2004); Andrews and Whittaker, *How to Break Web Software* (Addison-Wesley, 2006).

Metaphors can be a powerful guide for software testers.[2] This is the exact purpose we want to achieve: a metaphor that will act as a guide to help testers choose the right input, data, states, code paths, and environment settings to get the most out of their testing time and budget.

Testers must make many decisions while they are testing. There are big decisions, like how to obtain realistic data to simulate customer databases. There are small decisions, like choosing what string of characters to enter in a text box. Without the proper mindset and guidance, testers can end up wandering aimlessly around an application's interface looking for bugs that may or may not actually be there and gaining only poor coverage of the application in the process.

I often tell testers I work with that if it feels like you are on a ghost hunt during a testing session, you probably are.[3] If you feel like you are wandering around looking for shadows, stop testing and try to establish some better guiding goals for your effort.

This is where the metaphor can help by providing a strategy and a set of specific goals for software testers to follow, or at least keep in the back of their mind, as they are exploring an application. For an explorer, having a goal to pursue is better than just wandering around. A guiding metaphor should give testers a goal and then help them understand how to perform testing that fulfills that goal. If a metaphor yields goals that help testers make both big and small decisions, then a testers aren't just wandering aimlessly. The metaphor has helped them organize their testing to approach software's complexity and its broad range of features in a more methodical way. This chapter is about using a metaphor, specifically a tourism metaphor, to make large test decisions that will guide overall exploratory strategy and feature usage.

In finding a metaphor that works for exploratory testing, it is important to understand the spirit and intent of exploratory testing so that we ensure the metaphor is helpful. The goals of exploratory testing are as follows:

---

[2] However, the wrong metaphor can be distracting. It's an interesting piece of testing history that provides a case in point. The technique of estimating the number of fish present in a lake was used as a metaphor leading to the concept of *fault seeding* in the late 1980s and early 1990s. The idea was that to estimate the number of fish in a lake, one could stock a fixed number of a specific type of fish. After a bit of fishing (testing) where some number of real fish and some number of seeded fish are caught, one can estimate the number of real fish using the ratio of seeded fish caught to the total number of seeded fish. The fact that this technique has been relegated to the dusty libraries of testing past is enough proof that the metaphor was less than useful.

[3] Ghost-hunting television shows are popular in the U.S. Teams of paranormal experts (is such a thing possible?) search old buildings and graveyards for what they deem as evidence of the supernatural. My kids like the shows, and I often watch them in their company. The ghost stories are great, but the experts never confirm paranormal presence. They never rule it out either. This may work for entertainment, but it is not much use for testing. If you can neither confirm nor deny the presence of a bug in your software (or whether it is working as specified), you aren't doing a very good job testing. Perhaps, instead, you should start a television show about the process instead.

- **To gain an understanding of how an application works, what its interface looks like, and what functionality it implements:** Such a goal is often adopted by testers new to a project or those who want to identify test entry points, identify specific testing challenges, and write test plans. This is also the goal used by experienced testers as they explore an application to understand the depth of its testing needs and to find new unexplored functionality.
- **To force the software to exhibit its capabilities:** The idea is to make the software work hard and to ask it hard questions that put it through its paces. This may or may not find bugs, but it will certainly provide evidence that the software performs the function for which it was designed and that it satisfies its requirements.
- **To find bugs:** Exploring the edges of the application and hitting potential soft spots is a specialty of exploratory testing. The goal is purposeful, rather than aimless, exploration to identify untested and historically buggy functionality. Exploratory testers should not simply stumble across bugs, they should zero in on them with purpose and intent.

Even as real explorers seldom go about their tasks without some planning and a lot of strategy, exploratory testers are smart to do the same to maximize the potential that they look in places where functionality is complex, users are likely to tread, and bugs are more likely to exist. This is a broader mission that subsumes just breaking software, and it deserves a new metaphor. The one I think works best is that of a tourist trying to explore a new destination. I like to call this the "touring test" in honor of Alan Turing, who proposed the original Turing test.

The Tourist Metaphor

Suppose you are visiting a large city like London, England, for the very first time. It's a big, busy, confusing place for new tourists, with lots of things to see and do. Indeed, even the richest, most time-unconstrained tourist would have a hard time seeing everything a city like London has to offer. The same can be said of well-equipped testers trying to explore complex software; all the funding in the world won't guarantee completeness.

How does a savvy tourist decide whether car, underground, bus, or walking is the right method of getting around London? How can you see as much of the city as possible in the time allocated? How can you cover the most activities with the shortest commute between them? How can you make sure you see all the best landmarks and attractions? What if something goes wrong, who do you go to for help? Should you hire a guide or figure things out for yourself?

Such tours require some strategy and a lot of goal setting. Goals will affect how tourists plans their time and will determine what parts of the city they will see. A flight crew on an overnight layover will approach their tour much differently than the organizer of a troupe of visiting students. The purpose and goals of the tourist will weigh heavily in the actual touring strategy selected.

On my first trip to London, I was alone on a business trip and chose to simply walk the streets as my exploration strategy. I didn't bother with guidebooks, tours, or any other guidance beyond a vague notion of trying to find cool things. As it turns out, cool things are hard to avoid in London. But despite walking all day, I missed many major landmarks completely. Because I wasn't sure where anything was, I often saw things without appreciating them for what they were. That "awesome church" was actually Saint Paul's Cathedral, and its significance and history went unrecognized and unappreciated. When I tired of walking and resorted to the underground, I lost track of distances and haphazardly surfaced from the subway without really understanding where I was, where I had been, and how little ground I had actually covered. I felt like I had seen a lot but in reality barely scratched the surface. From a testing point of view, having such a false sense of coverage is dangerous.

My London tourist experience is a fairly common description of a lot of manual and automated testing[4] I see on a regular basis. I was a freestyle tourist, and had I not been lucky enough to return to London on many future occasions and explore it more methodically, I would have really missed out. As testers, we don't often get a chance to return at a later date. Our first "visit" is likely to be our only chance to really dig in and explore our application. We can't afford to wander around aimlessly and take the chance that we miss important functionality and major bugs. We have to make our visit count!

My second trip to London was with my wife. She likes structure, so she bought a guidebook, filled her (actually, my) pockets with tourist brochures, booked the Big Red Bus Tour, and paid for various walking tours guided by local experts. In between these guided tours, we used my method of wandering aimlessly. There is no question that the tours took us to more interesting places in much less time than my wandering. However, there was synergy between the two methods. Her tours often uncovered interesting side streets and alleys that needed additional investigation that my freestyle methods were perfectly suited as follow up, whereas my wandering often found cool places that we then identified guided tours to explore more thoroughly. The structure of the guided tour blended seamlessly with the freestyle wandering technique.

Tourism benefits from a mix of structure and freedom, and so does exploratory testing. There are many touring metaphors that will help us

---

[4] There is no fundamental difference in designing automated tests and designing manual tests. Both require similar design principles with the primary difference being how they are executed. Poor test design principles will ruin both manual and automated tests with automated tests simply doing nothing *faster*. Indeed, I maintain that all good automated tests began their lives as manual tests.

add structure to our exploration and get us through our applications faster and more thoroughly than freestyle testing alone. In this chapter, we discuss these tours. In later chapters, we actually use the tours as part of a larger exploratory testing strategy. Many of these tours fit into a larger testing strategy and can even be combined with traditional scenario-based testing that will determine exactly how the tour is organized. But for now, all the tours are described in this chapter to "get them inside your head" and as a reference for later when we employ them more strategically.

"Touring" Tests

Any discussion of test planning needs to begin with decomposition of the software into smaller pieces that are more manageable. This is where concepts such as feature testing come into play, where testing effort is distributed among the features that make up the application under test. This simplifies tracking testing progress and assigning test resources, but it also introduces a great deal of risk.

Features are rarely independent from each other. They often share application resources, process common inputs, and operate on the same internal data structures. Therefore, testing features independently may preclude finding bugs that surface only when features interact with each other.

Fortunately, the tourist metaphor insists on no such decomposition. Instead, it suggests a decomposition based on *intent* rather than on any inherent structure of the application under test. Like a tourist who approaches her vacation with the intent to see as much as possible in as short a period of time as possible, so the tester will also organize her tours. An actual tourist will select a mix of landmarks to see and sites to visit, and a tester will also choose to mix and match features of the software with the *intent to do something specific.* This intent often requires any number of application features and functions to be combined in ways that they would not be if we operated under a strict feature testing model.

Tourist guidebooks will often segment a destination into districts. There's the business district, the entertainment district, the theater district, the red light district, and so forth. For actual tourists, such segments often represent physical boundaries. For the software tester, they are strictly logical separations of an application's features, because distance is no real issue for the software tester. Instead, software testers should explore paths of the application that run through many features in various orders. Thus, we present a different take on the tourist guidebook.

We separate software functionality into overlapping "districts" for convenience and organization. These are the business district, the historical district, the tourist district, the entertainment district, the hotel district, and the seedy district. Each district and their associated tours are summarized here, and then tours through those districts are described in the sections that follow:

- **Business district:** In a city, the business district is bounded by the morning rush hour and evening commute and contains the productive business hours and after-work socials. In the business district, there are the banks, office buildings, cafes, and shops. For software, the business district is also "where the business gets done" and is bounded by startup and shutdown code and contains the features and functions for which customers use the software. These are the "back of the box" features that would appear in a marketing commercial or sales demo and the code that supports those features.
- **Historical district:** Many cities have historic places or were the setting for historic events. Tourists love the mystery and legacy of the past and that makes historical districts very popular. For software, history is determined by its legacy code and history of buggy functions and features. Like real history, legacy code is often poorly understood, and many assumptions are made when legacy code is included, modified, or used. Tours through this district are aimed at testing legacy code.
- **Tourist district:** Many cities have districts where only tourists go. Locals and those who live in the city avoid these congested thoroughfares. Software is similar in that novice users will be attracted to features and functions that an experienced user has no more use for.
- **Entertainment district:** When all the sites and historical places have been exhausted by a tourist (or have exhausted the tourist!), some mindless relaxation and entertainment is often needed to fill out the corners of a good vacation. Software, too, has such supportive features, and tours to test these features are associated with this district. These tours complement the tours through other districts and fill out the corners of a good test plan.
- **Hotel district:** Having a place for tourists to rest at night, recover from their busy day, or wait out lousy weather is a must for any destination city. As we shall see, software is actually quite busy when it is "at rest," and these tours seek to test those features.
- **Seedy district:** Seedy districts are those unsavory places that few guidebooks or visitors bureaus will document. They are full of people doing bad and illegal things and are better off left alone. Yet they attract a certain class of tourist anyway. Seedy tours are a must for testers because they find places of vulnerability that may be very unsavory to users should they remain in the product.

Tours of the Business District

Business districts for cities bustle during the morning and afternoon rush and over the lunch hour. They are also where work gets done. They contain banks, office buildings, and usually aren't interesting places for tourists to hang out.

This is not the case for the software tourist. The parts of the application that "get the business done" are the reasons that people buy and use software. They are the features that appear in marketing literature, and if you polled customers about why they use your software, these are the features they would quote.

Business District tours focus on these important features and guide testers through the paths of the software where these features are used.

The Guidebook Tour

Guidebooks for tourists often boil down the sights to see to a select (and manageable) few. They identify the best hotels, the best bargains, and the top attractions, without going into too much detail or overwhelming a tourist with too many options. The attractions in the guidebook have been visited by experts who tell the tourist exactly how to enjoy them and get the most out of a visit.

It is sheer speculation on my part, but I would imagine many tourists never wander beyond the confines created by the authors of these guidebooks. Cities must ensure that such attraction areas are clean, safe, and welcoming so that tourists will spend their money and return often. From a testing standpoint, hitting such hotspots is just as important, and that makes this tour a crucial part of every testing strategy. Like cities, we want users to enjoy their experience, and so the major features need to be usable, reliable, and work as advertised.

The analogous artifact for exploratory testing is the user manual, whether it is printed or implemented as online help (in which case, I often call this the *F1 tour* to denote the shortcut to most help systems). For this tour, we will follow the user manual's advice just like the wary traveler, by never deviating from its lead.

The guidebook tour is performed by reading the user manual and following its advice to the letter. When the manual describes features and how they are used, the tester heeds those directives. The goal is to try and execute each scenario described in the user manual as faithfully as possible. Many help systems describe features as opposed to scenarios, but almost all of them give very specific advice about which inputs to apply and how to navigate the user interface to execute the feature. Thus this tour tests not only the software's ability to deliver the functionality as described but also the accuracy of the user manual.

Variations of this tour would be the *Blogger's tour,* in which you follow third-party advice, and the *Pundit's tour,* where you create test cases that describe the complaints of unhappy reviewers. You'll find these sources of information in online forums, beta communities, user group newsletters, or if your application is big and widely distributed like Microsoft Office, on bookstore shelves. Another useful variant is the *Competitor's tour,* where you follow any of the above artifacts' advice for competing systems.[5]

The guidebook and its variants test the software's ability to deliver its advertised functionality. It's a straightforward test, and you should be alert for deviations from the manual and report those as bugs. It may end up that the fix is to update the manual, but in any event you have done a service for your users. The guidebook tour forces you to string together features of the software much the same way as a user would string them together and forces those features to interact. Any bugs found during this tour tend to be important ones.

In Chapter 6, "Exploratory Testing in Practice," several examples of the Guidebook tour are given.

The Money Tour

Every location that covets tourists must have some good reasons for them to come. For Las Vegas, it's the casinos and the strip, for Amsterdam it's the coffee shops and red light district, for Egypt it's the pyramids. Take these landmarks away and the place is no longer an attraction, and tourists will take their money elsewhere.

Software is much the same: There has to be some reason for users to buy it. If you identify the features that draw users, that's where the money is. For exploratory testers finding the money features means following the money, literally. And money usually leads directly to the sales force.

Sales folk spend a great deal of time giving demos of applications. One might imagine that because they get paid based on fulfilling their sales quota, they would be very good at it and would include any interesting nuances of usage that make the product look its very best. They also excel at shortcuts to smooth out the demo and often come up with scenarios that sell the product but weren't part of any specific requirements or user story. The long and short of it is that salespeople are a fantastic source of information for the *Money tour.*

Testers performing the Money tour should sit in on sales demos, watch sales videos, and accompany salespeople on trips to talk to customers. To execute the tour, simply run through the demos yourself and look for problems. As the product code is modified for bug fixes and new features, it may be that the demo breaks and you've not only found a great bug, but you've saved your sales force from some pretty serious embarrassment

[5] Testing your own application using the "guidebook" for a competing system is a novel approach to this tour. It works out very well in situations where the competing product is a market leader and you are trying to supplant it with your own. In these cases, the users who migrate to your application may well be used to working in the manner described in those sources, and therefore, you'll explore your application much the same way as (hopefully) lots of transitioning users. Better that such a tour happen with you as the tourist than to let your users discover whether your software meets their needs all on their own.

(perhaps even salvaging a sale). I have found enough bugs this way to privately wonder whether there is a case to be made for testers sharing in sales commissions!

A powerful variation of this tour is the *Skeptical Customer tour,* in which you execute the Money tour but pretend there is a customer constantly stopping the demo and asking "what if?" "What if I wanted to do *this?"* they may ask, or, "How would I do *that?"* requiring you to go off script and include a new feature into the demo. This happens a lot in customer demos, especially the serious ones where a purchase is imminent and the customer is kicking the tires one last time. It's a powerful way to create test cases that will matter to end users.

Once again, sitting in on customer demos by the sales force and having a good relationship with individual salespeople will give you a distinct advantage when you use this tour and will allow you to maximize the effect of this variation.

Clearly, any bugs you find on this tour are very important ones as they are likely to be seen by real customers.

In Chapter 6, several examples of the Money tour are given.

The Landmark Tour

As a boy growing up in the fields, meadows, and woods of Kentucky, I learned to use a compass by watching my older brother, who seemed to spend more time in the woods than he did anywhere else. He taught me how to orient myself by using the compass to pinpoint landmarks that were in the general direction we wanted to go. The process was simple. Use the compass to locate a landmark (a tree, rock, cliff face, and so forth) in the direction you want to go, make your way to that landmark, and then locate the next landmark, and so on and so forth. As long as the landmarks were all in the same direction, you could get yourself through a patch of dense Kentucky woods.[6]

The *Landmark tour* for exploratory testers is similar in that we will choose landmarks and perform the same landmark hopping through the software that we would through a forest. At Microsoft, we chose our landmarks in advance by selecting key features identified during the Guidebook tour and the Money tour. Choose a set of landmarks, decide on an ordering for them, and then explore the application going from landmark to landmark until you've visited all of them in your list. Keep track of which landmarks you've used and create a landmark coverage map to track your progress.

Testers can create a great deal of variation in this tour by choosing first a few landmarks and executing the tour, and then increasing the number of landmarks and varying the order in which you visit them.

---

[6] We once found a moonshine still this way, but that's one of the hazards of exploring rural Kentucky. Bugs will surface at a much faster rate than stills!

In Visual Studio, the first group at Microsoft to use the tours in production, this is the most popular and useful tour, followed closely by the Intellectual tour, which is described next.

The Intellectual Tour

I was once on a walking tour of London in which the guide was a gentleman in his fifties who claimed at the outset to have lived in London all his life. A fellow tourist happened to be a scholar who was knowledgeable in English history and was constantly asking hard questions of the guide. He didn't mean to be a jerk, but he was curious, and that combined with his knowledge ended up being a dangerous combination…at least to the guide.

Whenever the guide would talk about some specific location on the tour, whether it was Oscar Wilde's former apartment in Chelsea, details of the great fire, or what life was like when horses were the primary mode of transportation, the scholar would second guess him or ask him some hard question that the guide struggled to answer. The poor guide had never worked so hard on any past tour. Every time he opened his mouth, he knew he was going to be challenged, and he knew he had to be on his toes. He wasn't up to the task and finally admitted that he had only actually lived in London for five years, and he had memorized the script of the tour. Until he met the intellectual, his ruse had worked.

What a fantastic bug! The scholar actually managed to *break* the guide! I was so impressed I bought both the guide and the intellectual a pint when the tour ended at a pub (a place, incidentally, where the hapless guide was infinitely more knowledgeable than the scholar).

When applied to exploratory testing, this tour takes on the approach of *asking the software hard questions.* How do we make the software work as hard as possible? Which features will stretch it to its limits? What inputs and data will cause it to perform the most processing? Which inputs might fool its error-checking routines? Which inputs and internal data will stress its capability to produce any specific output?

Obviously, such questions will vary widely depending on the application under test. For folks who test word processors, this tour would direct them to create the most complicated documents possible, ones full of graphics, tables, multiple columns, footnotes, and so forth. For folks testing online purchasing systems, try to invent the hardest order possible. Can we order 200 items? Can we place multiple items on backorder? Can we keep changing our mind about the credit card we want to use? Can we make mistakes on *every* field in the data entry forms? This tour is going to be different for every application, but the idea is the same: Ask your software hard questions. Just as the intellectual did with the London guide, you are likely to find gaps in its logic and capabilities in the exact same manner.

A variation of this tour is the *Arrogant American tour* that celebrates a stereotype of my countrymen when we travel abroad. Instead of asking hard questions, we ask silly questions otherwise intended simply to annoy or impede the tour and draw attention to ourselves. We intentionally present obstacles to see how the software reacts. Instead of the most complicated word processing document, we make the most colorful, invert every other page, print only prime number pages, or place something in a location that makes little sense. On a shopping site, we'll seek out the most expensive items only to return them immediately. It doesn't have to make sense…we do it because we *can*. It isn't unheard of for your users to do the same.

This tour and its variants will find any number of types of bugs from high priority to simply stupid. It's up to the exploratory testers to rein themselves in. Try to separate the truly outrageous hard questions (like asking a London guide whether he founded the city on the north side of the river Thames or the south side; it's a hard question, but it doesn't have much purpose) from questions that really make the software work. Try to create *realistically* complicated documents, orders, or other data so that it is easier to argue that bugs you find really matter to the user and should be fixed.

The Intellectual tour is used in Chapter 6 by Bola Agbonile to test Windows Media Player.

The FedEx Tour

FedEx is an icon in the package-delivery world. They pick up packages, move them around their various distribution centers, and send them to their final destination. For this tour[7], instead of packages moving around the planet through the FedEx system, think of data moving through the software. The data starts its life as input and gets stored internally in variables and data structures where it is often manipulated, modified, and used in computation. Finally, much of this data is finally "delivered" as output to some user or destination.

During this tour, a tester must concentrate on this data. Try to identify inputs that are stored and "follow" them around the software. For example, when an address is entered into a shopping site, where does it gets displayed? What features consume it? If it is used as a billing address, make sure you exercise that feature. If it is used as a shipping address, make sure you use that feature. If can be updated, update it. Does it ever get printed or purged or processed? Try to find every feature that touches the data so that, just as FedEx handles their packages, you are involved in every stage of the data's life cycle.

David Gorena Elizondo applies the *FedEx tour* to Visual Studio in Chapter 6.

The After-Hours Tour

Even business has to stop at some point for workers to commute to their homes or head for the after-hours gathering spots. This is a crowded time

[7] This tour was first proposed by Tracy Monteith of Microsoft.

for cities, and many tourists choose to stay away from the business districts after hours.

But not the software tester! After hours, when the money features are no longer needed, many software applications remain at work. They perform maintenance tasks, archive data, and back up files. Sometimes applications do these things automatically, and sometimes a tester can force them. This is the tour that reminds us to do so.

A variation of this tour is the *Morning-Commute tour,* whose purpose it is to test startup procedures and scripts. Had this tour been applied on the Zune, we may well have avoided the infinite loop that bricked first-generation Zune devices on December 31, 2008.

The After-Hours Zune Bug

December 31 was the 366th day in the leap year of 2008. On that day, Microsoft's first-generation Zune froze and never recovered. The bug was an off-by-one error in a loop that only handled a year with 365 days. The result is that the loop never ended and the Zune froze, which is exactly what an infinite loop will cause software to do. The code looks like this:

```
year = ORIGINYEAR; /* = 1980 */
while (days > 365)
{
    if (IsLeapYear(year))
    {
        if (days > 366)
        {
            days -= 366;
            year += 1;
        }
    }
    else
    {
        days -= 365;
        year += 1;
    }
}
```

This code takes the clock information and computes the year and counts down from either 365 or 366 until it can determine the month and day. The problem is that 366 is too large a number to ever break out of the `while` loop (meaning that the loop never ends and the Zune goes off into never-never land). Because this script is in the startup code, once you turn the Zune on, it is caput. The solution requires that you need a new clock value on January 1 in order to reset the device: Therefore, the fix is to wait until the new year and pull the battery!

The Garbage Collector's Tour

Those who collect curbside garbage often know neighborhoods better than even residents and police because they go street by street, house by house, and become familiar with every bump in the road. They crisscross neighborhoods in a methodical manner, stopping at each house for a few moments before moving on. However, because they are in a hurry, they don't stay in one place very long.

For software, this is like a methodical spot check. We can decide to spot check the interface where we go screen by screen, dialog by dialog (favoring, like the garbage collector, the shortest route), and not stopping to test in detail, but checking the obvious things (perhaps like the Supermodel tour). We could also use this tour to go feature by feature, module by module, or any other landmark that makes sense for our specific application.

The *Garbage Collector's tour* is performed by choosing a goal (for example, all menu items, all error messages, all dialog boxes), and then visiting each one in the list by the shortest path possible. In Chapter 6, Bola Agbonile applies this tour to Windows Media Player, and Geoff Staneff applies it to Visual Studio.

Tours Through the Historical District

Historical districts within cities are areas that contain old buildings and places of historical note. In cities like Boston, they are distributed around the city and connected by marked walking trails. In Cologne, Germany, a small contiguous section of the city is called the "old town" to mark where the city stood before its modern expansion.

In software, historical district can be as loosely connected as in Boston or as contained as they are in Cologne. The historical district represents areas of legacy code, features that debuted in earlier versions, and bug fixes. The latter is particularly important because when it comes to bugs, history does indeed repeat itself, and it is important to retest previously buggy sections of code. Tours through the historical district are designed to test legacy functionality and verify bug fixes.

The Bad-Neighborhood Tour

Every city worth visiting has bad neighborhoods and areas that a tourist is well advised to avoid. Software also has bad neighborhoods—those sections of the code populated by bugs. The difference between real tourists and exploratory testers, however, is that the former try to avoid bad neighborhoods, and the latter are well advised to spend as much time in them as possible.

Clearly, we do not know in advance which features are likely to represent bad neighborhoods. But as bugs are found and reported, we can connect certain features with bug counts and can track where bugs are occurring on our product. Because bugs tend to congregate,[8] revisiting buggy sections of the product is a tour worth taking. Indeed, once a buggy section of code is identified, it is recommended to take a Garbage Collector's tour through nearby features to verify that the fixes didn't introduce any new bugs.

The Museum Tour

Museums that display antiquities are a favorite of tourists. The Smithsonian and various museums of natural history draw many thousands of visitors on a daily basis. Antiquities within a code base deserve the same kind of attention from testers. In this case, software's antiquities are legacy code.

Untouched legacy code is easy to identify by a quick perusal of the date/time stamps in the code repository or on project binary and assembly files. Many source repositories also maintain a modification record, so testers can do a little research to see what older code may contain some recent modifications.

Older code files that undergo revision or that are put into a new environment tend to be failure prone. With the original developers long gone and documentation often poor, legacy code is hard to modify, hard to review, and evades the unit testing net of developers (who usually write such tests only for new code). During this tour, testers should identify older code and executable artifacts and ensure they receive a fair share of testing attention.

The Prior Version Tour

Whenever a product is constructed as an update from a prior version, it is good to run all the scenarios and test cases that applied to the prior version. This will validate that functionality that users are used to is still supported in a useful and usable way in the new product. In the event that the newer version reimplements or removes some functionality, the tester should choose the inputs that represent the new way of doing things as defined by the latest version. Any tours that are no longer possible in the new version should be scrutinized to ensure that no necessary functionality was lost.

Tours Through the Entertainment District

On every vacation, tourists will need a break from their busy schedule of fighting crowds and seeing the sites. Visiting the entertainment district, taking in a show, or having a long quiet dinner out is a common way of doing this. Entertainment districts aren't about seeing sites, they fill in the gaps of a vacation and give a local flavor to relaxation.

---

[8] Bugs congregate in features for any number of reasons. Because developers tend to be assigned to a project based on feature ownership, a single feature will have a proportion of bugs based on the skill of the individual developer. Bugs also congregate around complexity; so features that are harder to code may end up with more bugs. The idea here is that after a feature is shown to be buggy, there are very likely more bugs to be found in that feature if only you keep looking for them.

Most software has features that serve these purposes. For example, the business district for a word processor is the set of features to construct the document, write text, and insert graphics, tables, and artwork. The entertainment district, on the other hand, is the filler features for laying out pages, formatting text, and modifying backgrounds and templates. In other words, the work is in making the document and the "fun" part is making it look nice and represents an intellectual break from the actual work.

Tours through the entertainment district will visit supporting rather than mainline features and ensure that the two are intertwined in useful and meaningful ways.

The Supporting Actor Tour

I'm glad I started this chapter using London as my analogy because London is full of interesting sites and really cool buildings. On one of the many guided walking tours I've taken through nearly all parts of the city, I couldn't help but to be more attracted to the buildings that the guide was *not* pointing out than the ones he was telling us about. As he described a famous church that had historical significance, I found myself drawn to a short row house of buildings with rounded doors barely more than 5 feet high. It was like the hobbit portion of the city. On another stop, he was telling the story of pelicans that had been granted tenure in one of the city's parks. I found the pelican uninteresting, but a small island in the pond had a willow tree with a root structure that looked like dragon's teeth. I was enthralled.

Whenever salespeople demo a product or marketing touts some feature of our application, users are liable to be tempted by features nearby those in the spotlight. The *Supporting Actor tour* encourages testers to focus on those features that share the screen with the features we expect most users to exercise. Simply their proximity to the main event increases their visibility, and we must not make the mistake of giving those features less attention than they deserve.

Examples include that little link for similar products that most people skip in favor of clicking on the product they searched for. If a menu of items is presented and the second item is the most popular, choose the third. If the purchasing scenarios are the bread and butter, then select the product review feature. Wherever the other testers are looking, turn your attention a few degrees left or right and make sure that the supporting actor gets the attention it deserves.

In Chapter 6, Nicole Haugen shows how she used the Supporting Actor tour on the Dynamics AX client software.

The Back Alley Tour

In many peoples' eye, a good tour is one in which you visit popular places. The opposite of these tours would be one in which you visited places no one else was likely to go. A tour of public toilets comes to mind, or a swing through the industrial section of town. There are also so-called "behind the scenes" tours at places like Disney World or film studios where one can see how things work and go where tourists ordinarily don't tread. In exploratory testing terms, these are the least likely features to be used and the ones that are the least attractive to users.[9]

If your organization tracks feature usage, this tour will direct you to test the ones at the bottom of the list. If your organization tracks code coverage, this tour implores you to find ways to test the code yet to be covered.

An interesting variation on this theme is the *Mixed-Destination tour.* Try visiting a combination of the most popular features with the least popular. You can think of this as the Landmark tour with both large and small landmarks intermixed. It may just be that you find features that interact in ways you didn't expect because developers didn't anticipate them being mixed together in a single scenario.

Feature Interaction

It's a frustrating fact of testing life that you can test a feature to death and not find bugs only to then see it fail when it interacts with another feature. In reality, one would have to test every feature of an application with every other feature in pairs, triplets, and so on to determine whether they interact in ways that will make the software fail. Clearly, such an exhaustive strategy is impossible, and for the most part it is not necessary. Instead, there are ways to determine if two features need to be tested together.

I like to frame this problem as a series of questions. Simply select two candidate features and ask yourself the following:

- **The input question:** Is there an input that gets processed by both features in question?
- **The output question:** Do the features operate on the same portion of the visible UI? Do they generate or update the same output?
- **The data question:** Do the features operate on shared internal data? Do they use or modify the same internally stored information?

If the answer to any of these questions is "yes," then the features interact and need to be tested together.

In Chapter 6, Nicole Haugen, David Gorena Elizondo, and Geoff Staneff all use the Back Alley tour for a variety of testing tasks.

---

[9] It would be fair to ask whether we should test these features at all, but I feel that it is important that we do so. If the feature has made it into the product, it is important to someone somewhere. At companies like Microsoft and Google, the user base is so large that even the less-popular features can be used millions of times in a single day. In such cases, there really is no such thing as an unimportant feature. However, it is wise to proportion a testing budget in accordance with usage frequency as much as it is possible to do so.

The All-Nighter Tour

Also known as the *Clubbing tour,* this one is for those folks who stay out late and hit the nightspots. The key here is *all night.* The tour must never stop; there is always one more club and one last drink. Such tours, some believe, are tests of the constitution. Can you last? Can you survive the all-nighter?

For exploratory testers, the question is the same: Can the app last? How long can it run and process data before it just collapses? This is a real challenge for software. Because of the buildup of data in memory and the constant reading and writing (and rereading and rewriting) of variable values, bad things can happen if given time to do so. Memory leaks, data corruption, race conditions…there are many reasons to give time to your testing. And because closing and opening an application resets the clock and clears out memory, the logic behind this tour is to *never close the app.* This also extends to using features continuously and keeping files open continuously.

Exploratory testers on the *All-Nighter tour* will keep their application running without closing it. They will open files and not close them. Often, they don't even bother saving them so as to avoid any potential resetting effect that might occur at save time. They connect to remote resources and never disconnect. And while all these resources are in constant use, they may even run tests using other tours to keep the software working and moving data around. If they do this long enough, they may find bugs that other testers will not find because the software is denied that clean reset that occurs when it is restarted.

Many groups use dedicated machines that never get turned off and run automation in a loop. It is even more important to do this for mobile devices that often do stay on for days at a time as a normal course of usage. Of course, if there are different stages of reset, such as a sleep mode or hibernation mode, these can be used at varying rates as long as the software itself retains its state information.

Tours Through the Tourist District

Every city that focuses on tourism has a section of town where tourists congregate. It's full of souvenir shops, restaurants, and other things to maximize spending and ensure the profits of the local merchants. There are collectibles for sale, services to be bought, and pampering to be had.

Tours through the tourist district take several flavors. There are short trips to buy souvenirs, which are analogous to brief, special-purpose test cases. There are longer trips to visit a checklist of destinations. These tours are not about making the software work, they are about visiting its functionality quickly…just to say you've been there.

The Collector's Tour

My parents possess a map of the United States with every state shaded a different color. Those states all started out white, but as they visited each state on vacation, that state was then colored in on the map. It was their goal to visit all 50 states, and they went out of their way to add to their collection. One might say they were collecting states.

Sometimes a tour involves freebies that can be collected. Maybe it's a wine tasting or a fair with booths for children to work on some craft. Whatever it may be, there is always someone who wants to do everything, collect everything. Perhaps it's the guy who has to take a picture of every single statue in the museum, a lady who wants her kid to meet every overstuffed character at Disney World, or the guy at the supermarket who must consume every free sample on offer. Well, this is just the kind of greed that will come in handy to the exploratory tester.

For exploratory testers also collect things and strive for completeness. The *Collector's tour* suggests collecting *outputs* from the software; and the more one collects, the better. The idea behind this tour is to go everywhere you can and document (as my parents did on their state map) all the outputs you see. Make sure you see the software generate every output it can generate. For a word processor, you would make sure it can print, spell check, format text, and so on. You may create a document with every possible structure, table, chart, or graphic. For an online shopping site, you need to see a purchase from every department, credit card transactions that succeed and ones that fail, and so on and so forth. Every possible outcome needs to be pursued until you can claim that you have been everywhere, seen everything, and completed your collection.

This is such a large tour that it is often good to take it as a group activity. Divvy up the features among members of the group or assign certain outputs to specific individuals for collection. And when a new version of the application is ready for testing, one needs to throw away all the outputs for the features that have changed and restart the collection.

The Collector's tour is demonstrated by Nicole Haugen in Chapter 6.

The Lonely Businessman Tour

I have a friend (whom I won't name given the rather derogatory title of this tour) who travels a great deal on business. He has visited many of the world's great cities, but mostly sees the airport, the hotel, and the office. To remedy this situation, he has adopted the strategy of booking a hotel as far away from the office he's visiting as possible. He then walks, bikes, or takes a taxi to the office, forcing him to see some of the sites and get a flavor of the city.

Exploratory testers can perform a variety of this tour that can be very effective. The idea is to visit (and, of course, test) the feature that is furthest away from the application's starting point as possible. Which feature takes the most clicks to get to? Select that one, click your way to it, and test it. Which feature requires the most screens to be navigated before it does anything useful? Select it and test it. The idea is to travel as far through the application as possible before reaching your destination. Choose long paths over short paths. Choose the page that is the buried deepest within the application as your target.

You may even decide to execute the Garbage Collector's tour both on the way to such a destination and once you get where you are going.

The Supermodel Tour

For this tour, I want you to think superficially. Whatever you do, don't go beyond skin deep. This tour is not about function or substance; it's about looks and first impressions. Think of this as the cool tour that all the beautiful people take; not because the tour is meaningful or a great learning experience. On the contrary, you take this tour just to be *seen.*

Get the idea? During the *Supermodel tour,* the focus is not on functionality or real interaction. It's only on the interface. Take the tour and watch the interface elements. Do they look good? Do they render properly, and is the performance good? As you make changes, does the GUI refresh properly? Does it do so correctly or are there unsightly artifacts left on the screen? If the software is using color in a way to convey some meaning, is this done consistently? Are the GUI panels internally consistent with buttons and controls where you would expect them to be? Does the interface violate any conventions or standards?

Software that passes this test may still be buggy in many other ways, but just like the supermodel…it is going to look really good standing at your side.

The Supermodel tour is used extensively in Chapter 6. Along with the Landmark tour and the Intellectual's tour, it was used on every pilot project at Microsoft.

The TOGOF Tour

This tour is a play on the acronym for Buy One Get One Free—BOGOF—that is popular among shoppers. The term is more common in the United Kingdom than the United States, but in either case it is not just for groceries and cheap shoes anymore. The idea isn't for the exploratory tester to buy anything, but instead to *Test One Get One Free.*

The *TOGOF tour* is a simple tour designed only to test for multiple copies of the same application running simultaneously. Start the tour by running your application, then starting another copy, and then another. Now put them through their paces by using features that cause each application to do something in memory and something on the disk. Try using all the different copies to open the same file or have them all transmit data over the network simultaneously. Perhaps they will stumble over each other in some way or do something incorrect when they all try to read from and write to the same file.

Why is it a TOGOF? Well, if you find a bug in one copy, you've found a bug in all of them! David Gorena Elizondo demonstrates how he applied this tour to Visual Studio in Chapter 6.

The Scottish Pub Tour

My friend Adam Shostack (the author of *The New School of Information Security*) was visiting Amsterdam when he had a chance meeting with a group of Scottish tourists. (The kilts betrayed their nationality as much as their accents.) They were members of a pub-crawling troupe with international tastes. He joined them on a pub tour of the city that he readily concedes consisted of venues he would never have found without their guidance. The pubs ranged from small, seedy joints to community gathering places buried in neighborhoods more than a little off the beaten path.

How many such places exist in my own town, I wonder? There are many places that you can find only by word of mouth and meeting the right guide.

This tour applies specifically to large and complicated applications. Microsoft Office products fit this category. So do sites such as eBay, Amazon, and MSDN. There are places in those applications that you have to know about to find.

This isn't to say they receive hardly any usage, they are just hard to find. Adam tells stories of many of the pubs on his Scottish tour fairly heaving with people. The trick is in finding them.

But testers can't depend on chance meetings at hotels with kilt-wearing guides. We have to meet the guides where they are. This means finding and talking to user groups, reading industry blogs, and spending a great deal of time touring the depths of your application.

Tours Through the Hotel District

The hotel is a place of sanctuary for the tourist. It is a place to get away from the hustle and bustle of the vacation hotspots for a little rest and relaxation. It is also a place for the software tester to get away from the primary functionality and popular features and test some of the secondary and supporting functions that are often ignored or under-represented in a test plan.

The Rained-Out Tour

Once again, my selection of London as my tourist base pays off because sometimes even the best tours get rained out. If you've taken a pub tour in London between the autumn and spring months, it can be a wet, rainy affair, and you may well find yourself tempted to cut the tour short at the second stop. For the tourist, I do not recommend this tactic. You are already wet, and that's just going to ensure that the next pub feels even better than the last once you manage to actually get there. But for the exploratory tester, I highly recommend use of that cancel button.

The idea behind the *Rained-Out tour* is to start operations and stop them. We may enter information to search for flights on a travel website only to cancel them after the search begins. We may print a document only to cancel it before the document is complete. We will do the same thing for any feature that provides a cancel option or that takes longer than a few seconds to complete.

Exploratory testers must seek out the time-consuming operations that their application possesses to use this attack to its fullest. Search capabilities are the obvious example, and using terms that make for a longer search is a tactic that will make this tour a little easier. Also, every time a cancel button appears, click it. If there is no cancel button, try the Esc key or even the back button for apps that run in a browser. There's always Shift-F4 or closing the X button to close the application completely. And try this, too: Start an operation, and then start it again without stopping the first.

The failures you will see on this tour are mostly related to the inability of the application to clean up after itself. There are often files left open, data left clogging up internal variables, and a state of the system that is no longer tenable for the software to do much else. So after you hit cancel (etc.), take some time to poke around the application to make sure it is still working properly. At the very least, you want to make sure that whatever action you canceled should be able to be exercised again and complete successfully. After all, one would expect a user to occasionally cancel something and then try again.

The Rained-Out tour is used extensively in Chapter 6.

The Couch Potato Tour

There's always one person on a group tour who just doesn't participate. He stands in the back with his arms folded. He's bored, unenergetic, and makes one wonder exactly why he bothered paying for the tour in the first place. However, on such tours, the guide is often prompted to work harder to try to draw the couch potato in and help him enjoy the tour.

From the tourist's perspective, it sounds like, and probably is, a waste of time. But it's exactly the opposite for software testers. Couch potatoes can make very effective testers! The reason is simple, even if it is not intuitive: Just because the tester isn't doing much does not mean that the software follows suit. Like the diligent tour guide, it's often the case that nonactivity forces software to work very hard because it is busy executing the "else" clauses in IF-THEN-ELSE conditions and figuring out what to do when the user leaves data fields blank. A great deal of "default logic" executes when a user declines to take the initiative.

A *Coach Potato tour* means doing as little actual work as possible. This means accepting all default values (values prepopulated by the application), leaving input fields blank, filling in as little form data as possible, never clicking on an advertisement, paging through screens without clicking any buttons or entering any data, and so forth. If there is any choice to go one way in the application or another, the coach potato always takes the path of least resistance.

As lazy as this sounds, and granted the tester does little real interaction, this does not mean the software is not working. Software must process default values, and it must run the code that handles blank input. As my father used to say (mostly during basketball games…I grew up in Kentucky, where the sport of hoops ruled), "That spot on the couch doesn't keep itself warm." And the same can be said of those default values and error-checking code: It doesn't execute itself, and missing default cases are far too common and very embarrassing in released products.

Tours Through the Seedy District

Much of the material presented in Chapter 3, "Exploratory Testing in the Small," would fit into this district if you could blend it into a tour. Inputs meant to break the software and do general harm are seedy in nature and fit the general purpose of these tours.

The Saboteur

This is the *Saboteur tour,* and during it we will attempt to undermine the application at every possible opportunity. We will ask the application to read from the disk (by opening a file or using some disk resource), but then sabotage its attempt to do so by rigging the file operations to fail (perhaps by corrupting the file in question). We will also ask it to do some memory-intensive operation when the application is either on a machine with too little memory or when other applications are operating in the background and consuming most of the memory resources.

This tour is simple to conceptualize:

- Force the software to take some action.
- Understand the resources it requires to successfully complete that action.
- Remove or restrict those resources in varying degrees.

During this tour, a tester will find that there are many ways to rig environments by adding or deleting files, changing file permissions, unplugging network cables, running other applications in the background, deploying the application under test on a machine that has known problems, and so forth. We might also employ the concept of *fault injection*[10] to artificially create errant environmental conditions.

The saboteur is very popular at Microsoft, using fault-injection tools and simpler mechanisms that are illustrated in Chapter 6. In particular, Shawn Brown has used this tour extensively on Windows Mobile.

The Antisocial Tour

Pub tours are one of my personal passions, and I enjoy them on my own or as part of a guided walk. I recall a specific tour in which a husband clearly had coerced his wife to accompany him. She wanted no part of the tour. When we went into a pub, she stayed outside. When it was time to leave the pub, she would walk in and order a drink. When we admired scenery or some landmark, she suddenly found a common squirrel fascinating. Everything the tour took in, she made it a point to do the opposite. She was so successful that at the end of the tour another tourist handed her husband his business card; that other tourist was a divorce attorney.

---

[10] The concept of runtime fault injection is covered in detail in *How to Break Software* from page 81 to 120, and again in Appendixes A and B.

An attorney with a sense of humor notwithstanding, I found her antisocial behavior absolutely inspiring from a test point of view. Exploratory testers are often trying specifically to break things; and being nice, kind, and following the crowd is seldom the best way to accomplish that goal. As a tester, it pays to be antisocial. So if a developer hands you the business card of a divorce attorney, you may consider it the highest of compliments.

The *Antisocial tour* requires entering either the least likely inputs and/or known bad inputs. If a real user would do *a,* then a tester on the Antisocial tour should never do *a* and instead find a much less meaningful input.

There are three specific ways to accomplish such antisocial behavior, which I organize here into subtours:

- The *Opposite tour* is performed by entering the least likely input every chance you get. Testers taking this tour select inputs that are out of context, just plain stupid, or totally nonsensical. How many of that item do you want in your shopping cart? 14,963. How many pages to print? –12. The idea is to apply the input that is the least likely input you can come up with for a specific input field. By doing so, you are testing the application's error-handling capability. If it helps, think of it as testing the application's patience!
- Illegal inputs are handled during the *Crime Spree tour,* and the idea here is to apply inputs that should *not* occur. You wouldn't expect a tourist to steal a pint on a pub tour, but on a crime spree that's the analogous behavior. You'll do the things that are not just antisocial, but downright illegal.

  Breaking the law as a tourist will land you in trouble or in jail; breaking the law as a tester will result in lots of error messages. Expect the Crime Spree tour inputs to invoke error messages, and if they do not, you may very well have a bug on your hands. Enter inputs that are the wrong type, the wrong format, too long, too short, and so forth. Think in terms of "what constraints are associated with this input," and then break those constraints. If the application wants a positive number, give it a negative number. If it wants an integer, give it a character. Keeping a tally of the error messages will be important for the next few chapters, where these tours will actually be used.
- Another aspect of antisocial behavior is embodied in the *Wrong Turn Tour*, which directs the tester to do things in the wrong order. Take a bunch of legal actions and mix them around so that the sequence is illegal. Try checking out before putting anything in your shopping cart. Try returning an item you didn't purchase. Try to change the delivery options before you complete your purchase.

The Obsessive-Compulsive Tour

I'm not quite sure such a tour in real life would be all that popular, and only its name made me put it in the seedy district. I can't actually imagine that a walking tour in which you can't step on any sidewalk cracks would gain many customers beyond the kindergarten demographic. Nor would a bus that drives only on a single street—just because the driver is desperate not to miss anything—find many riders. But being obsessive in testing can pay off.

OCD testers will enter the same input over and over. They will perform the same action over and over. They will repeat, redo, copy, paste, borrow, and then do all that some more. Mostly, the name of the game is repetition. Order an item on a shopping site and then order it again to check if a multiple purchase discount applies. Enter some data on a screen, then return immediately to enter it again. These are actions developers often don't program error cases for. They can wreak significant havoc.

Developers are often thinking about a user doing things in a specific order and using the software with purpose. But users make mistakes and have to backtrack, and they often don't understand what specific path the developer had in mind for them, and they take their own. This can cause a usage scheme carefully laid by developers to fall by the wayside quickly. It's better to find this out in testing than after release, which makes this an important tour for testers to complete.

Putting the Tours to Use

Tours give a structure to testing and help guide testers to more interesting and relevant scenarios than they would ordinarily come up with using only freestyle testing. By giving a goal to testers, the tours help guide them through interesting usage paths that tend to be more sophisticated than traditional feature-oriented testing where an individual tester will try to test a single feature in isolation.

Features are a common pivot for testers. A test manager may divide an application into features and distribute those features across her testers. Testing features in isolation will miss many important bugs that users, who mostly use features in combination and in sequence, will encounter. The tours are an important tool for testers to discover interesting ways of combining features and functionality in single test cases and in sets of test cases: The more interaction, the more thorough the testing.

Repeatability is another aspect of using the tours that I have noticed in practice. If two testers are told "go test this app," it is very likely that the two of them will test it in completely different ways. If the same two testers are told "go run this tour," they will tend to do very similar things and likely even identify the same bugs. The built-in strategy and goal of the tour makes them more repeatable and transferable among testers. It also helps a great deal in educating testers about what constitutes good test design as the tours guide testers through the question of *what should I test*.

Some tours are very likely to find many more problems than other tours, and if careful records are kept, the tours can be rank-ordered late in the cycle when every single test case counts. Testers should track which ones find the most bugs, take the least amount of time to execute, cover the most code/UI/features, and so forth. This is a side benefit of using actual strategy to organize testing; the tours provide specific categories of tests that we can rule in or out as better or worse in some situations. That way, over time, we can refine our methods and techniques and improve our testing from project to project. You'll only understand which tours are working if you pay attention and track your progress in finding bugs, discovering usability or performance problems, or simply verifying functionality in a cost- and time-effective manner.

The tours are an excellent way of distributing testing needs among members of a test team. As you gain comfort with the tours, patterns will emerge about which tours find certain classes of bugs and which are compatible with a specific feature. It is important that such knowledge gets documented and becomes part of the testing culture within your organization. Thus the tours not only become a way to test, they are also a way to organize testing and improve the spread and retention of testing knowledge across your team.

In many ways, that is what testing is all about: doing your best this time and making sure that next time you do even better. The tourist metaphor helps us organize according to this purpose.

Conclusion

Tours represent a mechanism to both organize a tester's thinking about how to approach exploring an application and in organizing actual testing. A list of tours can be used as a "did you think about this" checklist and also help a tester match application features to test techniques that will properly exercise them.

Furthermore, the tours help testers make the myriad decisions about which paths to choose, inputs to apply, or parameters to select. Certain decisions are simply more in the spirit of the selected tour than others and thus naturally emerge as "better" choices. This is testing guidance in its purest form.

Finally, at Microsoft, the tours are seen as a mechanism for gathering tribal knowledge, in that some tours will eventually establish a track record of success. In Visual Studio, the Landmark tour and the Intellectual tour have become part of the everyday language of our test community. Testers know what those tours are, how to apply them, and have a general idea of how much coverage and what types of bugs will ensue. It makes discussing testing easier and becomes part of the way we train new testers on our teams.

Exercises

1. Write your own tour! Using the tours discussed in this chapter as a guide, create your own tour. Your tour should have a name, a tie-in with the tourist metaphor, and you should use it on some software system and describe how the tour helps you test.
2. Find at least two tours that give similar testing advice. In other words, the tours might end up discovering the same bug or covering the same features in an application. Give an example testing scenario where the two tours cause a tester to do roughly the same test.
3. Using your favorite web application (eBay, Amazon, MySpace, and so on), write a test case for that application using any five of the tours discussed in this chapter as a guide.

CHAPTER 5
Hybrid Exploratory Testing Techniques

0110010110110001 0100

"When you have a good script you're almost in more trouble than when you have a terrible script."
—*Robert Downey, Jr.*

Scenarios and Exploration

As the preceding two chapters have shown, exploratory testing has a great deal of strategy associated with it. It is a good combination of structured thinking and freestyle exploration that can be very powerful for finding bugs and verifying correctness. This chapter shows how the exploratory testing mindset can be combined with more traditional scenario-based and scripted testing. This hybrid technique relaxes much of the rigidity ordinarily associated with scripting and makes good use of the exploratory testing guidance presented in the last two chapters. It also allows teams that are heavily vested in existing scripts to add exploratory testing to their arsenal.

Traditional scenario testing is very likely to be a familiar concept for the reader. Many testers write or follow some sort of script or end-to-end scenario when they perform manual testing. Scenario testing is popular because it lends confidence that the product will reliably perform the scenario for actual users. The more the scenario reflects expected usage, the more such confidence is gained. The added component that exploratory testing lends to this process is to inject variation into the scenario so that a wider swath of the product gets tested. Users cannot be constrained to just execute the software the way we intend, so our testing should expand to cover these additional scenario variants.

Scenario-based exploration will cover cases that simple scenario testing will not and more accurately mimics real users, who often stray from the main scenario: After all, the product allows many possible variations. We should not only expect that they get used, we should test that they will work.

The idea behind scenario-based exploratory testing is to use existing scenarios (we talk about where to get scenarios in this chapter) much as real explorers use a map to guide themselves through a wilderness or other unfamiliar terrain. Scenarios, like maps, are a general guide about what to do during testing, which inputs to select, and which code paths to traverse, but they are not absolutes. Maps may describe the location of your destination but offer multiple ways to get there. Likewise, the exploratory tester is offered alternate routes and even encouraged to consider a wide range of possible paths when executing a scenario. In fact, that's the exact purpose of this form of exploratory testing: to test the functionality described by the scenario, adding as much variation as possible. Our "map" isn't intended to identify the shortest route, it's intended to find *many* routes. The more we can test, the better; this leads to more confidence that the software will perform the scenario robustly when it is in the hands of users who can and will deviate from our expectations.

There is no formal definition of scenarios that I know of which really helps testers. Some scenarios are like maps, providing only general guidance, and others are more like printed driving directions with step-by-step instructions for every turn and intersection. In general, scenarios are written prose that follow no fixed format but describe how the features and functionality of the software under test work to solve user problems. A scenario can describe inputs, data sources, environment conditions (things such as Registry settings, available memory, file sizes, and so forth) as well as UI elements, outputs, and specific information about how the software under test is supposed to react when it is used.

The scenarios themselves often originate from outside the tester's domain. They can be gleaned from artifacts inherited from design and development. Requirements documents and specifications typically describe their purpose in the form of scenarios. Marketing departments sometimes work with scripts for product demos; some forms of agile development require the creation of user stories; requirements are often documented with example scenarios of expected usage. In many cases, testers don't need to write the scenarios as much as gather them. In fact, recordings made (using capture/replay tools, keystroke recorders, and so forth) during testing are also legitimate scenarios, and thus the tours of the previous chapter can be the source of a great number of high-quality scripts and scenarios. Any and all such scenarios can be used as the starting point for exploration.

In general, a useful scenario will do one or more of the following:

- **Tell a user story**

  Scenarios that tell user stories generally document a user's motivation, goals, and actions when using the software. User stories aren't often at the detailed level of "the users clicks here," but more general, as in "the user enters her banking information." It's the job of the tester to bring the scenario down to a level of detail appropriate for a test case.

  User stories are an excellent starting point for exploratory testing.

- **Describe a requirement**

  Requirements are capabilities that the software possesses, and written requirements are usually plentiful for software projects of any decent size. Scenarios that describe requirements should talk about how the product is used to perform that capability.

- **Demonstrate how a feature works**

  Scenarios that demonstrate features are usually pretty detailed and specific. They would specify which menus are used, which buttons are pressed, and what data is entered at a fine level of detail. These often appear in online help or printed instructions for users.

- **Demonstrate an integration scenario**

  Products that integrate with other applications or share information often have integration or end-to-end (abbreviated e2e) scenarios defined for them. In this case, scenarios document how features work together and how a user would use those integrated features on some real task.

- **Describe setup and installation**

  Instructions that describe initial installation procedures, setup and configuration, account creation or other administrative tasks, optional installation flags, and customization can readily be used as scenarios for exploratory testing. Guidance from user manuals and online help systems are an excellent source of scenarios for setup and installation.

- **Describe cautions and things that could go wrong**

  Documents that describe troubleshooting and maintenance procedures make very good scenarios. Because these are the features a user would exercise in the event something goes wrong, it is important that they work correctly. Artifacts such as threat models or attack trees that describe tampering attempts are also a good source of such "negative" usage scenarios.

Exploratory testers should work hard to ensure they gather as many scenarios as possible from all of these categories. It is then our task to follow the scenarios and inject variation as we see fit. It is how we choose to inject this variation that makes this task exploratory in nature and that is the subject we turn to next.

Applying Scenario-Based Exploratory Testing

Testers often use scenarios that describe user intent to test the software. Scenario testing works because it mimics the way a real user would behave, and thus it finds bugs that, if they survived testing, would plague actual users.

But seldom do real users confine themselves to usage of the software as described by the scenario. Users are free to vary from the scenario by adding steps or taking them away, and they do so according to their own schedules and timetables. It is our task to second-guess such variation and ensure they get tested because they represent some of the most likely ways in which the software will be used after it has been released.

Injecting variation into scenarios is what this form of exploratory testing is all about. A single written scenario can be turned into many individual test cases by methodically considering choices in input selection, data usage, and environmental conditions. Two main techniques are used to accomplish this: scenario operators and tours.

Introducing Variation Through Scenario Operators

Exploratory testing can be combined with scenario testing to help a tester explore minor and even major variations on a specific scenario. Where a scenario describes specific actions for a tester to take, the techniques described next can be used to permute those actions and create deviations from the scenario that will test different states and code paths. Where a scenario describes general activity, these techniques can be used to select among the possible choices and allow a tester to consider alternate paths in a more methodical manner.

We introduce the concept of *scenario operators* to achieve this goal. Scenario operators are constructs that operate on steps within a scenario to inject variation into the scenario. When we apply a scenario operator to an existing scenario, we get a new scenario that we call a *derived scenario.* A tester can apply one or more scenario operators to a given scenario and even apply operators to derived scenarios. The amount and number of such operators is, in true exploratory fashion, up to the individual tester and can be performed in advance of testing or, my preference, on-the-fly.

The scenario operators in the following subsections are the ones most testers will find useful.

Inserting Steps

Adding additional steps to a scenario can make them more diverse and allow them to test more functionality. Inserting one or more steps into a scenario creates more opportunity for the software to fail. Code paths may be executed with different data, and the state of the software will be varied in ways that are different from what the original scenario allowed. The additional steps can be

- **Adding more data:** When the scenario asks for, say, 10 records to be added to a database, the tester should increase that to 20 or 30 records or even more if it makes sense to do so. If the scenario requires an item to be added to the shopping cart, add that item and then some additional items on top of that. It is useful also to add related data so that if the scenario calls for a new account to be created, we may also add information to that account over and above what the scenario calls for.

The tester should ask herself, "What data is used in this scenario and how would it make sense to increase the amount of data I enter?"

- **Using additional inputs:** When the scenario calls for a series of inputs to be entered, find more inputs that can be added. If the scenario asks that the tester create a product review for some online shopping site, the tester can choose to add ratings for other customer reviews, too. The idea is to understand what additional features are related to the features in the scenario and add inputs to test those new features as well.

  The tester should ask herself, "What other inputs are related to the inputs used in the existing scenario?"

- **Visiting a new part of the UI:** When the scenario calls for specific screens and dialog boxes to be used, the tester should identify other screens or dialogs and add those to the scenario. If the scenario calls for a tester to pay a bill on a financial services website, the tester could choose to also visit the pages to check account balances before submitting the payment.

  The tester should ask herself, "What other parts of the UI are related to the parts used in the existing scenario?"

Eventually, the steps need to loop back into the original scenario. It helps to keep in mind that the idea is to enhance the scenario, not to change it from its fundamental purpose. If the scenario was meant to add records to the database, that should still be its primary purpose, and that goal should not change. What the tester is doing in this scenario operator is adding inputs, data, or variation that makes the scenario longer but does not alter its core purpose.

Removing Steps

Redundant and optional steps can also be removed with the idea being to reduce the scenario to its shortest possible length. The derived scenario may then be missing steps that set preconditions for other steps, testing the application's ability to recognize missing information and dependent functionality.

A tester can apply this scenario operator in an iterative fashion, removing one step at a time. In this case, the scenario actually gets executed against the software under test each time a step is removed until the minimal test case ends the cycle. For example, a scenario that requires a tester to log on to a shopping site, search for items, add them to a shopping cart, enter account info, complete the purchase, and finally log off would be eventually reduced to just logging on and logging off (an interesting and important case to test!) with a single step being removed each time the test case is run.

Replacing Steps

If there is more than one way to accomplish some specific step in a scenario, this scenario operator is the way to modify the scenario to accomplish that. It's really a combination of the preceding two operators in that replacement is the same thing as removing and then adding.

The tester must research alternate ways of performing each of the steps or actions in a scenario. For example, instead of searching for an item to purchase, we might simply use its item number to look it up directly. Because the software under test provides both of these as options, we can create a derived scenario to test the alternative. Similarly, we might use keyboard shortcuts instead of the mouse or choose to bypass creating an account and just purchase an item without registering on the site. Testers need to be aware of all the different options and functionality that exists within their application to be truly effective at applying this scenario operator.

Repeating Steps

Scenarios often contain very specific sequences of actions. This operator modifies such a sequence by repeating steps individually or in groups to create additional variation. By repeating and reordering steps, we are testing new code paths and potentially finding bugs related to data initialization. If one feature initializes a data value that is used by another feature, the order in which the two features is executed matters, and reordering them may cause a failure.

Often, certain actions make sense to repeat. For example, if we are testing a financial services website for the general scenario of log in to an account, check the balance, pay bills, make a deposit, and then log out, we may repeat the "check the balance" action after we pay the bills, and then again after making the deposit. The general scenario is the same, but we have repeated an action that a user is also likely to do. The same can be said of actions such as "view the shopping cart," which could happen over and over during a scenario for an online shopping site.

Repetition can also occur with multiple actions, so that we pay one bill, check the balance, pay another bill, check the balance, and so forth. The tester's task is to understand the variability and create repetitive sequences as appropriate.

Data Substitution

It is often the case that a scenario will require a connection to some database, data file, or other local or remote data source. The scenario then specifies actions that the tester performs to cause that data to be read, modified, or manipulated in some way. Testers need to be aware of the data sources that the application under test interacts with and be able to offer variations.

Are there backup databases, alternate test databases, real customer databases, and so forth that are accessible to testers? If so, use those when testing the scenarios instead of the default. What if the data source is down or otherwise unavailable? Can we create or simulate that situation so that we can test how the system under test reacts? What if the data source holds ten times as many records? What if it only holds one record?

The idea here is to understand the data sources the application connects to or uses and to make sure that interaction is robust.

Environment Substitution

As discussed in Chapter 3, "Exploratory Testing in the Small," testing is necessarily dependent on the environment in which the software resides when we run our test cases. We can run billions of tests successfully when the software is in one environment only to have them all fail when the software is put into a different environment. Therefore, this operator is used to ensure those alternate environments receive testing.

The simple part of this operator is that the scenarios themselves don't actually change, only the system on which the software is running when the scenario is applied. Unfortunately, understanding which parts of the environment to change, and actually enacting that change, is very difficult. Here are some considerations:

- **Substitute the hardware:** The easiest part of the environment to vary is the hardware on which the application under test case runs. If we expect our users to have a range of hardware from fast and powerful to antiquated and slow, we need to acquire similar machines for our test lab and ensure that we have beta customers willing to help us with testing and pre-release validation. Of course, this is an excellent use of virtual machines as well.
- **Substitute the container:** If our application runs inside a so-called container application (like a browser), we need to ensure that our scenarios run in all the major containers we expect our user to have access to. Browsers like Internet Explorer, Firefox, Opera, and Chrome or platforms like Java or .NET or even animation tools like Flash and Silverlight will impact the way our applications run.
- **Swap out the version:** All the previous containers also have earlier versions that still enjoy market share. How does your app run in the earlier versions of Flash?
- **Modify local settings:** Does your application use cookies or write files to user machines? Does it use the local Registry? What happens when users modify their browser settings to limit these types of activity? What happens if they change your application's Registry settings directly (without going through your app)? If you don't test these things, your users likely will, and their doing so may bring a nasty post-release surprise to your engineering team. It's better to find out for yourself before the app ships how it will handle these things.

When using any of these operators to create derived scenarios, it is generally the case that we try to stay as true to the original scenario as possible. Using too many operators or using operators in such a way as to make the origin of the derived scenarios unrecognizable is usually not useful. But don't take my word for it. If you try it and it finds good bugs, then it's a useful technique! However, such broader based modification of tours is the job of the second technique to inject variation in scenarios: tours. This is the subject we turn to next.

Introducing Variation Through Tours

At any point in the execution of a scenario, one can stop and inject variations that will create derived scenarios. The scenario operators described above are one way to do this, and using the tours is another. I like to think of this use of tours as *side trips*. The idea is simple: A tester reviews the scripts looking for places where decisions can be made or places where it is possible to fork the logic within the script and go in a completely different direction before returning to the main path dictated by the script.

I like to use the analogy of a car tour or even a hike in the woods on foot. It's often that on such a trip there is some scenic overlook at which one can park the car and take a short walk to some monument or beautiful view before returning to the car and continuing the voyage. That short side trip represents the tour, and the longer car ride is the scenario. This is a useful technique for adding variation to scenarios.

The key difference between scenario operators and tours is that tours end up creating longer side trips, in general, than operators. Operators focus on small, incremental changes and optional steps in a scenario, and tours can actually create derived scenarios that are significantly longer and broader in scope. Just as some side trips can turn into a destination all their own, it may be that the tours overwhelm the original scenario, and this can actually be a very desirable effect. It's good to always remember that exploratory testing is about variation, and when scenarios are combined with tours, the result can add significant variation. It's up to the tester to determine whether the variation is useful, and it is often the case that one has to build up some history to determine which tours are most effective for a given application.

Here is a list of tours that are effective as side trips during scenario-based exploratory testing. I suggest rereading the actual tour as presented in Chapter 3 along with the additional description here. After you practice the tours a few times, you should be able to determine how to best follow this advice for your particular situation.

The Money Tour

Can any major features not already used in the scenario be easily incorporated into the scenario? If so, modify the scenario to include the use of a new feature or features. Assuming that the original scenario already included some features, this will help test feature interaction in a scenario-driven way. If the scenario was a realistic user scenario, it's even better because we are mimicking the user including another feature into his existing work habits (as represented by the scenario). There are many users who will learn a feature, master it, and then move on to new features as their familiarity with the application grows. This technique mimics that usage pattern.

The Landmark Tour

Start with a scenario and pick specific feature landmarks out of the scenario. Now randomize the order of the landmarks so that it is different than the original scenario. Run some tests with the new order of landmark features and repeat this process as often as you think is necessary. Obviously, that will depend on how many landmarks you are dealing with; use your own judgment. This combination of the Landmark tour within a structured scenario has been very valuable at Microsoft.

The Intellectual Tour

Review the scenario and modify it so that it makes the software work harder. In other words, *ask the software hard questions.* If the scenario requires the software to open a file, what is the most complicated file you can give it? If the software asks for data, what is the data that will make it work the hardest? Would very long strings do the trick? What about input that breaks formatting rules (for example, Ctrl characters, Esc sequences, and special characters)?

The Back Alley Tour

This is an interesting variation on the Money tour. Both tours suggest we inject new features into the scenario, but the Back Alley tour suggest the least likely or least useful features instead. Granted, this variation will find more obscure bugs, but if an application is widely used, there may be no such thing as least likely because every single feature will get used by someone, and all paying customers are important.

The Obsessive-Compulsive Tour

This one is straightforward: Repeat every step of the scenario twice. Or three times. Be as obsessive as you like!

Specifically, any step in a scenario that manipulates data is a good one to repeat because it will cause internal data to be manipulated and internal state to be set and then changed. Moving data around the software is always an effective way to test and to find important bugs.

The All-Nighter Tour

This one is best when a scenario can be automated or even recorded and then played back. Just run the scenario over and over without ever exiting the application under test. If the scenario specifies that the software be shut down, remove that clause and keep the scenario running over and over again. Choose scenarios (or even derived scenarios) that make the software work hard, use memory and the network, and otherwise consume resources that might over time cause problems.

The Saboteur

Scenarios are a great start for sabotage. Review the scenario or derived scenario and make a note every time it uses some resource (another computer, the network, file system, or another local resource) that you have access to, and then when you execute the scenario, sabotage that resource when the scenario calls for it to be used.

For example, if a scenario causes data to be transmitted over a network, unplug the network cable (or disconnect it via the OS or turn off the radio switch for wireless connections) just before or while you are executing that particular step of the scenario. Document all such sabotage points and execute as many of them as sensible or prudent.

The Collector's Tour

Document every output you see as you execute scenarios and derived scenarios. You can even score scenarios based on the number of such outputs they force. The more outputs, the higher the score for that scenario. Can you create (or derive) new scenarios that cause outputs that are not in any of the other scenarios? Can you create a super scenario that causes the absolute maximum number of outputs possible? Make a game out of it and let your testers compete to see who can generate the most outputs, and give prizes to the winners.

The Supermodel Tour

Run the scenario but don't look past the interface. Make sure everything is where it is supposed to be, that the interface is sensible, and watch particularly for usability problems. Choose scenarios that manipulate data, and then cause it to be displayed on the UI. Force the data to be displayed and redisplayed as often as possible and look for screen-refresh problems.

The Supporting Actor Tour

I think of this as the *Nearest-Neighbor tour,* in that instead of exercising the features as described in the script, the testers find the nearest neighboring feature instead.

For example, if a scenario specifies an item on a drop-down menu, choose the item above or below the one specified. Whenever a choice is presented in the scenario, choose not the one suggested but one right next to it (either by proximity on the interface or close in semantic meaning). If the scenario specifies using italics, use boldface; if it wants you to highlight some text, highlight other text instead, always choosing that which is "nearest" in whatever way makes the most sense.

The Rained-Out Tour

This is the tour that not only makes good use of the cancel button (press it whenever you see it while running the scenario) but also in starting and stopping execution. Review the scenarios for time-consuming tasks such as complicated searches, file transfers, and the like. Start those features, and then cancel them using provided cancel buttons, hitting the Escape key and so forth.

The Tour-Crasher Tour

This tour is new for this chapter and didn't appear earlier when the tourist metaphor was first described. Indeed, it is specific to scenario-based testing. The concept is based on those people who don't pay for the tour when it begins, but join it in progress by simply melting into the crowd and acting like they've been there all the time. They not only crash a tour, but they also may even hop from tour to tour as they encounter other groups (in a museum or some historical building where tours are continuous) of tourists.

We're going to adopt this process for hopping from scenario to scenario as a way of combining two or more scenarios into a single scenario of mixed purpose. Review your scenarios and find ones that operate on common data, focus on common features, or have steps in common. It is this overlap that will allow you to seamlessly leave one scenario and pick up the remainder of another. Just like the guy who peels himself away from one tour and melts into the crowd of another. He's able to do it because for some small period of time, the two tour groups are sharing the same space on the museum floor. We're able to do it as testers because the scenarios both go through the same part of the application. We'll follow one scenario to that place but then follow the other when we leave it.

Conclusion

Static scenario testing and exploratory testing do not have to be at odds. Scenarios can represent an excellent starting point for exploration, and exploration can add valuable variation to otherwise limited scenarios. A wise tester can combine the two methods for better application coverage and variation of input sequences, code paths, and data usage.

Exercises

1. Name the two ways to create derived scenarios from existing scripts or scenarios as described in this chapter. Which one do you think would be likely to find the most bugs? Justify your answer.
2. Name and describe at least three software development artifacts from which scenarios can be gathered. Can you come up with a way to create a scenario that is not described in this chapter?
3. When creating derived scenarios, what is the primary difference between using tours and using scenario operators? Which will yield the most variation from the original scenario?
4. Which scenario operator is related to the Obsessive-Compulsive tour? How would one get the same derived scenario from this operator and the OCD tour?
5. Pick a tour from the previous chapter that is not used in this chapter and see whether you can reason about how it might be used effectively in scenario-based exploratory testing.
6. What properties of a scenario would make it a good candidate for the All-Nighter tour? Why?

CHAPTER 6
Exploratory Testing in Practice

0110010110110001 0100

"Not all who wander are lost."

—*J. R. R. Tolkien*

The Touring Test

A testing technique is nothing until it leaves home and makes a name for itself in the real world. It is one thing to talk of adventure and travel, and quite another to live it. This chapter was written by the first testers to apply the tourism metaphor purposefully on real projects and under real ship pressure.

The in-the-small and especially in-the-large techniques were born within the Developer Division of Microsoft and saw their first use within our teams in Redmond, Washington, and our India Development Center at the hands of David Gorena Elizondo and Anutthara Bharadwaj, respectively. They saw their first public unveiling at EuroSTAR 2008 in Den Haag, Netherlands,[1] in November 2008. Since then, I am personally aware of some dozens of groups outside Microsoft who have made them work.

Later that same month, two efforts were launched inside Microsoft to take the tours "on tour." A formal effort within Visual Studio was started that is still ongoing at the time of this writing. At the same time, a broader grassroots effort began companywide. I began it by sending an email to the Test Managers and Test Architects in the company, those testers of the highest level and broadest reach within Microsoft, asking to be referred to talented testers, regardless of their experience. I specifically asked for promising manual testing talent.

I was flooded with responses and whittled down the pool with personal interviews, frankly by choosing those who seemed most enthusiastic. I like working with passionate people! Then we began training, and each tester read and edited this text. After that, we began touring.

---

[1] You can find information about EuroSTAR at http://qualtechconferences.arobis.com/content.asp?id=91.

Many product lines were involved, from games to enterprise, mobile to cloud, operating system to web services. I've selected five of the most informative to appear here. The remainder are still ongoing, so don't be surprised if there are follow-ups on Microsoft blogs or elsewhere.

As you will see in this discussion, many of the tours survived being put into practice intact and were applied exactly how they were documented in Chapter 4, "Exploratory Testing in the Large." However, many variations were crafted on-the-fly, and in some cases new tours were created from scratch. Not only is this acceptable, it's desirable. I expect any team to find tours that work for them and tours that don't. That's why this chapter is here: to show how the tours work in practice.

The experience reports that follow are from the following Microsoft testers and appear with their permission:

- Nicole Haugen, Test Lead, Dynamics AX Client Product Team
- David Gorena Elizondo, SDET, Visual Studio Team Test
- Shawn Brown, Senior Test Lead, Windows Mobile
- Bola Agbonile, Software Development Engineer in Test, Windows
- Geoff Staneff, SDET, Visual Studio Team System

Touring the Dynamics AX Client

By Nicole Haugen

My team is responsible for testing Dynamics AX's client. Dynamics AX is an enterprise resource planning, or ERP, solution that was implemented more than 20 years ago in native C++ and was acquired when Microsoft purchased Navision. As the client team, we are considered to be a "foundation" team that is responsible for providing forms, controls, and shell functionality that the rest of the application is built on. Prior to this, my team was primarily testing public APIs, so Dynamics AX was a mind shift to testing through a GUI. When we made this transition, we learned several things:

- Many of the bugs that we found were not being caught by the test cases that we had identified in our test designs.
- Testing through the GUI introduced a seemingly infinite number of scenarios and complex user interactions that were not easily captured using automated tests.
- Whether a test is automated or manual, it is a regression test that must be maintained. My team has thousands of tests, so we must constantly consider the return on investment associated with adding a new test case to our regressions.
- Dynamics AX is a massive application and there was a lot about it we did not know, let alone how it should be tested.

Exploratory testing helped us to address all of the proceding issues. As a result, we have incorporated it into our process in the following ways:

- Before each feature is checked in, a tester performs exploratory testing on the code; this is to find important bugs fast and preferably, before they are ever checked in. We also follow this same practice for check-ins related to fixes of critical or high-risk bugs.
- Exploratory testing is used to help with the development of test cases while writing our test designs. It helps us to discover new scenarios that may have been missed in requirements.
- During our manual test pass, we use the test scripts as a jumping-off point to inject exploratory testing, as described in Chapter 5, "Hybrid Exploratory Testing Techniques." It has been my personal experience that the manual tests as they are written rarely detect new issues; however, with even the slightest detour from the test, many bugs are found.
- During bug bashes, we perform exploratory testing, which has helped lead us to investigate other areas outside of the current feature area to discover related issues.

Useful Tours for Exploration

The concept of tours makes exploratory testing much more concrete, teachable, and repeatable for us. This section describes a few tours that have been particularly useful for finding bugs in Dynamics AX.

Taxicab Tour

When traveling by mass public transportation, there is always risk that travelers may board the wrong route or get off at the wrong stop. Another drawback is that it is often impossible to take a direct route to a desired location. In the rare case that it is, the exact same route is usually taken over and over, with no variety to offer those that have visited the destination more than once. One surefire alternative is to travel by taxicab. While the fare of a taxicab costs more, the old adage "you get what you pay for" definitely applies. In a city such as London, where there are more than 25,000 streets, cab drivers must take rigorous exams to ensure that they know every route possible to get from point A to point B within the city. You can bet your bottom dollar (or should I say pound) that cab drivers know which route has the shortest distance, which offers the shortest amount of travel time, and even which is the most scenic. Furthermore, each and every time, passengers will consistently arrive at their specified location.

This same type of tour is also applicable to testing software applications. To reach a desired screen, dialog, or some other piece of functionality, there are often myriad routes that the user can take. As a result, testers have the same responsibility as taxicab drivers, in that they must educate themselves on every possible route to a specified location. Testers can then leverage this knowledge to verify that each route consistently delivers users to their target destination. In some situations, the state of the target destination may be expected to vary depending on the route, which should also be verified. Notice that this tour is a derivative of the Obsessive-Compulsive tour, in that the ultimate goal is to repeat a specific action; however, rather than exercising the exact *same* path to the action over and over, the key difference is that this tour concentrates on exercising *different* paths.

Consider an example using Microsoft Office's Print window. To open this window, users have various options:

- They can send the Ctrl+P hotkey.
- They can select the Print menu item through the Office menu button.
- They can click the Print button on the toolbar of the Print Preview window.

No matter which of these routes the user chooses, the end result should be the same: The Print window opens.

Conversely, there is also the concept of the *Blockaded Taxicab tour.* The objective of this tour is to verify that a user is consistently blocked from a destination regardless of the route taken. There are many different reasons why a user may be prevented from accessing functionality within an application, whether it is because the user does not have sufficient permissions or it is to circumvent the application from entering into an invalid state. Regardless, it is important to test each and every route because it is surprising how many times a developer overlooks ones.

Although the preceding example involving the Print window is becoming somewhat contrived at this point, let's continue with it for the sake of simplicity. Suppose that a user should be prohibited from printing hard copies. Because we know that there are many different ways to access the Print window, it is important to verify that no matter how the user tries to access this window that the user is consistently prevented. This means that at a minimum, the Ctrl+P hotkey should result in a no-op and that the Print menu item and toolbar button should become disabled.

Multicultural Tour

One great aspect of London is the sheer diversity of people that it encompasses. Without leaving the city, let alone the country, a tourist can experience cultures from around the world. For example, a tourist might choose to visit London's Chinatown, where the delicious aroma of Chinese cuisine can be smelled and traditional Chinese scripture can be viewed throughout. Similarly, a tourist may opt for an Indian restaurant tucked within one of London's busy streets, where diners enjoy smoking tobacco out of hookahs. Tourists can choose to submerse themselves into many different cultures as an exciting and wonderful way to spend a vacation in London.

The *Multicultural tour* applies to testing because it is important that testers consider the implications of providing software that is localized to different countries around the world. It is essential that language, currency, formatting of dates, types of calendars, and so forth be adapted appropriately to the end users' region. In addition, it is important that functionality continues to work as expected, regardless of the locale.

Although testing a product's localization can be very complex, here are a few basic ideas to get you started. Notice that you do not necessarily need to be fluent in a different language to perform these types of tests:

- A basic aspect of localization is that no text should be hard-coded (and thereby prohibiting it from being translated to the appropriate language). A great way to test this is simply to change the application's and operating system's language and verify that labels, exception messages, tooltips, menu items, window captions, and so on no longer appear in English. Also, it is likely that there are specific words that should *not* be translated, which should also be verified, such as words that are part of a brand name.
- Try launching the application under test in a right-to-left language, such as Arabic; verify that controls and windows behave correctly. With right-to-left languages, it is interesting to change the size of windows and make sure that they repaint correctly. Also, test controls, especially custom-implemented controls, and make sure that they still function as they did in left-to-right mode.

This list is obviously far from being comprehensive but at least gives an idea of general aspects of an application to verify without necessarily getting language-specific.

The Collector's Tour and Bugs as Souvenirs

This section is dedicated to the bugs that have been collected as souvenirs while traveling throughout Dynamics AX using the Taxicab and Multicultural tours. While these tours have helped to find many bugs, here are a few of my favorites.

A Bug Collected Using the Blockaded Taxicab Tour

Dynamics AX has a known limitation: Only eight instances of the application's workspace can be opened simultaneously.[2] Any more than eight will cause the entire application to crash (which, by the way, is an issue that could have been caught by using the *Test One, Get One Free tour*). Because of the complexity involved with fixing this issue, it was decided that users should simply be prevented from opening more than eight workspaces so that they never get into the situation where the application crashes.

When I learned of this behavior, the Taxicab tour immediately came to mind. Specifically, I began to think of all the possible ways that a user can open up a new workspace. Like any experienced taxicab driver, I came up with several routes:

[2] Note that although multiple application workspaces are created, in this scenario they are tied to a single Ax32.exe process.

- Clicking the New Workspace button on the Dynamics AX toolbar
- Sending the Ctrl+W hotkey
- Executing the New Workspace menu item under the Dynamics AX Windows menu
- Clicking the New Workspace button that exists in the Dynamics AX Select Company Accounts form

Once I was equipped with all the possible routes, I then proceeded to open seven application workspaces. With seven workspaces open, my first objective was to verify that an eighth workspace could be opened using each of the routes. As it turned out, each route was successful in doing so.

Next I applied the *Blockaded Taxicab tour.* Now that I had eight workspaces open, my objective was to verify that the user was blocked from opening a ninth workspace. I attempted to travel the first three possible routes, and in each case I was prevented. However, when I got to the fourth route, it was still possible to create a new workspace. As a result, I was able to launch a ninth workspace, which caused the application to crash.

A Bug Collected Using the Taxicab Tour

Like most applications, Dynamics AX provides several common menus to the user, such as View, Windows, and Help. To test Dynamics AX menu behavior, I executed each menu item to ensure that the desired action was performed. This, of course, is a pretty straightforward approach; so to make it more interesting, I decided to apply the *Taxicab tour.* Specifically, I executed menu items by traveling the following routes:

- Clicking the menu and menu item with the mouse
- Sending the hotkey that corresponds to the menu item
- Sending the menu's access key followed by the menu item's accelerator key

Sure enough, I discovered a bug when I used the third route (using the access and accelerator keys to execute the menu item). For example, to execute the Help menu's Help menu item, I attempted to send the Alt+H access key to open the menu, followed by the H accelerator key to execute the menu item. Surprisingly, I did not get that far because the Help menu failed to even open. On the bright side, this was an important accessibility issue that was identified and fixed before the product was shipped.

Bugs Collected Using the Multicultural Tour

Dynamics AX is shipped in many different languages, including right-to-left languages, so it is important to verify that the application supports globalization and localizability. The *Multicultural tour* has helped to discover many bugs in this area.

Example 1

One bug that I discovered while using the *Multicultural tour* involves the tooltips that display menu access key information to the user. Consider the Windows menu tooltip, which in English is displayed as Windows <Alt+W>.

I opened Dynamics AX in various languages, such as Italian, and noticed that the Windows menu tooltip displayed Finestre <Alt+W>. Although the name of the Windows menu had been properly translated, the access key had not. Instead, it should have displayed Finestre <Alt+F>.

Example 2

A majority of Dynamics AX controls are custom, so it's very interesting to run the application in right-to-left languages and verify that the controls behave correctly. In fact, a great example of a bug found by one of my colleagues involves the Dynamics AX Navigation Pane, which can be put in either an expanded (see Figure 6.1) or collapsed state (see Figure 6.2) by the user:

FIGURE 6.1 Expanded Navigation Pane.

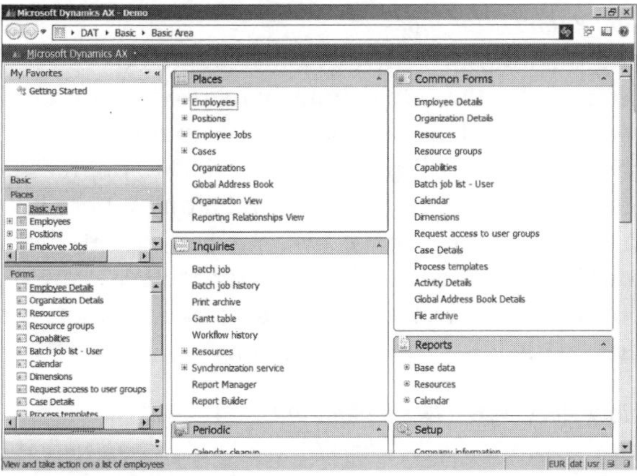

FIGURE 6.2 Collapsed Navigation Pane.

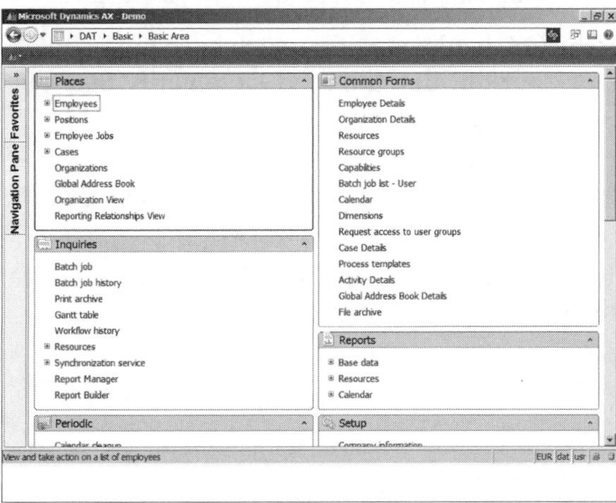

Notice that the << and >> buttons at the top of the Navigation Pane are used for changing the pane's state. When my colleague launched Dynamics AX in a right-to-left language, clicking the << arrow button simply failed to collapse the Navigation Pane; however, these buttons worked fine in left-to-right languages.

Both of these bugs would have gone undiscovered if we had not taken the *Multicultural tour* through Dynamics AX.

Tour Tips

While applying the tours described in Chapter 4, I compiled the following list of tips as a "traveling" companion for the savvy tester.

Supermodel Tour

When we are testing a product with a GUI, the *Supermodel tour* is vital to eliminating glaring flaws in the interface. A useful tip for using this tour to find even the most subtle flaws is to combine it with some of the other tours described in Chapter 4.

Combine with Supporting Actor Tour

While perusing the interface, always take care to look beyond the current window or control that you are primarily focused on to see how the rest of the application appears. This technique is comparable to the *Supporting Actor tour,* where you must "turn your attention 10 degrees left or right" to get the full effect. For instance, I once found a bug where I opened a pop-up window on a form and the title bar became grayed-out, thereby making it appear as though the entire form had lost focus. While my main attention was on the pop-up window, by taking a step back to look at the entire form, I caught a very subtle bug with the title bar.

Combine with Back Alley\Mixed Destination Tour

The main premise of the *Back Alley\Mixed Destination tour* is to test how different features interact with one another. With respect to a GUI, it's important to verify how features of the external environment affect the appearance of an application. Here are a few examples:

- Modify the OS display settings, such as to high contrast, and take a *Supermodel tour* through the product to verify that all controls, icons, and text display properly.
- Use Terminal Services to remote into the machine that has the application installed and verify that there is no painting or flickering issues as windows in the application are drawn.
- Run the application with dual monitors and verify that menus and windows display in the correct monitor.

Because most first impressions are based on looks alone, bugs involving the appearance of an application can lead to perceptions of an unprofessional, poorly engineered product. Unfortunately, these types of bugs are often deemed as low priority to fix. A handful of appearance-related bugs in an application may seem harmless, but together they often have a cumulative effect on usability and therefore should *not* be ignored.

Rained-Out Tour

The *Rained-Out tour* concentrates on terminating functionality and verifying that the application continues to behave correctly. The two tips that I provide for this tour are actually already mentioned in Chapter 4; however, I want to emphasize them here because they truly are very helpful in detecting bugs.

First, it is important to change the state of the object under test *before* canceling out of it. Let's use a form as an example: Do not just open a form and immediately close it. Instead, alter either the form's or application's state before closing it. To demonstrate this, here are some actual bugs that I have found in Dynamics AX using this technique:

- I opened a form and then opened a pop-up window that was parented by the form. With the pop-up window still open, I clicked the form's X button to close it. As a result, the application crashed because the form failed to properly close the pop-up window before closing itself.
- After opening the User Setup form, I left the form open and switched to a different module in the application. Next, I clicked the User Setup form's Cancel button, which caused the application to crash.

Second, it is imperative to reattempt the same scenario after canceling out of an operation. I used this very technique recently while performing exploratory testing for a new feature planned for the 6.0 release of Dynamics AX and found yet another client-crashing bug. This new feature ensures that creates, updates, and deletes for inner/outer joined data sources occur within a single transaction. While testing updates, I decided to cancel (discard) these changes by clicking the Restore button on the form's toolbar. As a result of clicking Restore, my changes were discarded and replaced by values in the database table. I then reattempted to update the same record again, and lo and behold Dynamics AX crashed.

Landmark Tour

Some applications are so large, such as ERP solutions, that it's overwhelming to even think where to start with the *Landmark tour,* simply because there are so many features. In some cases, testers may not even be very familiar with other features outside their primary area of responsibility. A tip for combating this issue is to pair up with another person who is an expert in a complementary feature area.

Using Tours to Find Bugs

By David Gorena Elizondo

I started working for Microsoft as soon as I graduated from college. (I had done a summer internship for Microsoft a year prior.) I joined as a Software design engineer in Test, and I was part of the first version of Visual Studio Team System in 2005. My job at the time included testing the tools within Visual Studio for unit testing, code coverage, remote testing, and so forth. I am a tester who tests testing tools!

Throughout my four years at Microsoft, I became involved with the different testing approaches and methodologies used inside and outside the company, from test automation to script-based testing, E2E testing, and exploratory testing. I have experimented with a lot of different test techniques. It is in learning and performing exploratory testing that I found my testing passion. I've now been using exploratory tours for over a year. Organizing my thinking around the tourist metaphor has substantially increased the number of fixable bugs that I find in features that I'm responsible for testing.

Although all the tours have been valuable to me at one time or another, I've seen through experience that certain tours work best under specific circumstances. I will try to share some of my thoughts on when to use them, and the kinds of bugs that I've found while testing the test case management solution that I've been working on for the last year.

Note that all the bugs I describe here have been fixed and will be unable to plague any users of our test case management system!

Testing a Test Case Management Solution

I used the exploratory tours with the test case management system that we've been developing for the past year and a half on my team. Before I describe how I used the tours, I will describe our product because its features and design affect the way I chose and executed the tours.

The test case management client works hand in hand with a server, from which it basically pulls what we call "work items"; things such as test cases, bugs, and so forth to display for a user to manipulate. Without the server, the client can basically do nothing. Just by knowing this piece of information, you can easily tell that tours such as the *Rained-Out tour* and the *Saboteur* yielded a lot of bugs. Imagine canceling a server operation halfway through its completion, or just getting rid of the server itself. Then if you think about it a bit deeper, you realize that a work item (or anything on the server) can be modified at the same time by more than one client. So, the *TOGOF tour* yielded a good amount of bugs, as well. Updates are happening all the time throughout the application, so the *FedEx tour* is also one to target.

Complete books on the tours presented in this book could be written. Until then, here are some of my bug-finding experiences.

The Rained-Out Tour

When you're working with a client application that works closely with a server, you can assume that any unexpected server activity can cause weird things to happen (both on the server and on the client). Interrupted requests to a server is tricky business, as is refreshing client-side data. Think about it: If you open a page that starts loading information from a server, and you immediately click Refresh, one action is canceled, and a new one starts immediately. The software on both sides of such a transaction needs to be on its toes. That's why this tour finds tons of bugs. A few of my favorites are (using the exact titles that were entered into our bug management system) as follows:

- **Bug: If we cancel initial connect to a project, we can no longer connect to it manually.**

  Whenever our test case management system is launched, we remember the previous server (that contains the test case and test data repository) that the user was connected to and initiate an automatic connection to this data store. If users want to connect to a different store, they have to cancel this operation. It turns out that the developers didn't think through the cancellation scenario well and caused an environment variable to be deleted under certain circumstances; so when I loaded a new version of the test data repository, the connection to the server was lost.

- **Bug: When deleting a configuration variable and canceling or confirming, you get prompted again.**

  This would have been a nasty bug to ship with. It happened whenever I tried to delete an existing test repository variable and then canceled the request at a certain UI prompt. Because the *Rained-Out tour* makes a tester conscious of recognizing complex and timing-sensitive actions, it led me to naturally think of this test case.

  The *Rained-Out tour* makes us think beyond explicit actions. There are times when a feature or a product has to implicitly cancel an action that has already started (often for performance reasons). This was exactly the case for this bug.

- **Bug: Plan Contents: Moving between suites does not cancel the loading of tests.**

  It turns out that whenever we chose a test repository, the application would start loading the test cases that were associated with it. The tour led me to think that there had to be an implicit cancel action whenever I quickly chose a different repository, and if not, there would be performance issues. It turned out to be true; we were not canceling the action properly, and performance was really bad.

  The *Rained-Out tour* makes it clear to the tourist: Cancel every action you can, and cancel it many times and under many different circumstances. It is raining, so scream and yell for everyone to cancel their plans! This strategy led me to bugs like the next one.

- **Bug: Time to refresh starts growing exponentially as we try it several times.**

  Knowing that a refresh action will basically cancel any in-progress activity, I decided to click that Refresh button many times (quickly), and this actually caused horrible performance issues in the product.

  The strategy used to find this next bug was exactly the same one mentioned in the previous one.

- **Bug: Stress-refreshing test settings manager crashes Camano.**

  However, the result was much better for a tester's perspective: a crash! Clicking the Refresh button like a maniac actually caused the application to die.

The Saboteur

The *Saboteur* forces you to think though the application's use of resources so that you can vary the amount of resources available, and thus potentially find scenarios that will cause it to fail, as discussed here:

- **Bug: Camano crashes when trying to view a test configuration when there is no TFS connection.**

  TFS is the server used to store test cases and test data. The *Saboteur* caused me to think through many scenarios where availability of TFS was crucial and where good error-handling routines needed to be in place. Making the server unavailable at the right places sometimes found serious crashing bugs, and the resulting fixes have made our product robust with respect to server connection problems.

  In this next bug, the strategy was the same one: looking for a resource that the application uses.

- **Bug: Camano crashes at startup time if Camano.config becomes corrupt. Camano continually fails until the config file is corrected.**

  The resource in this case was a configuration file that the application uses to persist data between sessions. The *Saboteur* requires that all such state-bearing files be tampered with to see whether the application is robust enough to handle it when those persistent resources are corrupt or unavailable. Playing around with these persistent files not only found some high-severity bugs, it was also fun and had me anticipating when and where the crash would occur. Given that no one else on our team had thought to try these scenarios made me happy to have the *Saboteur* in my tool kit.

  This next bug shows the exact same strategy as the previous one but with a new twist.

- **Bug: Camano crashes when config file is really large.**

  Finding this particular bug consisted of playing around with the configuration file and creating variants of it and modifying its properties. The

Saboteur suggests making it read-only, deleting it, changing its type, and so forth. But the property that worked for me was its size. When I created a very large config file, the application was simply not able to cope with it.

The FedEx Tour

Our test case management solution processes a great deal of data that flows freely between the client and the server: bugs, test cases, test plans, test plan content, and so on. All this information has to be refreshed appropriately to remain in sync, and this is not easy for an application where multiple activities work with the same artifacts simultaneously. The *FedEx tour* is tailor-made to help a tester think through such scenarios. The following bugs show some defects that the *FedEx tour* found.

- **Bug: Test plan not refreshing automatically after coming back from a work item.**

  The test plan contents show the actual test cases in the test plan. The strategies that the tour led me to were actually modifying properties on test cases (and the test plan itself) and ensuring that all these were refreshed appropriately. It turns out that if we modified the *name* of a test case, and came back to view the test plan, you had to manually refresh the activity for the test case to show the updated name.

  We found a number of bugs similar to this next one.

- **Bug: When a test plan is selected in the TAC, and we modify one of its artifacts, Camano crashes.**

  In this particular scenario, modifying a property (such as configuration name) of a test plan, while showing that same property on another activity, would crash the application because it would not be able to cope with the property change. If you think about it, this bug was found using the exact same strategy as the previous one: modifying properties and artifacts, and making sure they were refreshed correctly somewhere else.

  This next one was an interesting bug.

- **Bug: Camano will crash forever and ever if we have a test plan that uses a build that has been deleted.**

  Our test plans can be bound to builds, meaning that we can link a test plan to a particular build. However, if we deleted the build that a test plan was bound to, the application would crash every time we opened that particular test plan. Here the *FedEx tour* is helping us identify those types of data dependencies and guiding us through thinking about such associations between data elements in a methodical manner.

The TOGOF Tour

The *TOGOF tour* will find bugs in applications that can be used by multiple simultaneous users. We found the following bug while having multiple users active within the application at the same time.

- **Bug: Test Configuration Manager: Camano crashes when you "Assign to new test plans" if the configuration is not up-to-date.**

Test configurations have a Boolean property called "Assign to new test plans" (which can be toggled on or off). It turns out that if user A and user B were looking at the same exact copy of any given configuration (with say, the Boolean property set to true), and user A changed the property to false (and saved it), whenever user B tried to make any change to the configuration and saved it, his application would just crash. This shows a bug that would have been very difficult to catch if only one user was testing the application. The *TOGOF tour's* strategy is very clear in these kinds of scenarios: Test different instances of the application at the same time to find bugs that will be difficult to find otherwise.

The Practice of Tours in Windows Mobile Devices

By Shawn Brown

In 2000, Microsoft shipped a product that could fit on a device to be carried around and perform many of the same functions that a full-size PC could perform. This device was called the Pocket PC and started a series of releases of Windows Mobile. Throughout the releases of Windows Mobile, more and more functionality was added, and therefore the ecosystem to test became more and more complex: from the first, nonconnected PDA-style device, to the multiconnected GSM/CDMA, Bluetooth, and WiFi devices that could stay connected and provide up-to-date information without the user even having to make a request.

During this evolution, the testing of these devices also had to evolve. Constraints such as memory, battery life, CPU speed, and bandwidth all had to be considered when developing and testing for this platform. In addition, being the first multithreaded handheld device allowed for more functionality and more applications working together to give the user more "smart" behavior, and hence the name Smartphone came into the picture. Now, take that environment and add an additional "unknown" variable into the picture called ISVs (independent software vendors). ISVs may use an SDK (software development kit) to create applications on this platform to expand its capabilities and to a buck or two for themselves through revenue, and may thus cause a new testing challenge. These creative and smart ISVs may not abide by certain development practices that internal-to-Microsoft developers are trained to do, or may want to push the boundaries of what the platform can do, and therefore they may potentially cause unexpected issues when deploying their applications to the devices. Some global measures can be put into place, but as a tester on a Mobile platform with a fairly extensive SDK, we cannot ignore the potential of one of these add-ons to affect the overall health of the platform with respect to all the categories of test. Given the fluidity and the overall challenges of testing Windows Mobile, this is a great product to hone testing skills on.

During my career with Windows Mobile, I have owned the testing of Connection Manager, certain Office applications in the earlier releases, and one of my favorites, the phone functionality.

I catch myself hunting for areas of the product that go unnoticed for lengths of time and capitalize on their neglect. When I find a flaw in a product, it creates a sense of accomplishment and job satisfaction. As my career in test evolved, I took notice that in addition to being able to discover new and creative ways to break my product, I was also taking a closer look at how to prevent bugs from getting into the product and was paying more attention to the end-to-end solution of the system. Bug prevention starts with testing the initial design. Roughly 10 percent of all of the bugs found over the years are spec issues. Looking back, this 10 percent, if they had made it into the product, could have caused more bugs as well as more time to complete the project. As you can understand, finding these issues early helps the product and the schedule.

My Approach/Philosophy to Testing

My philosophy to testing is quite basic. Find the weaknesses of the product before anyone else does, and ensure the product's strengths are highly polished. This approach requires a continual watch on the product and the environment around it that can affect the performance or functionality. How can you look at the environment you are positioning yourself to test in a way that encompasses everyone who is going to interact with it? Then, how do you prioritize your attack?

Independent of the test problem, I begin by defining the problem statement. What is the desired end goal? I determine the variables. I formulate an approach (keeping it simple). After a simple solution is defined, I determine the reusability and agility of the solution. Where are the solution's trade-offs and weak points? I have used this approach in developing and testing hardware as well as software.

One example of my use of this methodology is when I was developing a shielding technique to enable electronic components to be used in the bore of an MRI. This violent magnetic environment was never meant to have metallic objects inside (because of safety and because of the potential to disrupt the sensitive readings). Knowing the problem statement was "create a method for housing electronics in the bore of an active MRI unit without disrupting the readings more than 5%," I started by gaining a better understanding of the environment: the strength of the magnetic field, the frequency of the gradient shifting when the unit is in active mode, the method of the readings, and the requirements around what the electronics inside the bore were expected to do. This information narrowed the solution to two main options:

1. Create a shield to prevent the magnetic from penetrating into the housing of the electronics.

   or

2. Create a shield that prevented the RF from escaping from the housing.

After researching the known methods for both, one being a ferrous metal that would prevent the magnetic fields from entering the box, and the other, a highly permeable metal to shield the RF from escaping from the box, I realized that traditional shielding methods would not fit this goal. (Because the RF that would be generated by either material upon placing them inside the bore during active mode would most likely degrade the reading beyond the 5 percent margin.) In addition, the ferrous material could cause more of a hazard to anyone in the room, given the highly concentrated and erratic magnetic field being produced could cause any ferrous metal to be hurled through space at a deathly rate. Therefore, one more option was removed from the equation. Given the material for shielding could not be a solid plate (because of the RF induced by the environment), it had to be unconnected loops. After I calculated the penetration of the RF, the end results were to create a <1cm grid of nonconnecting loops of copper, which would prevent the RF from escaping from the box and would mostly prevent the RF from entering or being generated by the material itself. My approach led to the shielding technique being a success, and I continue to use this process when testing software.

Testing is a continually growing domain, much like any other engineering discipline. To keep increasing your product's quality, expose how you test to your developers/designers. The more they know about how you are going to test it, the more they will try to create a design that will account for the methods you will use to exploit the gaps in their design. Testing can be difficult, because even though you want to maintain the edge on being able to break any product, you also want to help your developers write better code. Therefore, you must always be one step ahead of your developers. As they learn how you test and you learn how they approach solving algorithm problems, your ability to break their code becomes more and more difficult, Success! However, it is still your job to find the bugs in the product.

Interesting Bugs Found Using Tours

Using the Rained-Out Tour

While performing exploratory testing on a previous release of Windows Mobile, I caught a race condition with "smart dial" functionality. In this instance, it was known that a side process was being used to do a background search on the search criteria to aid with performance. The larger the data set, the longer it takes this process to complete. This turned out to be an excellent opportunity to use the *Rained-Out tour.* After loading more than

4,000 contacts onto the device under test, I entered a search string that was expected to end in no results. As the side process was churning away in the background, I changed the search string by deleting one character. The expected result was to still have no matches, but the side process was not done with checking the entire data set, and therefore the next filter, which is designed to check the results of the initial side process, was passed the data that was not checked yet. This resulted in an incorrect IF statement, and data that did not match the search clause was displayed incorrectly. If this bug had not been caught early and through exploratory testing, it could have caused more downstream design challenges.

Another example of using the *Rained-Out tour* is in an issue found and then fixed in the Bluetooth bonding wizard in Windows Mobile. After creating bonds with a few headsets and peripherals, I proceeded to use the *Rained-Out tour* during the connection-request phase. When the listed peripherals were all disconnected, there was an option to connect one of them to the phone. I selected one of the BT peripherals and selected the Connect option. I then noticed a time delay between when the connection request was made and when the connection or the failure dialog was actually shown. During this time, I tried all the available menu items. They all functioned properly during this state. It wasn't until I moved focus away from the existing item, then back to the item with the current connection request, that I noticed that the connection option became available again. So as a tester using the *Rained-Out tour,* I selected that option. Doing so keyed up another connection request to the same peripheral. I performed the same steps a few more times in quick succession before the initial connection request completed, and voilà, a sequence of failure dialogs popped up. Ultimately, the code was able to handle this situation, but there was no need to be able to continue to make multiple connection requests to the same peripheral, and therefore the bug was fixed.

Using the Saboteur

A contact list is linked to a number of other functionalities (call history, text messaging, speed dial, and so on). Knowing this, I used a *Saboteur* and created a list of contacts and some speed-dial entries. Now for the unexpected situation to be triggered: A sync error was simulated where the contacts on the device were all removed from one of the linking databases on the device, but the device still thought they were synced (because they still existed on the device). Therefore, syncing was seemingly successful, but the database that housed the links to the speed dial did not exist anymore, and therefore a blank speed dial was shown.

Using the Supermodel Tour

Here is an example of when I used the *Supermodel tour* on a Windows Mobile device and explored UI centering and anchor points using different resolutions. After booting an image with a resolution that I knew was not used a lot, I navigated around the device performing simple user tasks (for example, creating contacts, checking email, and checking calendar events). During the calendar event navigation, I noticed that when I selected to navigate to a specific date, the calendar week view centered itself onscreen. A number of views could be used, and so I inspected each view. Not until I got to the month view did I see a centering issue. After I changed which month to view via the month picker, the repainting of the month that was selected was centered in the middle of the screen, instead of being top justified like every other view. This incorrect centering occurred because of a missing flag in this one view.

Example of the Saboteur

A good time to use the *Saboteur* is when testing an application that utilizes data connectivity. Data connectivity is a fickle beast and can come and go when you least expect it. Using this tour, I was able to find a problem with a device-side client who requires a connection to provide its functionality. Not only was this application coupled to connectivity, it also had an impact on other locations where the user's entity can be used. I'm speaking of Instant Messenger, of course. I successfully configured this application and signed in. Now, knowing my device is a 2.5G device, which means it can handle only one data pipe at a time, I then called the device from another phone, thus terminating the active connection, which, on Windows Mobile on GSM, puts the device connection into a suspended state. Then I signed in to the same account on my desktop, attempting to fully sever the connection to that service on the device. Voilà, the device-side client never got the notification that it was signed in to another location but it also appeared to be signed out. However, in the menu options, the option to Sign Out was still available (because it never was told it was signed out).

Another way to be a saboteur is to turn the device's flight mode on, which turns off all radios (for when the user goes on an airplane but still wants to use the device). Many times, applications do not listen to radio on/off notifications, and this can cause a limbo state to occur. Sure enough, signing on to IM on the device and then turning off the cellular radio, which in turn removes all GSM connectivity, was not detected by this application, and the application is in a perpetual "connected" state, which is quite confusing to the user.

Example of the Supermodel Tour

An example of a bug found by using the *Supermodel tour* coupled with focus specifically on usability and intuitiveness of designs is as follows. While traversing through a connected mapping application on Windows Mobile, I decided to see how easy it was to get directions from my current location to another location, such as a restaurant. I launched the application, the device found my current location, and then I decided to select the option to get Directions from A to B from the menu. In this UI, there was no intuitive way to select my current location as my starting point. Given that I did not know the address where I currently was, I just then decided to enter the point B location and hit Go. An error appeared stating it needed to know where I was starting from. Interesting, because upon entering the application, it made it a point to tell me where I was. This lack of completeness can cause much pain when using the application, and a simple addition to prepopulate this field could be the difference between someone using this application all of the time versus it getting slammed in a review on the Web.

The Three-Hour Tour (or Taking the Tours on Tour)

by Shawn Brown

I found a fun way to use the tours to build teamwork and increase morale and find a lot of great bugs in the process. Given that our product is meant to travel, we assembled the team and headed off campus on a testing adventure. We brought our devices, chargers, tools, and tours and drove around looking for bugs. We set a goal of finding 20 bugs in 3 hours and to have a lot of fun. The result, we found 25, and no one was ready to return to the office! Here's the report.

Applications can function perfectly in a controlled test environment, but when put in the hands of an end user, coupled with its interactions with other applications or protocols on a mobile device, is when it gets interesting; and it is critical to be correct. In the ever-increasing mobile environment, technology is being put in awkward situations, which makes end-to-end testing more and more critical. Many years ago, a computer would sit in a dedicated room and not move around, which made "environment" testing not as critical. Yes, you would have to take into consideration changes in bandwidth if connectivity was available, and different users, but even so, the user segment was more adaptable to this new technology. As technology grew, it became more interesting, and the more interesting it got, the more it fell into the hands of users who were not prepared, nor wanted, to understand how it works; they just wanted it to work. As a technology's user segment evolves, our testing strategies also have to evolve to ensure that what is important to the end user is at the forefront of our minds when we create a test plan. This does not mean that we abandon the tried-and-true methods and "test buckets"; although we may have to approach and prioritize how we use these buckets depending on the technology being tested.

With that said, being mobile and staying connected has become a necessity in a lot of regions. This new environment variable needs to be taken into consideration when defining a test strategy or plan. For the sake of brevity, this discussion focuses on Windows Mobile. Windows Mobile is composed of many moving parts, and its customers can be anyone from a teenager in high school to a retired businessperson who wants to keep current with news, email, and so on...wherever he/she goes.

Knowing that our end users use devices in a variety of ways, a small set of test engineers set out to accomplish some predefined tasks that mobile devices can do in the wild. We used multiple tours and uncovered a number of bugs in a short amount of time. We found the *Supermodel tour,* the *Saboteur,* and the *Obsessive-Compulsive tour* most useful, although we could have leveraged just about any tour. The *Supermodel tour* was primarily used in the mobile platform during this "tour of tours" to flush out interoperability and integration between applications and tasks. While taking these tours on tour to accomplish the tasks, each attendee also had their "attention to detail" radar cranked up. In addition, we paid extra attention to certain requirements of the device because they have been proven time and time again to aggravate users when malfunctioning and delight users when "it just works." These requirements related to always-on connections, performance in accomplishing tasks, or navigating (especially via an error message or a dialog to guide users back on track after something went wrong).

As we took the tours on tour, we uncovered new bugs that might not have been found this early in a static testing environment. Using the *Obsessive-Compulsive tour,* we discovered that attempting to use every WiFi hot spot in the area to browse the Web eventually caused IE to unexpectedly stop working. This could be due do an authentication error or a protocol that has not been accounted for. In addition, this tour also uncovered an authentication page that IE could not render and therefore could never be successfully used.

The *Saboteur* happened to be one of the more fun tours during a team outing such as this one. As testers, we want to break things, and this notion of being a saboteur of the device just fits. As we were out in public, there were many discussion of "what if" this happens or that happens, such as, "I wonder what will happen if I'm in a call with you, and I attempt to play a song?" If that functioned properly, the next question would have been this: "How about we pull the storage card that the song resides on and see what happens?" This constructive destruction was like a snowball rolling down a hill picking up speed. In addition to finding a number of new issues in the product in just three hours, it was a team-building outing that enabled brainstorming to teach each other new ways of thinking.

During the entire time, the *Supermodel tour* was at the forefront of our minds. Each attempted task was put under high scrutiny, and within just a few hours, a large number of fit and finish bugs were discovered (for example, error dialogs that really were not helpful, and messages that could not be sent because of either network reliability or as a result of our sabotage [and which were never sent, even after connectivity was reestablished]). In addition, bugs were found where the input panel covered the edit field, which can be quite annoying or confusing to the end user.

The Practice of Tours in Windows Media Player

By Bola Agbonile

I am a graduate of the University of Lagos, Nigeria, where I attained an MBA (1996) and a Bachelor's degree in Electrical Engineering (1990). I presently work on the Windows Experience (WEX) platform with the Windows Media Player team as a Software Development Engineer in Test (SDET), a role that I continue to relish daily.

As an SDET, my role is primarily to work with others on my team to ensure that a high-quality product is what we present to our customers. To achieve this, one of my key roles as an SDET is to validate that the finished product satisfies what our target-market customers require and adheres to the written specifications as outlined by the Program Manager. Another one of my primary roles is to ensure that the product can withstand rigorous tests thrown at it.

Windows Media Player

In the Windows Experience division, on the Windows Media Experience (WMEX) team, I have worked with others at enhancing Windows Media Player (WMP) from previous versions, with the sole aim being to satisfy our target market by providing a solid, robust, functional, media player. For instance, it was with WMP 10 that we first introduced being able to synchronize *to* devices, and with WMP 11 we took it one step further by adding greater support for Media Transfer Protocol (MTP) devices, including the ability to have an automatic sync partnership and allowing for synchronization *from* the device. WMP allows for sync, burn, rip, and playback of numerous file types, including pictures and DVDs. WMP 12 introduces a lightweight player mode for quick, easy, and clutter-free playback with practically no UI chrome.

WMP is an application that is UI-centric. As such, the tours relevant to this kind of application are the ones I use. To be specific, WMP's input sources are via text boxes, check boxes, option buttons, and "shiny discs" (CDs, DVDs, and CD-R[W]s), while its output is as audio, video, and dialogs displayed to the user.

Following are the tours that I use for testing WMP 12, with examples of things that I have encountered along the way that I consider to be interesting.

The Garbage Collector's Tour

Garbage collectors are systematic, house to house, driveway to driveway. Some testers might, as Chapter 4 suggests, be systematic by testing features that are close together in an application. I apply it a bit differently and arrange features in buckets according to their similarity. For WMP, the first categorization bucket could be "All UI Objects." The next bucket will be "Dialogs," followed by "Text Boxes," "Boundaries," and so on. Then, the garbage collector can begin her systematic collection.

WMP buckets look something like this:

1. WMP's Player mode
    a. Transport control
        1. Shuffle
        2. Repeat
        3. Stop
        4. Back
        5. Play
        6. Next
        7. Mute
        8. Volume
    b. Buttons
        1. Switch to Library mode
        2. Switch to Full Screen mode
        3. Close WMP
        4. Minimize WMP
        5. Maximize WMP
    c. Seek bar
    d. Title bar
    e. Right-click context menu
        1. Spelling of labels
        2. Persistence of user's choice
        3. Navigation using keyboard
    f. Hotkey functionality
        1. Alt+Enter
        2. Ctrl+P
        3. Ctrl+H
        4. Ctrl+T
        5. Ctrl+Shift+C
    g. Dialogs
        1. Options
            Tabs
            Options buttons
            Check boxes
            Text boxes
            Command buttons

2. Enhancements
    - Next button
    - Previous button
    - Hyperlinks
    - Option buttons
    - Check boxes
    - Labels
    - Hover tooltips
    - Sliders
    - Mouse pointer
    - Drop lists
3. Default language settings
    - Drop list
    - Arrow-key navigation
    - Command buttons

h. List pane

i. Center pane
1. Play all music shuffled
2. Play again
3. Continue playlist
4. Go to Library
5. Play previous playlist

j. External links
1. Windows Help and Support
2. Download visualizations
3. Info Center view

One of the benefits of this tour is that with the categorization of the application, the tester can systematically walk through and identify features that might otherwise be overlooked. For example, while taking this tour and looking WMP over, I came across a bug that I have now logged. The bug is that in the center pane, "Play previous playlist" does not actually start playback unlike "Play all music shuffled" and "Play again." A user would expect consistent behavior, and if I had not applied the *Garbage Collector's tour,* I would have missed this difference.

The *Garbage Collector's tour* made me take a long hard look at WMP and systematically categorize all the buttons available in the center pane (for instance) and then test each item's functionality for consistency when compared with other items in a similar bucket.

The Supermodel Tour

This tour should be on your list when success is to be measured by the quantity of bugs found. For example, if there is to be a bug bash, and there are no restrictions on which feature gets tested, it is beneficial to be one of the first people on the ground when the whistle blows. Examples of supermodel bugs that I classify as "low-hanging fruit" are typographical errors. Early on in the product cycle is when this category of bugs is more common. To effectively spot text bugs, one should read *each* word and then count to *two* before reading the next word. In my opinion, this is the secret to spotting typos and grammatical errors.

Figure 6.3 is an example of a bug that I found on a WMP dialog. Take a look at the dialog and see whether you can spot the typo in it.

FIGURE 6.3 An easy bug to miss.

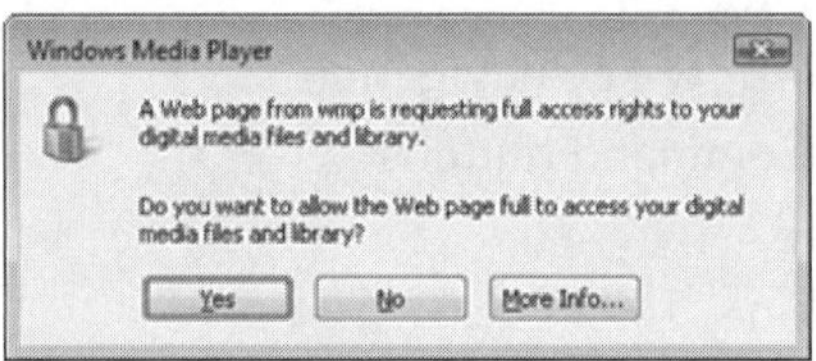

Spot the bug? It is in the second paragraph. "Do you want to allow the Web page full *to access your....*" This should be, "Do you want to allow the Web page full access to your...." It is easy to read too fast and correct the sentence in your head while not seeing the error in front of you.

The Intellectual Tour

When running manual tests, it pays to keep asking "What if?" For instance, when looking at the Player versus Library mode of WMP, one could ask this: "What if the Library mode is busy and then WMP is expected to be in the Player mode?"

Having asked this question, one would then investigate possible answers by performing a task that is exclusively for the Library mode (such as ripping an audio CD) and then performing a task that is exclusively for the Player mode (such as DVD playback). The whole purpose of this is to see whether this scenario has been handled or whether one would get the undesirable situation of WMP running in *both* modes (see Figure 6.4).

FIGURE 6.4 One application running in two different modes.

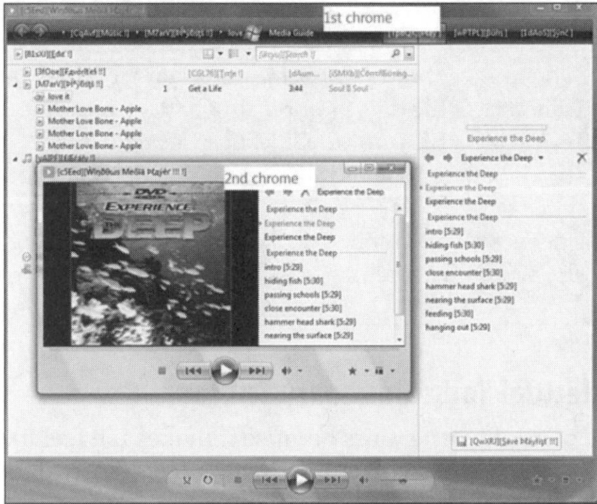

> ### Twenty-Five Examples of Other WMP-Related "What If?" Questions
>
> *What if a user decides to…*
>
> - Burn via Shell *and* via WMP concurrently?
> - Change options from one to another?
> - Change view from smaller to larger UI object?
> - Delete via WMP a file that is already gone?
> - Double-click a UI object?
> - Exit from Full Screen mode with ongoing playback?
> - Exit WMP with an ongoing process (sync, rip, playback, burn, transcode, and so on)?
> - Insert an audio CD with auto-rip enabled while a context menu is displayed?
> - Place an ampersand (&) in an editable field?
> - Play back content over the network, and then disable network connectivity?
> - Play back an expired DRM track after moving back the system clock?
> - Play back two DVDs concurrently, one with WMP and one with a third-party app?
> - Play back two DVDs using WMP concurrently from different ROM drives?
> - Press a keyboard key during an ongoing process?
> - Read Web Help?
> - Repeat a hotkey sequence?

- Sync content to an already full device?
- Sync/burn/rip content on a PC with no hard drive space?
- Synchronize to two devices concurrently?
- Synchronize/burn/playback, and then hibernate the PC?
- Transcode a file on a laptop using battery power?
- Transcode a file prior to DRM license acquisition?
- Turn *off* an option, and then verify whether the option is in the off state?
- Uncheck *all* the options on a dialog (like Customize Tree View)?
- Use word wheel search, and then drag and drop?

The Intellectual Tour: Boundary Subtour

This is one of my favorite tours because it makes me feel like a real detective. The *Boundary tour* involves conducting tests close to the upper and lower boundaries, all the while looking for a breaking point. It's a specific case of the *Intellectual tour* that suggests that we ask the software hard questions.

Classic examples include the following:

- Filling a text box with its maximum number of characters or null
- Creating a very deep folder hierarchy, and then placing a media file in the last folder and attempting to play back the media file in WMP
- Clicking a button very close to its outer edges to see whether the click command will still be recognized

For example, in WMP, after I attempted to type characters in a text box meant for only numbers, the mitigation taken was to ensure that a user can type in only numbers (see Figure 6.5).

FIGURE 6.5 Mitigation taken to prevent non-numeric inputs.

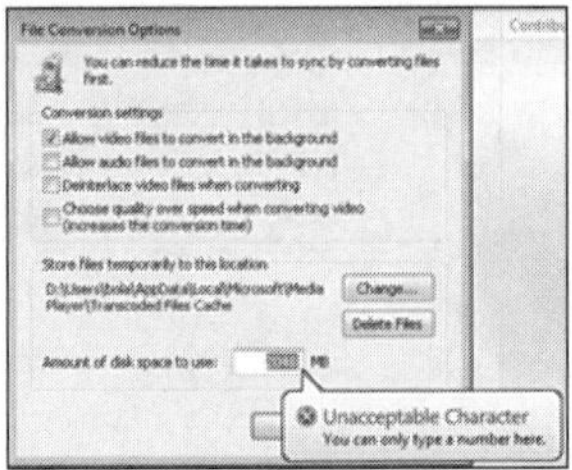

Conducting more tests on a different tab unearthed a dialog with bad indentation (see Figure 6.6).

FIGURE 6.6 Dialog with bad text indentation.

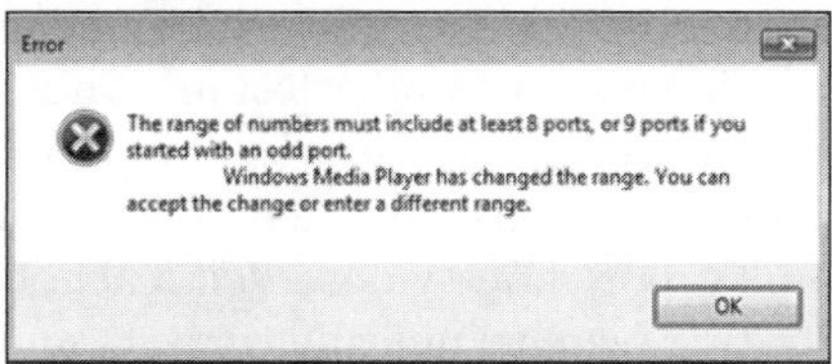

The bugs found while on the *Boundary subtour* are varied in nature, including buffer overruns, bad handling of data, and UI formatting errors.

The Parking Lot Tour and the Practice of Tours in Visual Studio Team System Test Edition

By Geoff Staneff

In 2004, I came to Microsoft with zero programming experience, but a Ph.D. in Materials Science from the California Institute of Technology. I spent the first nine months taking computer science courses and test training in the mornings while working on the Windows event log in the afternoons. By the end of the first year, I owned 50k lines of native test code, filed 450 bugs, and had an 80 percent fixed rate. Since moving to Visual Studio, my focus has changed tremendously. Our work, both the product we test and the test code we write, contains predominantly managed code, and most of our regular testing is manual or semi-automated. Although the particulars of the day-to-day work are vastly different, the act of testing is the same. I keep a lab book at my desk to track identified and reproduced defects and to note interesting areas of investigation that bear future attention.

Tours in Sprints

Our development and test teams work closely during each sprint. It is standard practice for the test team to build new bits between check-ins from our developers and participate in code reviews for the same. As such, we have some uncommon advantages in knowing where certain kinds of defects are likely to be found. Instead of jumping right into these known risk areas, I take a more methodical approach ingrained by my years of studying experimental science. The first thing I do with a new application (or version) is take a brief *Parking Lot tour* to get the lay of the land. As I learn how the various parts of the application are supposed to work together, I take notes on which areas deserve in-depth attention and follow-on tours. The next wave of tours focuses on individual features, typically with an imposed bias such as accessibility, expose all error dialogs, or force all default values (permutations pulled straight out of *How to Break Software* and summarized in Chapter 3, "Exploratory Testing in the Small," of this book).

Between the *Parking Lot tour* and the *Breaking Software tour,* I generally pick most of the "low-hanging" fruit in terms of obvious bugs.

My final wave of tours is a much more targeted endeavor. After a couple days observing how the product under test responds, it is time to go for more abusive tours that challenge the assumptions of implementation. The ones I end up using the most are the *Back Alley tour* and the *Obsessive-Compulsive tour,* built on previously observed reactions in the product (observations or behavior that were technically correct, but perhaps incomplete or narrow) or conversations with the developer about his implementation.

Over the course of two such tight sprints, I identified about 75 defects in each, of which all but 5 were fixed before the end of the week in which they were identified. We were working in what we call "low-overhead mode," such that if development could address the issue before the end of the week, test would not formally log the bug. This arrangement was great from both sides of the dev-test relationship; product quality was quickly improved, and no one had to deal with bug-reporting and -documenting overhead. Had the turnaround on bugs been days rather than hours, this arrangement would not have been appropriate, because details of the observed bug could have been lost.

Keeping the pace brisk was facilitated by a cut time each day when a new build would be produced and tested. This had a dual impact. First, development would communicate the fixes we should expect prior to the cut time each day, focusing the testing effort to newly implemented or repaired features. Second, the regular testing start time provided regular feedback to development about the state of their progress. Developers were eager to get their fixes into the next day's testing effort, causing them to work with test to ensure they'd make the test deadline each day, which helped keep the features to spec with limited creep. We maintained a very high rate of code churn and a tight loop of checking in and testing, which allowed us to stay on top of defects and find the important ones early. Testing during these sprints lent itself to exploratory tours, as the testing cycle was iterative and short. Returning to a general tour such as the *Money tour* or the *Guidebook tour* every few days helped ensure that we didn't let any new work slip through undetected. I do not recall any new bugs in those features over the last four months, despite regular use by our team and others.

Reviewing the bugs identified over one of these testing efforts shows a breakdown by detecting tour:

- 9% *Taxicab tour* (keyboard, mouse, and so on)
- 9% *Garbage Collector's tour* (checking resources after releasing/removing them)
- 15% *Back Alley tour* (attempting known bad actions, such as closing a dialog twice)
- 18% *Obsessive-Compulsive tour*
- 19% *Landmark tour*
- 30% *Supermodel tour*

While most of the *Supermodel tour* defects were not recall class, nearly all the *Back Alley* and *Garbage Collector's tours* would have forced a recall or patch on a released product. Although the *Supermodel tours* didn't directly reveal the more severe issues, they did identify places where more-focused tours could follow up and deal real damage. One such example was the identification of keyboard acceleration for the Cancel button in a wizard. This observation identified a bug immediately. Wizards do not typically accelerate the Cancel button with a lowercase *L;* instead, they usually reserve the Esc key for that, without any visual indicator. A follow-up *Back Alley tour* exploited this keyboard acceleration to cancel the wizard several times. This exposed an unhandled exception and a UI timing issue where a modal dialog was hidden behind the UI element waiting on it. Of course, canceling the same wizard instance more than once should also have not been possible.

Whenever I revisit a feature we've previously tested, I run another *Parking Lot tour*. Just recently, using this method I observed two defects in functionality that had been verified not two weeks earlier. Even when I wasn't planning to test this particular part of the feature, just by revisiting the bounds of the code under test, a broken link and an unhandled exception presented themselves for observation. Following a strict script and just getting in and getting your work done as efficiently as possible would have missed these opportunities, leading to increased mean time to detection for new defects in the system.

Parking Lot Tour

The *Parking Lot tour* was born of countless family vacations, where distances on the map didn't look nearly as imposing as they did after driving from place to place. Such ambitious plans often saw the family arrive at a venue after closing time, leaving nothing to do but tour the parking lot and try to make the next stop before it too closed. I used a *Parking Lot tour* to find a usability bug and an app crash during my interview for my current team:

- **Primary objective:** Identify the entry points for all features and points of interest within the scope of testing.
- **Secondary objective:** Identify areas where specific tours will be helpful.
- **Targets of opportunity:** Enumerate any show-stopping bugs on the first pass.

In a way, the *Parking Lot tour* is like a mixture of a *Landmark tour* and a *Supermodel tour.* The first pass isn't going to look too deep and is really more interested in how the code under test presents itself than anything the code under test does.

Test Planning and Managing with Tours

By Geoff Staneff

When testers express an interest in exploratory testing, this can often be interpreted by their managers as a rejection of rigor or planning. Through the use of the touring metaphor, managers can gain repeatability and an understanding of what has been tested, while testers can maintain their autonomy and exploratory imitative. This section outlines some of the strategies and techniques that will prove useful when managing a tour-driven test process.

Defining the Landscape

Two concerns frequently arise when discussing exploratory testing from the standpoint of the person who isn't using it right now in his own work. First, there are concerns about what will be tested. How can we know what we've covered and what we've not covered when the testers decide where and how to test while they are sitting with the application under test? Second, there are concerns about the transferability of that knowledge. What happens when the exploratory tester becomes unavailable for further testing efforts on this feature or product? Both of these concerns can be addressed through the utilization of testing tours.

What is a testing tour but a description of *what* and *how* to test? By taking a well-defined tour, for instance the *Supermodel tour,* and pointing your defect observer (the tester) at a particular feature or product, you can know that a test pass has been scheduled to review said feature or product to survey the state of fit and finish class defects. Although the tester may, under his or her own initiative, find other kinds of defects, the entire testing act has been biased to detect those defects that make the product look bad.

Where heavily scripted testing may specify precisely which defects to confirm or deny the existence of in a given product, the tour specifies a class of behavior or defect and leaves it to the tester to determine the best route to confirming or denying the existence. This leaves management free to set the testing strategy, without impairing the tester's ability to choose tactics suitable to the feature or session of exploration.

The second question is perhaps a more difficult question for test as a discipline and not just exploratory testing. As testers gain experience, they improve their understanding of software systems, how they are typically constructed, and how they typically fail. This has the advantage of making experienced testers more efficient at finding typical software defects, or even defects typical of a given piece of software through the various stages of development, but this increased value makes the temporary or permanent loss all the more damaging to the overall test process. Testers will become unavailable throughout the course of development: They can take time off, be transferred to another project or team, change their role within the organization, leave the company entirely, or any number of other things may arise that conspire to deprive your test effort of its most experienced testers. This is where touring really shines, because it defines *what* and *how,* such that any rational agent should be able to perform a similar tour and detect similar defects. Tours will not help testers detect subtle changes in typesetting, but tours can inform a tester that they ought to be concentrating on that sort of defect as they traverse the features they've been assigned.

A successful tour is one that intentionally reveals a particular class of defect, providing enough detail to bias the detection, but not so much as to narrow the focus too tightly either in feature scope or defect class. As such, it becomes even more important to record side trips and ancillary tours that were spawned by the scheduled tour. It should not be uncommon for your testers to pass up bug-finding opportunities but note them for further study when they can dedicate their focus to this unplanned area of interest. Touring, therefore, instills some discipline on the testing process. No matter if you choose to take the side trip now and resume the tour later, or mark the POI on your map and return after your tour, by making the distinction between on- and off-tour, one can come along later and understand which combination of tours should reveal all the defects observed. It is at this point when a decision can be made to either expand the set of regularly scheduled tours, or to run with the normal set and track whether these side-trip opportunities present themselves to other testers in the future.

Expanding the set may be helpful if you have a wide product and need to split work between new resources. By expanding the set, one is withholding some of the decision-making process from those doing the testing, but this can be critically important to avoid overlap and redundancy in a testing effort.

Tracking the recurrence of side trips in the future makes sense if you will have several opportunities to test different versions of the same application or same kind of application. In the event that a specific side trip does not present itself, it can be assigned as a special tour just to ensure that there really were not any such significant defects present in this testing effort. The subsequent sections walk through the use of tools through various points of an application development life cycle.

Planning with Tours

Before setting foot in a new city, prepared travelers will have acquired some basic information about their destination. It's good to know such things as what language is spoken there, if they will accept your currency, and whether they treat foreigners kindly, before you find yourself in unfamiliar surroundings with no plan in place to mitigate the challenges you'll encounter. This might mean taking one of the survey tours (*Landmark* or *Parking Lot*) yourself to get an overview of the key features you'll be expected to report on throughout the development and maintenance of the application. At the end of the cycle, you'll want to be able to report any show-stopper defects as well as how wide the happy path for users actually is through your application. This means providing tours aimed at covering well the core scenarios and providing opportunistic tours with great breadth across the application to pick up abnormalities in out-of-the-way corners of the application.

Many tours fit into the start or end of a development cycle naturally. A tour capable of detecting improper implementation of controls, such as a *Taxicab tour,* should come earlier than one focused on fit and finish, such as the *Supermodel tour.* Although the individual testers needn't have any privileged information about the data or class structure of the application under test, they are still capable of revealing defects that are sensitive to these structures. It is therefore important to find systematic errors early, such as misuse of a classes or controls, before the application has had a chance to solidify around this peculiar behavior and fixing the defect becomes too risky, or time-consuming, or the repercussions of the change too poorly understood to undertake a fix.

Early-cycle objectives include the following:

- Find design defects early.
- Find misuse of controls.
- Find misuse of UI/usability.

These objectives lend themselves to *tours of intent:* those explorations that focus on getting something done rather than doing that thing in any particular way. Tours of intent include the *Landmark tour* and the *Taxicab tour.* At the start of the cycle, a testing effort will usually attempt to identify big problems.

Late-cycle objectives include the following:

- Ensure public functions function.
- Ensure user data is secure.
- Ensure fit and finish is up to expectation.
- Characterize the width of the functional feature path.
- Confirm previous defects are not observable.

These objectives lend themselves to *tours of specifics:* those explorations that focus on a particular something in a particular way. Tours of specifics include the *Back Alley tour, Garbage Collector's tour, Supermodel tour,* and *Rained-Out tour.*

Permutations on tours should be intentional and planned ahead of time. Thinking about taking a *Landmark tour,* but only using the mouse to navigate your application? Make that decision up front.

At the end of the day, one must still plan and martial testing resources effectively from the start to secure the opportunity to succeed for one's team, regardless of the testing techniques employed. Often, realizing that a delay exists between development and test, test will undertake a testing effort over parts of the application in isolation rather than biting off an incomplete end-to-end scenario. Even when the application is nearly complete, when it is handed over to test as a full unit, it makes sense to begin with the early-cycle tours because they help identify opportunities for more in-depth tours and allocation of testing resources.

Letting the Tours Run

While exploration and permutation are important parts of the exploratory testing process, it is important that the tour and the tour guide stay on target for the duration of the tour. Staying on target means sticking within the intent of the tour. For example, if your current tour is scheduled to hit *N* major features, make sure you cover those *N* major features. This advice applies not just to the tester, but also to the test manager: Letting the planned tour run is important to identify the various side trips and follow-up tours that will help guide the next iteration of testing. Tours are meant to be repeated, by different testers, with different permutations in focus.

Because each tour is meant to be short, comprising a session of a few hours, there isn't much to gain from interrupting the tour. There is, however, much to lose from interrupting a tour in the way of knowing what you were looking for during that session. Testers will find bugs in products. This is not a surprise and isn't anything out of the ordinary. Figuring out how and why they found that bug might be something to talk about. With a guided tour, you have a framework under which another tester may be able to find similar defects. This is special and should be leveraged in subsequent tour assignments. When testers go off-tour, for whatever reason, they may find defects, but we already expect them to find defects on the tour they were experiencing. By leaving the tour, they will have lost the focus and observational bias granted by that tour, which makes scheduling a sensible follow-up tour much more difficult. A tester who chases down a promising side trip of "good bugs" might not get through the balance of the tour, leaving an even larger risk area in a completely unknown state. Without the confidence to come back to an area despite knowing bugs are ready to be found right now, you'll put yourself in a state of not knowing what you don't know at the end of the tour.

Analysis of Tour Results

Because tours impart a bias to the observer (for example, the tester is interested in specific kinds of observations with respect to the features comprising the tour), it provides great information about both the toured portion of the software and the need for additional tours through those parts of the software. Touring testers will report both opportunities for side trips and defects that were strictly "off-tour" but prominent enough to stand out despite the testing focus elsewhere. This provides several opportunities to involve the testers, helping them to take ownership in the entire process. The opportunities for side trips are clear and can lead directly to specific in-depth tours or additional broad tours in this previously missed feature area. Reports of bugs that reside outside the focus of the tour are indicators that a tour similar to the last but with a focus more attuned to the unexpected bug detected should be performed.

Finally, when multiple testers have taken the same tour, some overlap will occur as to the bugs they report. Because the tour is providing a bias to the act of bug detection, the overlap, or lack thereof, should provide some insight into how many of those kinds of bug remain undetected in the product—or if further tours in this area should be scheduled until such time as the reported bugs from different tourists converge. Assigning multiple testers to the same tour is not actually a waste of resources (in contrast to assigning multiple testers to the same scripted test case, which is a waste of resources). Because the tour leaves many of the tactical decisions of test to the individual, variation will exist between testers despite the similarity in the testing they have performed. Although this might run counter to the claim that a tour will improve reproducibility in a test pass across testers and time, so long as the tour reveals a particular kind of defect with great regularity it is not incompatible with the discovery of different bugs (for example, a variety of manifestations will point back to the same root cause of failure).

Making the Call: Milestone/Release

When the time comes to report on product quality, a tour-based testing effort will be able to report on what works in the product and how well it works. A tour-based testing effort will be able to report on what fraction of the planned work actually works, in addition to how wide the path to each working feature actually is. From a high level, test will be able to report how likely additional bugs will exist in given features, remaining to be discovered. Likewise, they will be able to report how unlikely certain types of defects will occur along the tour paths taken during testing. While the number of bugs detected per hour might not differ from other testing methods, the tour-based effort should be able to prioritize which types of bugs to find first, and thus provide early detection of assumed risks.

In Practice

Your circumstances may dictate much of your strategy for breaking down work and running a tour-based testing effort. Some test teams may be involved during the feature design stages and provide input on usability and testability of features before they are implemented, or your team might have no direct contact with the developers, only interacting with "complete" projects thrown over the wall in your general direction.

No matter what deadline you are under, you will want to start with a wider or overview tour to help identify where opportunities for in-depth exploration reside and specific tours to schedule. The feedback loop between these first explorations and the second wave is the most critical, as this is where you will begin to identify the overall allocation of testing resource to the product you have in front of you. Therefore, it is important to have great discipline early in sticking to the tour and identifying places to return with subsequent investigations. First, map the space for which you are responsible, and then go about focusing on particular points of interest or hot spots of trouble.

Conclusion

The touring concepts applied at Microsoft have helped software testers to better organize their approach to manual testing and to be more consistent, prescriptive, and purposeful. All the testers involved in these and other case studies have found the metaphor useful and an excellent way to document and communicate test techniques. They are now focused less on individual test cases and more on the higher-level concepts of test design and technique.

Exercises

1. Pick any bug described in this chapter and name a tour that would find it. Is there a tour, other than the one cited by the author in this chapter, that would also find the bug?
2. Pick any two bugs in this chapter at random and compare and contrast the bugs. Which one is more important in your mind? Base your argument on how you think the bug would impact a user who stumbles across it.
3. The *Supermodel tour* has been cited as a good tour for UI testing. Can you describe a way in which this tour might be used to test an API or other such software that has little or no visible UI?

CHAPTER 7
Touring and Testing's Primary Pain Points

0110010110110001 0100

"One man's crappy software is another man's full time job."

—Jessica Gaston

The Five Pain Points of Software Testing

Never in the history of mankind has society depended so completely on a product that is often so deeply flawed. Not only does software control our systems of government, law enforcement, banking, defense, communication, transportation, and energy, but it also holds the key to the computationally intensive solutions that will one day remake this planet. How will we tame our economic markets, achieve clean energy, or control our changing climate without the computing power of software? Beyond the innovative spirit of the human mind, is there a single tool that is more important to the future of mankind than software?

Yet software, more than any other product in history, is famous for its ability to fail. Newsreels overflow with stories of stranded ships, region-wide power failures, malfunctioning medical devices, exploding spacecraft, financial loss, and even human death. Minor inconveniences are so commonplace that it is a joke at Microsoft that employees act as the help desk for all their nontechnical friends and family. Computers and the software that makes them do useful things are a wonder, but their complexity is too much for the way we develop software today.

It is *testing* that the industry relies on as the check-and-balance between innovation and dependability. The complex nature of software development and the fallibility of the humans who write code combine to virtually guarantee the introduction of errors. But as a process to manage and minimize these errors, testing has some serious drawbacks. The five most concerning pain points are the subject of this chapter, and we must solve these issues to have any hope that software of the future will be any better than the software of today.

This chapter comes last, after the tours have been thoroughly discussed, to lead the reader into using the tours to relieve these pain points. The five pain points are as follows:

- Aimlessness
- Repetitiveness
- Transiency
- Monotony
- Memorylessness

Each is discussed in order next.

Aimlessness

Much has been written about the evils of a life without purpose, but it is *tests without purpose* and the aimlessness of much of our modern testing practice that are creating a major testing pain point. Testing is not simply something that we *can just go do.* It requires planning, preparation, strategy, and adaptable tactics for it to be performed successfully. But far too many software organizations ignore proper preparation in favor of *just doing it.* Testing is too important to treat it so casually.

When I was a professor at Florida Tech, I taught software testing, and one semester my class was much too large for my liking. I decided to run an experiment that would scare off a few of the less-serious students. On the first day, I convened the class in a computer lab and instructed the students to identify an application to test and work in pairs to test it. I gave them no further instruction on how to carry out such testing, but as an incentive, I told them that if they impressed me with their technique, they could stay in the class. If they did not, I would see that they were automatically dropped (not something I intended to do, but the threat was sufficient for my purpose).

I prowled the lab, which had the effect of increasing the tension in the room, and occasionally stopped a pair of students and demanded to know how they intended to find a bug. Each time I rendered such questioning, I got some variation of "not sure, doc, we're just hoping it fails." Finally, some astute student would realize that those answers weren't working and get a bit closer to something that indicated strategy. In fact, I remember the exact statement that caused me to admit the first pair of students and send them on their way: "We're going through all the text boxes entering long strings, hoping to find a place where they are not checking string length.[1]"

Bingo! Perhaps this is not the best or most important strategy, but it *is* a strategy, and as such it helps counter aimlessness. Software testers are far too often without strategy and specific goals as they are running tests.

---

[1] They found one, too. See attack 4 on page 35 of *How to Break Software.*

When testing manually, they wander the app in an ad hoc manner. And when writing automation it is simply because *they know how to write it;* whether the automation will find worthwhile bugs, will stand the test of time, and be worth the cost of maintenance isn't part of the picture.

This aimless nature of software testing must stop. How often will test managers provide the meaningless advice of *just go and test it* before we create a better way? Stop this aimless process now one team a time.

I know, it's easier said than done. After all, there are an infinite number of tests possible for even the simplest of applications. But I argue that there are a finite number of testing *goals.*

Define What Needs to Be Tested

Software testing usually occurs by partitioning an application into sections based on a component (defined by structural boundaries like code files and assemblies) or feature (specific functionality of a component) basis and assigning individual testers or teams of testers to a component or feature. Many companies I have worked with have *feature teams* or even assign separate test leads to each large component.

But such a partitioning does not really support good testing practice. Users don't care about components and features, and if we want to find bugs that real users are likely to stumble upon, we will benefit by following their lead. Users care about *capabilities* and use various components and features to exercise a desired capability. If we test according to capabilities, we can more closely align our testing to real-world usage.

For example, I can choose a set of capabilities to test as an ensemble or focus on a single one. I can purposefully explore the capabilities across a number of features or stick to the capabilities of a single feature. I can exercise capabilities that cross component boundaries or choose to stay within a component. I can rely on architecture documentation or written specs to build a component/feature/capability map to guide my testing and ensure that I cover the interesting combinations to the extent possible. Focusing on more fine-grained capabilities rather than higher-level notions of components and features puts me in a position to better understand what needs to be tested. To test a feature, I must exercise its capabilities in varying degree and order. By explicitly calling out the capabilities, I make this job more purposeful and can more easily account for progress and coverage.

Determine When to Test

The idea of decomposing features into capabilities can help organize a test team to focus on testing real-world concerns of users. In the best case, manual testers should be free to find subtle but important bugs by forcing an application to perform tasks it might be faced with when in the hands of a real user. However, the extent to which this is possible requires that prior testing must be effective at reducing the overall level of "bug noise."

Bug noise is what I call the niggling bugs and issues that keep testers from being productive. If all testers are doing is finding technical issues like an input field allowing characters when it should only allow numbers or constantly finding the same bug over and over again, productivity will fall. In the best case, all of these issues have already been found by prior developer testing, unit test, code reviews, and so forth. If not, a great deal of effort in manual testing will be spent finding them, and that means fewer cycles to run more tours and find more subtle but probably more impactful issues.

This means that over time it is important to understand how the bug-finding efforts in each testing phase matches the actual bugs being found. At Microsoft, this is part of the bug triage process: For every bug found, explicitly determine *when the bug should have been caught*. That way we can learn how to focus review effort, unit testing effort, and so forth based on historical bug data. It takes a few project cycles to perfect this process, but it pays off in the long run.

Determine How to Test

As the prior point was focused on the *testing phase,* this point is about *testing type,* meaning specifically manual versus automated testing. In Chapter 2, "The Case for Manual Testing," I spent a great deal of effort describing the differences between the two, and I will not rehash that here. However, within manual testing, it is also useful to classify how certain bugs were found. Was it ad hoc testing, scripted, or exploratory? Was a specific tour responsible for guiding the tester to the bug in question? If so, document this.

Teams that take care to match technique to bug have gone a long way toward answering the question *how.* Ultimately, a collective wisdom of sorts will emerge in the group in that certain bug types will be linked with certain tours or techniques, and testers will know that "this function/feature is best tested this way."

This is where the tours come in. Tours are a way to identify higher-level test techniques and over time understand the relationship between tours and features they are good at testing and bugs they are likely to find. As teams establish a base set of simple and advanced tours, they will have the link between feature type and bugs that they can use to make testing far less aimless than before.

Repetitiveness

We test and then we test some more. As our application grows in features, we run old tests on the existing features and new tests on the new ones. As the product grows over its life cycle, however, the new tests soon become old ones, and all of them eventually become stale.

Even stale tests have their role to play. As bugs are fixed, features and functionality must be retested, and existing test cases are seen as the least expensive way to retest the application. Indeed, it is foolish to waste any test case, and the idea of disposable test assets is a repugnant one for busy and overworked testers. The industry has found test case reuse such a useful paradigm that we've given the activity special names such as *regression tests* or even *regression suites* (to make them sound more thorough?) to highlight their role and purpose. For an application of any size and longevity, regression test cases can sometimes number in the millions.

Let's put aside the problem of maintaining such large test suites and focus on the repetition problem. Treading over already well-worn paths and data/environment combinations has only limited utility. It can be useful to verify a bug fix, but not to find new bugs or to test for potential side effects of a code change, and they are of no use whatsoever in testing new or substantially modified features. Worse still is the fact that many testers and developers put unwarranted faith in such tests, particularly when they are large in number. Running a million test cases sounds nice at face value (at least to managers and vice presidents), but it is what's *in* those test cases that really matters. Is it good news or bad news that a million plus members of a regression suite have executed clean? Are there really no bugs, or is the regression suite just incapable of finding the bugs that remain? To understand the difference, we must have a firmer grasp on what testing has already occurred and how our present and future testing will add to the whole.

Know What Testing Has Already Occurred

When a regression suite executes clean, we can't be sure whether this is good news or bad news. Boris Beizer called this phenomenon the *pesticide paradox,* and I can frame it no better than he did. If you spray a field of crops with the same pesticide, you will kill a large number of critters, but those that remain are likely to develop strong resistance to the poison. Regression suites and reused test cases are no different. Once a suite of tests finds its prescribed lot of bugs, those bugs that remain will be immune to its future effects. This is the paradox: The more poison you apply, a smaller percentage of bugs are killed over time.

Farmers need to know what pesticide formula they are using and understand that over time its value decreases. Testers must know what testing has already occurred and understand that reusing the same tired techniques will be of little bug-finding value. This calls for intelligent variation of testing goals and concerns.

Understand When to Inject Variation

Solving the pesticide paradox means that farmers must tinker with their pesticide formula, and for testers it requires *injection of variation* into test cases. That is a bigger subject than this book covers, but an important part of it is woven throughout the whole tours concept. By establishing clear goal-oriented testing techniques and understanding what types of bugs are found using those techniques, testers can pick and choose techniques that better suit their purpose. They can also vary the techniques, combine the techniques, and apply them in different orders and in different ways. Variation of testing focus is the key, and the methodology in this book provides the tools to achieve a consistent application of effective and ever-changing "pesticide."

Of course, simply changing the formula is a process that can be improved, too. Farmers know that if they match the right pesticide for their specific crop and the bugs they expect to combat, they achieve even more success. Your scenarios and tours are your pesticide and inject variation in the scenarios, as described in Chapter 5, " Hybrid Exploratory Testing Techniques," and using the tours in a variety of orders and with varying data and environments can help ensure that the ever-changing formula is one that potential bugs will never get used to.

Real pesticides have labels that show what crops they are safe for and what critters they target. Can we say the same about our tests? Not yet, but pesticide makers got where they are only by a lot of trial and error and by learning from all those trials. Software testers can and should do a lot of the same.

Transiency

Two communities regularly find bugs: the testers who are paid to find them, and the users who stumble upon them quite by accident. Clearly, the users aren't doing so on purpose, but through the normal course of using the software to get work (or entertainment, socializing, and so forth) done, failures occur. Often, it is the magic combination of an application interacting with real user data on a real user's computing environment that causes software to fail. Isn't it obvious then that testers should endeavor to create such data and environmental conditions in the test lab to find these bugs before the software ships?

Actually, the test community has been diligently attempting to do just that for decades. I call this process *bringing the user into the test lab,* either in body or in spirit. Indeed, my own Ph.D. dissertation was on the topic of statistical usage testing, and I was nowhere near the first person to think of the idea, as my multipage bibliography will attest. However, there is a natural limit to the success of such efforts. Testers simply cannot be users or simulate their actions in a realistic enough way to find all the important bugs. Unless you actually *live in the software,* you will miss important issues. And most testers do not live in their software; they are transients, and once the application is shipped, they move on to the next one.

It's like homeownership. It doesn't matter how well the house is built. It doesn't matter how diligent the builder and the subcontractors are during the construction process. The house can be thoroughly inspected during every phase of construction by the contractor, the homeowner, and the state building inspector. There are just some problems that will be found only after the house is occupied for some period of time. It needs to be used, dined in, slept in, showered in, cooked in, partied in, relaxed in, and all the other things homeowners do in their houses. It's not until the teenager takes an hour-long shower while the sprinklers are running that the septic system is found deficient. It's not until a car is parked in the garage overnight that we find out the rebar was left out of the concrete slab. And time matters, as well. It takes a few months of blowing light bulbs at the rate of one every other week to discover the glitch in the wiring, and a year has to pass before the nailheads begin protruding from the drywall. How can a home builder or inspector hope to find such issues?

These are some number of bugs that simply cannot be found until the house is lived in, and software is no different. It needs to be in the hands of real users doing real work with real data in real environments. Those bugs are as inaccessible to testers as nail pops and missing rebar are to home builders.

The tours and other exploratory constructs in this book are of limited value in fighting transience. Getting users involved in testing will help, getting testers involved with users so that they can create tours that mimic their actions will help, too. But at the end of the day, testers are transients. We can do what we can do and nothing more. It's good to understand our limitations and plan for the inevitable "punch lists" from our users. Pretending that when an application is released the project is over is simply wrong headed. There is a warranty period that we are overlooking, and that period is still part of the testing phase. I approach this topic in the next chapter, which explores the future of testing.

Monotony

Testing is boring. Don't pretend for a moment that you've never heard a developer, designer, architect, or other nonquality-assurance-oriented role express that sentiment. In fact, few QA people I know wouldn't at least agree that many aspects of what they do day in and day out are, if not boring, monotonous and uncreative.

As exhilarating as the hunt for bugs is early in one's career, for many it gets monotonous over time. I see this period of focusing exclusively on *the hunt* as a rite of passage, an important trial by fire that helps immerse a new tester in testing culture, technique, and mindset. However, if I had to do it for too long as the main focus of my day, I'd go bonkers. This monotony is the reason that many testers leave the discipline for what they see as the more creative pastures of design and development.

This is shortsighted because testing is full of interesting strategic problems that can entertain and challenge: deciding what to test and how to combine multiple features and environmental consideration in a single test; coming up with higher-level test techniques and concepts and understanding how a set of tests fits into an overall testing strategy. All of these are interesting, strategic problems that often get overlooked in the rush to test and test some more. The tactical part of testing, actually running test cases and logging bugs, is the least interesting part, yet it is the main focus of most testers' day, week, month, and career.

Smart test managers and test directors need to recognize this and ensure that every tester splits their time between strategy and tactics. Take the tedious and repetitive parts of the testing process and automate them. Tool development is a major creative task at Microsoft, and is well rewarded by the corporate culture.

For the hard parts of the testing process, such as deciding what to test and determining test completeness, user scenarios, and so forth, we have another creative and interesting task. Testers who spend time categorizing tests and developing strategy (the interesting part) are more focused on better testing and thus spend less time running tests (the boring part).

Testing remains an immature science. A thinking person can make a lot of insights without inordinate effort. By ensuring that testers make time to step back from their testing effort and find insights that will improve their testing, teams will benefit. Not only are such insights liable to improve the overall quality of the test, but the creative time will improve the morale of the testers involved.

This book addresses this need for creativity using *tours* as a higher-level representation of test cases. The act of recognizing, documenting, sharing, and perfecting a tours-based approach to testing has been widely cited at Microsoft as a productive, creative, and fun way to do more effective testing.

Memorylessness

I have a habit of doing paired testing at Microsoft, where I sit with another tester and we test an application together. I vividly recall one such session with a tester who had a good reputation among his peers and was idolized by his manager for his prolific bug finding.[2] Here's how the conversation went in preparation for the paired testing session:

> ME: "Okay, we just installed the new build. It has some new code and some bug fixes, so there is a lot to do. Can you give me the rundown on what testing you did on the prior builds so that we can decide where to start?"

---

[2] See my blog entry for "measuring testers" in Appendix C, "An Annotated Transcript of JW's Microsoft Blog," to see what I think of counting bugs as a way to measure a tester's value.

HIM: "Well, I ran a bunch of test cases and logged a bunch of bugs."

ME: "Okay, but what parts did you test? I'd like to start off by testing some places you haven't covered a great deal."

And from this I got a blank stare. He was doing a lot of testing, but his memory of where he had been, what he had tested, and what he had missed was nonexistent. Unfortunately, he's not unique in his lack of attention to his past. I think it is a common trait of modern testing practice.

Testing is a present-oriented task. By this I mean that testers are mostly caught in the moment and don't spend a lot of time thinking about the future. We plan tests, write them, execute them, analyze them, and quickly forget them after they have been used. We don't spend a lot of time thinking about how to use them on future versions of our application or even other testing projects.

Test teams are often even worse about thinking toward future efforts. Tests are conceived, run, and discarded. Features are tested without documenting the insights of what worked and what did not work, the good tests versus the bad. When the testing has finished, what has the team really learned?

Even the industry as a whole suffers from this amnesia. How many times has an edit dialog been tested over time and by how many different testers? How many times has the same function, feature, API, or protocol been tested? What is it about testing, that we don't take collective wisdom seriously?

Often, the memory of good tests and good testing resides in the head of the testers who performed it. However, testers move from project to project, team to team, and company to company far too often for them to be a useful repository of knowledge.

Test cases aren't a good currency for such memory either. Changes to an application often require expensive test case maintenance, and the pesticide paradox lessens the value of preexisting tests.

Tours are somewhat better because a single tour can represent any number of actual test cases, and if we are diligent about mapping tours to features and to bugs, we will create a ledger for our product that will give the next set of testers a great deal of insight into what we did that worked and what was less effective.

Conclusion

The industry's approach to manual testing has been either to overprepare by writing scripts, scenarios, and plans in advance or underprepare by simply proceeding in an ad hoc manner. Software, its specs, requirements, and other documentation change too much to over-rely on the former and is too important to entrust to the latter. Exploratory testing with tours is a good middle ground. It takes the testing task up a level from simple test cases to a broader class of test strategy and technique.

Having a strategy and a set of prescriptive techniques allows testers to approach their task with much more purpose, directly addressing the problem of aimlessness. Tours also force a more variable approach to test case creation, so that the problems of repetitiveness and monotony are attacked head on. Furthermore, the tours provide a structure to discuss test technique and create a tribal knowledge and testing culture to address both transiency (as much as it can be addressed without real users in the loop) and memorylessness. Tour usage can be tracked, and statistics about their coverage and bug-finding ability can be compiled into more meaningful and actionable reports that testers can learn from and use to improve their future efforts.

Exercises

1. Think about the software you use every day. Write a tour that describes the way you use it.
2. If testers could acquire data from their users and use it during testing, we would likely find more bugs that users would care about. But users are often uncooperative in sharing their data files and databases. Can you list at least three reasons why?
3. How can a tester keep track of what parts of the application have been tested? Can you name at least four things a tester can use as the basis for completeness measures?

CHAPTER 8
The Future of Software Testing

"The best way to predict the future is to invent it."

— *Alan Kay*

Welcome to the Future

Modern software testing is a far cry from the discipline as practiced in the past. It has evolved and changed a great deal since the middle part of the last century, when the first programs were being written.

In the early days of computer programming, the same people who wrote software were the ones who tested it. Programs were small and by today's standards very simple. They were algorithms, physics problems really, that were often completely specified (as most mathematical algorithms tend to be), meant only to be run on a single computer in a very controlled environment and used by people who knew what they were doing. Such control of complexity, the operational environment, and usage patterns is a far cry from modern software that must run on nearly any computer and be used by nearly any user and that solves problems much more diverse than the physics problems and military applications that dominated the birth of computing. Today's software truly requires professional test engineers.

But somewhere between the dawn of computing and the time of this writing, software testing took a fateful turn. There was a point at which the need for software applications outpaced the ability of trained programmers to produce them. There simply were not enough coders. One of the many solutions to this problem was to separate the roles of developer and tester. To free up time of those trained to code, the problem of testing that code was put into the hands of a new class of IT professionals, the software testers.

This was not a partition of the existing developer community into dev and test, that would not have served to increase the number of developers; instead, software testing became more of a clerical role, with the reasoning that because they didn't have to program, testers did not need to be as technical.

Obviously, there were exceptions, and places like IBM, DEC, and the new player on the block Microsoft hired programming talent for testing positions, particularly within groups that produced low-level applications such as compilers, operating systems, and device drivers. But outside these islands of ISVs, the tradition of hiring nontechnical people for testing roles became pervasive.

Modern testers still come from the nontechnical (or at least non–computer science) ranks, but there is a great deal of training and on-the-job mentoring available now, and this trend is slowly reversing. In my opinion, however, the slow evolution of our discipline is not enough to keep pace with the major advances in computing and software development. Applications are getting much more complicated. Platforms are becoming much more capable, and their complexity is mushrooming. The applications of the future that will be built on these new platforms and that were discussed in Chapter 1, "The Case for Software Quality," will require a level of testing sophistication that we do not currently possess. How will we as a test community rise to the challenges of the future and be in a position to test these applications and help make them as reliable and trustworthy as they need to be? In a world where everything runs on computers and everyone depends on software, are we confident that the way we test now is good enough?

I am not. In fact, in many ways the applications of the future are just not testable given our current toolset and knowledge base. The rate of failure of most all of our current software systems makes it hard to argue that what we have now in testing is enough for today's applications, much less tomorrow's. To have some degree of optimism in the quality of tomorrow's software, we are going to need some new tools and techniques to help us get there.

That's what this chapter is about: painting a picture of the future of software testing that will actually work to deliver the highly reliable applications of tomorrow. These are a collection of ideas and visions about what software testing ought to be.

The *Heads-Up Display* for Testers

The tester sits in her office, papers full of printed diagrams, prose, and technical information scattered haphazardly across her workspace, a full dozen folders open on her desktop containing links to specifications, documentation, and bug databases. With one eye, she watches her email and instant message clients waiting for answers from her developers about bug fixes. With the other eye, she watches the application under test for symptoms of failure and her test tools for progress indicators. Her mind is a hodgepodge of test cases, bug data, spec data...so much information that she's overwhelmed with it and yet not enough information to do her job properly.

Contrast the tester's predicament with that of the computer (or console) gamer. Gamers have no need for workspace. That area can be used for empty soda cans and chip wrappers; every piece of information they require about their video game is provided by the video game itself. Unlike the tester who must sit and wonder what the application is doing behind the interface, gamers can see their entire world laid out in front of them. Thanks to their heads-up display, information seeps into their consciousness automatically.

Consider the wildly popular World of Warcraft online game and its heads-up display. In the upper-right corner of the screen, a mini map of the world pinpoints the hero's exact location. Across the entire bottom of the screen, every tool, spell, weapon, capability, and trick the hero possesses is laid out for easy access. In the upper left, information about objects in the world, adversaries, and opportunities stream into view as the hero moves about the world. This information, called the "heads-up display," overlays the users' view of the game world, making them more effective without reducing their ability to play and enjoy it.

This parallels nicely with software testing, I think, to produce a nice vision for our future—a future in which information from the application and the documents and files that define it are seamlessly displayed in a configurable skin that overlays the application under test: the *tester's heads-up display*, or *THUD* for short.

Imagine a heads up display that allows the tester to hover the cursor over a UI control and a window into the source code materializes. Don't want to see the source? That's fine because you can also view the code churn (fixes and modifications to the source code) information and bug fix history, and view all the prior test cases and test values for that control and any other information relevant to the tester. It is a wealth of information at your fingertips, presented in a noninvasive manner to be consumed by the tester as needed. Useful information painted on the canvass of the application under test.

Information is important enough that the THUD allows any number of overlays. Imagine a game world where targeting information is grafted over adversaries so that they are easier to shoot. The tester can see architectural layer dependencies overlaid on top of the UI *while the application is running*, quickly spotting hotspots and understanding the interaction between the inputs she applies and architectural and environmental dependencies. You could experience the interaction between a web app and its remote data store, much like Master Chief of the *Halo* Xbox series conquers a level. You could watch inputs trickle through two levels of stored procedures, or see the interaction between an API and its host file system through a visual experience that mirrors the game world experience of today.

From this knowledge will come much better guidance than what we have now. As we play our video game called software testing, we will know when bugs get fixed and what components, controls, APIs, and so forth are affected. Our heads-up display will tell us. As we test, we will be reminded of prior inputs we applied and past testing results. We'll be reminded of which inputs are likely to find problems and which ones already have been part of some automated suite or even a prior unit test. The THUD will be a constant companion to the manual tester and a font of knowledge about the application under test, its structure, its assumptions, its architecture, its bugs, and entire test history.

The existence of the THUD will be to testers what the HUD is to gamers now. You simply don't play a video game with the HUD turned off. Without the information the HUD provides, you'd never manage to navigate the complex and dangerous world of the game. HUD-less, you could have but one strategy: *Try everything you can think of and hope for the best.* That pretty much sums up what a lot of THUD-less software testing is today. Without the right information, displayed when and how we need it, what else are we supposed to do?

In the future, the experience of the software tester will be unrecognizable from what it is today. Manual testing will become much more similar to playing a video game.

"Testipedia"

The THUD and the technology it will enable will make testing much more repeatable, reusable, and generalize-able. Testers will be able to record manual test cases to have them automatically converted to automated test cases. This will increase the ability for testers across different teams, organizations, or even companies to share test experiences and test assets. The development of resources to access and share these assets is the obvious next step. I call these resources *Testipedia* in deference to its analogous predecessor Wikipedia.

Wikipedia is one of the most novel and useful sites on the Internet and often the very top result of an Internet search. It's based on the idea that all the information about every concept or entity that exists is in the head of some human being. What if we got all those human beings to build an encyclopedia that exposed that knowledge to everyone else? Well, that happened, and the result is www.wikipedia.org.

Now, let's apply the Wikipedia concept to testing. I conjecture that every function you can test has already been tested somewhere and at sometime by some tester who has come before you. Need to test a username and password entry dialog? It's been tested before. Need to test a web form that displays the contents of a shopping cart? It's been tested before. Indeed, every input field, function, behavior, procedure, API, or feature has been tested before. And if not the exact feature, something so close that whatever testing applied to that prior product also applies to yours to some greater or lesser extent. What we need is a Testipedia that encapsulates all this testing knowledge and surfaces the test cases in a form usable by any software tester.

Two main things have to happen for Testipedia to become a reality. First, tests have to be reusable so that a test that runs on one tester's machine can be transported to another tester's machine and execute without modification. Second, test cases have to be generalized so that they apply to more than just a single application. Let's talk about these in order and discuss what will have to happen to make this a reality.

Test Case Reuse

Here's the scenario: One tester writes a set of test cases and automates them so that she can run them over and over again. They are good test cases, so you decide to run them, as well. However, when you do run them, you find they won't work on your machine. Your tester friend used automation APIs that you don't have installed on your computer and scripting libraries that you don't have either. The problem with porting test cases is that they are too specific to their environment.

In the future, we will solve this problem with a concept I call *environment-carrying tests.* Test cases of the future will be written in such a way that they will encapsulate their environment needs within the test case using virtualization.[1] Test cases will be written within virtual capsules that embed all the necessary environmental dependencies so that the test case can run on whatever machine you need it to run on.

The scope of technological advances we need for this to happen are fairly modest. However, the Achilles heel of reuse has never been technological so much as economic. The real work required to reuse software artifacts has always been on the consumer of the reused artifact and not on its producer. What we need is an incentive for testers to write reusable test cases. So, what if we create a Testipedia that stored test cases and paid the contributing tester, or their organization, for contributions? What is a test case worth? A dollar? Ten dollars? More? Clearly they have value, and a database full of them would have enough value that a business could be created to host the database and resell test cases on an as-needed basis. The more worthy a test case, the higher its value, and testers would be incentivized to contribute.

Reusable test cases will have enough intrinsic value that a market for test case converters would likely emerge so that entire libraries of tests could be provided as a service or licensed as a product.

But this is only part of the solution. Having test cases that can be run in any environment is helpful, but we still need test cases that apply to the application we want to test.

---

[1] Virtualization plays a significant role in my future testing vision, as you will see later in this chapter.

Test Atoms and Test Molecules

Microsoft, and other companies I have worked for, is really like a bunch of smaller companies all working under the same corporate structure. SQL Server, Exchange, Live, Windows Mobile…there are a lot of testers writing a lot of test cases for a lot of applications. Too bad these test cases are so hard to transfer from application to application. Testers working on SQL Server, for example, don't find it easy to consume test cases from, say, Exchange even though both products are large server applications.

The reason for this is that we write test cases that are specifically tied to a single application. This shouldn't come as any big surprise given that we've never expected test cases to have any value outside our immediate team. But the picture I've painted of the future requires exactly that. And if you accept the argument that test cases have value outside their immediate project, there will be financial incentive to realize that value.

Instead of writing a test case for an application, we could move down a level and write them for features instead. Any number of web applications implement a shopping cart, so test cases written for such a feature should be applicable to any number of applications. The same can be said of many common features such as connecting to a network, making SQL queries to a database, username and password authentication, and so forth. Feature-level test cases are far more reusable and transferable than application-specific test cases.

The more focused we make the scope of the test cases we write, the more general they become. Features are more focused than applications, functions and objects are more focused than features, controls and data types are more focused than functions, and so forth. At a low enough level, we have what I like to call "atomic" test cases. A *test atom* is a test case that exists at the lowest possible level of abstraction. Perhaps you'd write a set of test cases that simply submits alphanumeric input into a text box control. It does one thing only and doesn't try to be anything more. You may then replicate this test atom and modify it for different purposes. For example, if the alphanumeric string in question is intended to be a username, a new test atom that encoded the structure of valid usernames would be created. Over time, Testipedia entries for thousands (and hopefully orders of magnitude more) of such test atoms would be collected.

Test atoms will be combined into *test molecules,* as well. Two alphanumeric string atoms might be combined into a test molecule that tests a username and password dialog box. I can see cases where many independent test authors would build such molecules and then over time the best such molecule would win out on Testipedia, and yet the alternatives would still be available. With the proper incentives, test case authors would build any number of molecules that could then be borrowed, leased, or purchased for reuse by application vendors that implement similar functionality.

An extremely valuable extension of this idea is to write atoms and molecules in such a way that they will understand whether they apply to an application. Imagine highlighting and then dragging a series of 10,000 tests onto an application and having the tests themselves figure out whether they apply to the application and then running themselves over and over within different environments and configurations. At some point, there would exist enough test atoms and molecules that the need to write new, custom tests would be minimal.

Virtualization of Test Assets

Environment-carrying test cases are only the tip of the iceberg when it comes to the use of virtual machines in the future of software testing. One of the major complexities a tester faces, as discussed in Chapter 3, "Exploratory Testing in the Small," is the availability of actual customer environments in which to run her test cases. If we are shipping our application to run on consumer machines, how do we anticipate how those machines will be configured? What other applications will be running on them? How do we get the machines in our test labs configured in a similar manner so that our tests are as realistic as possible?

At Microsoft, they have an amazing tool called "Watson" that gives insight into what user machines look like and how our applications fail in actual user situations. Watson is built in to applications that run on user machines. It detects catastrophic failures and allows the user to choose whether to package up information about the failure and send it to Microsoft where it can be diagnosed and fixed. (Fixes are delivered through Windows Update or other similar update services by other vendors.)

Virtualization technology could be used in the future to improve this process and to contribute customer environments to Testipedia for reuse. Imagine that instead of just sending the bug report to Microsoft or some other vendor, the entire machine (minus personal information obviously) is virtualized and sent to the vendor over the Internet. Developers could debug a problem from the actual point of failure on the user's machine. Debugging of field failures would be reduced dramatically, and over time a cache of virtual machines representing thousands of real customer environments would be stored. With the right infrastructure, these VMs could be made available as part of a virtual test lab. A trade in buying, selling, and leasing test labs would supplement Testipedia and relegate test lab design and construction to the dustbin of twentieth-century testing history.

Visualization

The availability of reusable test labs and test cases will make the job of future software testers much more of a design activity than the low-level test case construction activity that it is today. Testers will be collecting prebuilt artifacts and using sophisticated lab management solutions to organize and execute their tests. There exists the distinct possibility that without the proper oversight and insight, all this testing could miss the mark by a wide margin.

This points to the need for better software visualization so that testers can monitor testing progress and ensure that the tests are doing the job that needs to be done.

But how does one visualize software? What indeed does software look like? Software is not a physical product, like an automobile, that we can see, touch, and analyze. If an automobile is missing a bumper, it's easy to see the defect, and everyone associated with building the car can agree on the fix and when the fix is complete. With software, however, this scenario is not quite that easy. Missing and broken parts aren't so readily distinguished from working parts. Tests can execute without yielding much information about whether the software passed or failed the test or how new tests contribute to the overall knowledge pool about application quality. Clearly, visualization tools that expose important software properties and allow useful images of the software, both at rest and in use, to assist testers of the future would fill an important gap in our testing capability.

Visualizations of software can be based on actual software assets or properties of those assets. For example, inputs, internally stored data, dependencies, and source code are all concrete software assets that can be rendered in ways useful for testers to view. Source code can be visualized textually in a code editor or pictorially as a flow graph. For example, Figure 8.1 is a screen shot of a testing tool used in Microsoft's Xbox and PC games test teams to help a tester visualize code paths.

Instead of seeing paths as code artifacts, the visual displays the flow in terms of which screen in the game follows other screens.[2] It's a sequence of UI elements that allows testers to look ahead and understand how their inputs (in this case, the input is steering the car through Project Gotham Racing II) take them through different paths of the software. This visual can be used to drive better coverage and can help testers select inputs that take them to more interesting and functionally rich places in the game.

Visualizations can also be based on properties of the application, like churned (changed) code, coverage, complexity, and so forth. When the visualizations are based on information used to guide testing decisions, that's when they are most useful. For example, if you wanted to test, say, the components that are the most complex, how would you decide how to choose the right components?

During the testing of Windows Vista, a visualization tool was constructed to expose such properties in a way that is consumable by software testers. The screen snap in Figure 8.2 is one example of this.

---

[2] This particular image is taken from the testing of Project Gotham Racing II and is used with permission of the Games Test Org at Microsoft.

FIGURE 8.1 A UI visualization tool from the Microsoft Games Test Org.

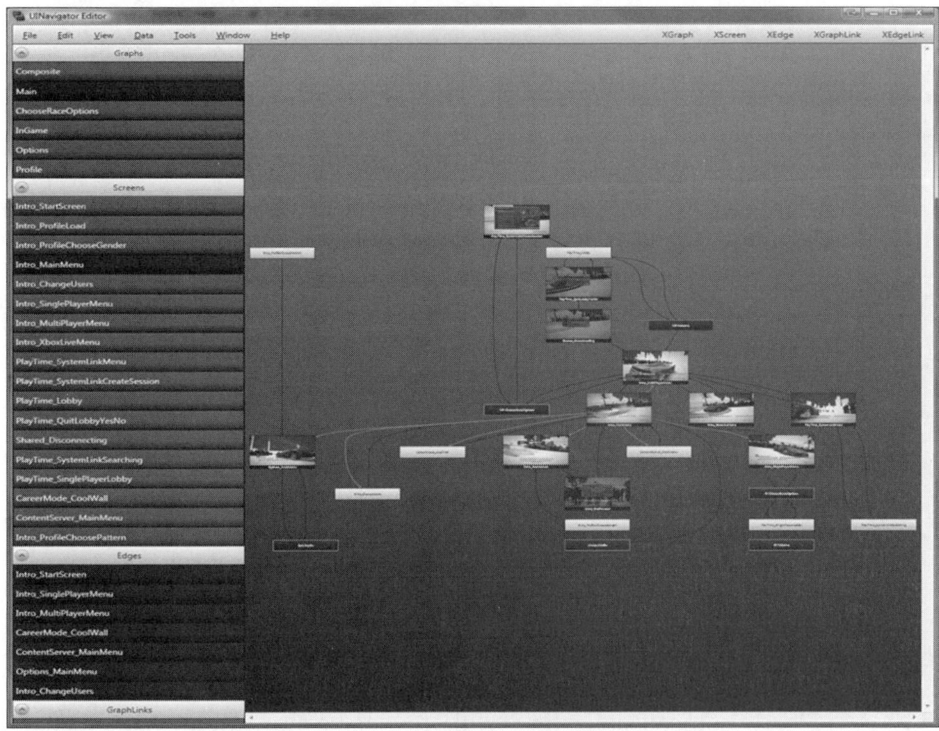

FIGURE 8.2 A reliability analysis tool used to visualize complexity.

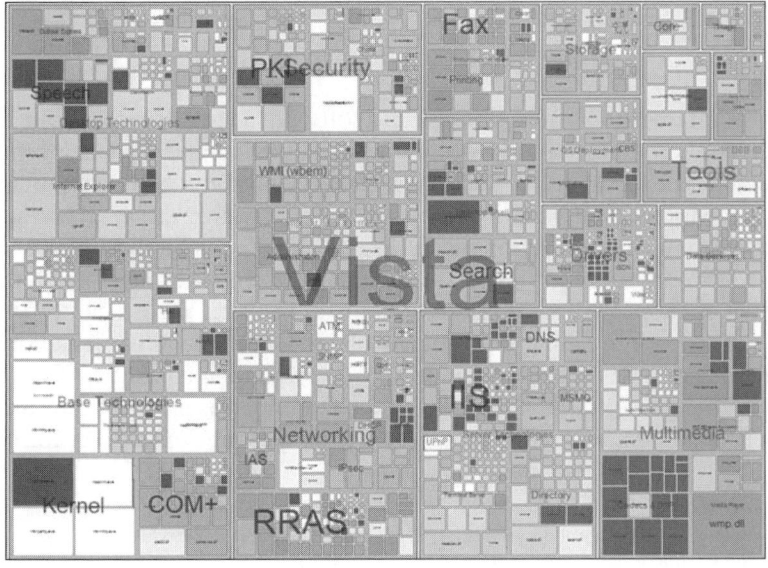

Figure 8.2 is a visualization of the components of Vista and their relative complexity.[3] Note that each labeled square is a component grouped according to the feature set to which the component belongs. The size of each square represents one of the numerous complexity measures the Windows group has defined, and the color represents a different complexity measure. Thus, bigger and darker squares represent more complex features. If our goal were to focus testing on complexity, this visual would be an excellent starting point.

Good visualizations will require support from the runtime environment in which the target software is operating. Interactions between the system under test and its external resources, such as the files, libraries, and APIs, can no longer be something that happens privately and invisibly and that only complicated tools like debuggers can reveal. We need the equivalent of X-ray machines and MRIs that bring the inner workings of software to life in three dimensions. Imagine a process similar to medical dye injection where an input is injected into a working system and its path through the system is traced visually. As the dyed input travels through the application's components, its impact on external resources can be monitored and experiments conducted to isolate bugs, identify performance bottlenecks, and compare various implementation options. It will be this level of transparency, scrutiny, instrumentation, and analysis that will enable us to achieve the level of sophistication in software that is currently enjoyed in medical science. Software is both complicated enough and important enough that such an investment is needed.

Clearly, some visualizations will prove to be more useful than others, and in the future we will be able to pick and choose which ones we need and when. As we gain experience using visualizations, best practice will emerge to provide guidance on how to optimize their usage.

Testing in the Future

So what does the future hold for the software tester? How will the THUD-like tools and Testipedia work with virtualization and visualization tools to remake the future of the software tester? Here's how I envision it.

Imagine a software development organization. Perhaps it is a start-up developing an application meant to run on GPS-enabled cellular phones or the IT department in a giant financial institution building a new line of business app. Perhaps it is even Microsoft itself building a cloud-based application interacting with a small client-side managed application. Any of these vendors will build their application and then contract with a test designer. For either the start-up or the IT shop, this is likely to be an external consultant, whereas Microsoft may use full-time employees for this task.

[3] This tool was developed by Brendan Murphy of Microsoft Research Cambridge and is used with permission.

In either case, the test designer will analyze the application's testing requirements and interfaces and document the testing needs. She will then satisfy those needs by identifying the test assets she needs to fulfill the testing requirements. She may lease or purchase those assets from commercial vendors or from a free and open source like Testipedia.[4]

The result will be any number of virtualized operational environments; I imagine tens of thousands or more, and millions of applicable test cases and their variants. These environments would then be deployed on a cloud-based virtual test lab, and the test cases would be executed in parallel. In a matter of a few hours, the amount of testing would exceed centuries of person-year effort. Coverage of application's source code, dependent libraries and resources, UI, and so forth would be measured to quality levels far beyond our current technology and likely contain every conceivable use case. All this will be managed by visualization, measurement, and management tools that will provide automated bug reporting and build management so that little human monitoring will be necessary.

This future will be possible only after some years or decades of developing and collecting reusable test assets. What it will eventually mean for software testers is that they will no longer be consumed by the low-level tasks of writing test cases and executing them. They will move up several layers of abstraction to the point where they will be designing test plans and picking and choosing among relevant existing test cases and automation frameworks.

For the start-up developing cell phone apps, they would be able to acquire virtual environments representing every conceivable cell phone their customers would use. LOB app developers would be able to simulate user environments with every conceivable configuration and with thousands of potentially conflicting applications installed. Microsoft would be able to create test environments for its cloud-based application that would meet or exceed the complexity and diversity of the real production environment.

Test atoms and test molecules numbering in the hundreds of millions would, over time, be gathered and submitted individually and in groups. These tests will scour the application looking for every place where they apply, and then execute automatically, compiling their own results into the larger test monitoring system so that the human test designer can tweak how the automation is working and measure its progress. Over hours of actual time, centuries of testing will occur, and as bugs are fixed, the tests will rerun themselves at the exact moment the application is available.

By the time the application is released, every conceivable test case will have been run against every conceivable operational environment. Every

[4] Reusable test assets, both virtualized operational environments and test cases/test plans, are likely to have good commercial value. I can envision cases where multiple vendors provide commercial off-the-shelf-test assets coexisting with a Testipedia that provides a bazaar-like open source market. Which model prevails is not part of my prediction; I'm only predicting their general availability, not the acquisition and profit model.

input field will have been pummeled with legal and illegal input numbering in the millions. Every feature will be overtested, and every potential feature conflict or application compatibility issue will have been checked and double-checked. All possible outputs that the application can generate will be generated numerous times, and its state space will be well covered. Test suites for security, performance, privacy, and so forth will have run on every build and intermediate build. Gaps in test coverage will be identified automatically and new tests acquired to fill these gaps.

And all this is before the application ships. After it ships, testing will continue.

Post-Release Testing

Even in the face of centuries of testing that we can achieve, testing can never really be complete. If we're not done testing when the product releases, why should we stop? Test code should ship with the binary, and it should survive release and continue doing its job without the testers being present to provide ongoing testing and diagnostics.

Part of this future is already here. The Watson technology mentioned earlier (the famous "send/don't send" error reporting for Windows apps) that ships in-process allows the capture of faults when they occur in the field. The next logical step is to do something about them.

Watson captures a fault and snaps an image of relevant debug info. Then some poor sap at the other end of the pipe gets to wade through all that data and figure out a way to fix it via Windows update. This was revolutionary in 2004, still is actually. In two to five years, it will be old school.

What if that "poor sap" could run additional tests and take advantage of the testing infrastructure that existed before the software was released? What if that poor sap could deploy a fix and run a regression suite in the actual environment in which the failure occurred? What if that poor sap could deploy a production fix and *tell the application to regress itself?*

He would no longer be a poor sap, that's for sure.

To accomplish this, it will be necessary for an application to remember its prior testing and carry along that memory wherever it goes. And that means that the *ability to test itself* will be a fundamental feature of software of the future. Our job will be to figure out how to take our testing magic and embed it into the application itself. The coolest software feature of the future could very well be placed there by software testers!

Conclusion

The world of the software tester is full of information. Information flows from the application we are testing, the platform and environment the application runs in, and from the development history of the application itself. The way testers consume and leverage this information will ultimately determine how well applications are tested and subsequently the quality levels of the applications that make up the software ecosystem. The only successful future for software testers is one where we master this information and use it in the ways previously prescribed failing to do so will mean the same levels of low quality our industry has historically achieved.

Any number of industries have successfully harnessed such a large amount of information, and we should look to those industries for inspiration. The one I think represents the best model for software testing is the video gaming industry, where the sheer amount and complexity of information is just as overwhelming as the body of information software testers must handle. However, gamers can handle this information simply and elegantly through their collection of tricks, tips, cheats, and the almighty heads-up display. It really boils down to information at the gamer's fingertips and a shared set of strategies and guidance available to all so that new gamers can rapidly become experts through the experiences of old gamers.

In fact, the gaming world has been so successful that their processes, tools, and techniques have built incredibly engaging products that have created their own complex economies and changed society in some very fundamental ways. Surely, if they can take information and guidance that far, so can software testers!

The processes, techniques, and guiding principles of the gamer are a compelling model for the software tester to mimic. In the future, information should flow seamlessly and conveniently from the application under test, its environment, and its history of use directly to the tester in the most simple-to-consume form: a heads-up display for testers. Testers will be as equipped as gamers to navigate a complex world of inputs, outputs, data, and computation.

Testing stands to gain a substantial amount in terms of productivity, precision, and completeness. And, who knows, if testing is like playing a video game, it might just be more fun as well.

Exercises

1. Name five things you'd want on a tester's heads-up display.
2. Name five things you'd want on an exploratory tester's heads up display.
3. If you had to write a business plan for Testipedia, how would you argue its utility?
   a. Write a summary of how Testipedia could be used as a free community asset.
   b. Write a summary of how Testipedia could be used to make a profit.

4. In Chapter 3, testing in the small was broken into input, state, code paths, user data, and environment issues. Besides environment, which of these issues is the best possible candidate for using virtualization? Explain how virtualization could be used to support better testing of this issue.
5. Figure 8.2 is often called a "heat map" and shows two aspects of the application under test: size and complexity. Name two additional properties of software that would be useful to visualize in this manner. Explain how these properties might be used to guide a tester.
6. Could the infrastructure for post-release testing be misused by a hacker? Give a case that might be a problem. Can you name another concern a user might have with a post-release testing infrastructure? How might these problems be overcome?
7. Have a class/team/group discussion about whether human testers might one day become obsolete. What parts of the future of testing still require a human tester to be present? What would have to happen for software companies to no longer be required to employ large numbers of in-house testers?

APPENDIX A
Building a Successful Career in Testing

"If you have a job without any aggravations, you don't have a job."

—*Malcolm Forbes*

How Did You Get into Testing?

I made the transition from software developer to software tester in 1989, when I was a graduate student at the University of Tennessee. It was not a transition I made by choice. One fateful morning, my professor[1] confronted me about my missing too many development meetings. The meetings, I explained, were inconveniently convened on a Saturday morning, and as a new graduate student living away from home for the first time in my life, this particular time slot was problematic.[2] Interestingly enough, my punishment was not a pink slip, but a sentence to be the sole tester of the group and to have no interaction with the development team at all.[3]

How fateful this decision was for my career, which has produced dozens of papers on testing, tools so numerous I can't even remember them all, five books, and countless happy hours at work. Testing has been a creative, technically challenging, and fulfilling career for me; but the same cannot be said of everyone. Granted, my introduction to the field was an intensive, graduate school immersion, and there are certain advantages to that. But moreover, I think there is a *testing hump* that exists between the novice and expert stages that people need help climbing, through a combination of mentoring, access to information, and general guidance. It's easy

---

[1] I worked on a well-funded development project using Cleanroom Software Engineering under the direction of Professor Jesse Poore of the University of Tennessee and the supervision of Harlan D. Mills, who was at Florida Tech at that time and was the inventor of the Cleanroom methodology.

[2] The time slot was complicated by the fact that I had met and was living with a girl who considered Saturday to be off limits for work. Given that I eventually married and had kids with that girl, one could say I got into testing to improve my love life.

[3] Cleanroom requires complete independence of developers and testers.

to become a novice tester, and not too hard to become proficient. It's climbing the hump from proficient to expert that this chapter is about.

Back to the Future

Time has stood still on the discipline of software testing. We do things in the twenty-first century much the same as they were done last century. Bill Hetzel's 1972 collection[4] of testing knowledge is still very relevant today, and my own *How to Break Software* series first published in 2002 has yet to be supplanted as the chief resource for actual software testing techniques.

Indeed, if it were possible to transport testers from the 1970s to the present, I expect that we'd find their skills adequate for testing of modern software. They'd have to learn about the Web and various protocols, but the techniques they possess for actual testing would translate fairly well. Take one from the 1990s, and almost no training at all would be required.

The same cannot be said of developers, whose last-century skills would be almost completely obsolete. Ask anyone who hasn't coded for a while to take the practice up again and see what kind of reaction you get.

It bothers me more than a little that we can hire bodies off the street and they can test and be productive from day one. Can it really be that easy? Or are our expectations simply that low? It bothers me even more that we can't take decent testing talent from being productive to being an expert in any predictable fashion. Can testing really be that hard?

It's that hump again. The price of entry is low, but the road to mastery is difficult.

On the approach to the testing hump, we rely on the fact that many aspects of testing are easy to master. Most anyone can learn to be decent at it. Apply even a little common sense to input selection and you will find bugs. Testing at this level is real fishing-in-a-barrel activity, enough to make anyone feel smart. But after the approach, the path steepens sharply, and testing knowledge becomes more arcane. We find that some people are good at it, and we call them "naturals" and praise their instincts.

But must they be instincts? Is the path across the hump navigable by more than just those who seem born to do it? Is testing teachable in a way that more experts can be created? I think the hump is navigable, and this chapter is my notes on how to go about doing just that in your own career. It's not a recipe because a career is no cookbook. But you can do some things to accelerate your career. But, as you might have guessed, they are easier to talk about than to actually do.

---

[4] W. Hetzel (editor), *Program Test Methods*, Englewood Cliffs, NJ: Prentice-Hall, 1972.

The Ascent

Early in a testing career is the time to prepare for the long ascent up the testing hump. The best advice I can give is to think in halves. For every project you do, there are two sets of (not necessarily equal) tasks. The first task is doing what it takes to make the current testing project succeed. The second task is learning what you need to do to make the next testing project easier. I call this *testing for today's project while preparing for tomorrow's.* If every project is split into two such halves, one has almost guaranteed consistent improvement so that with each project you do, you'll be a better tester because of it.

So let's concentrate on the second task, preparing for the next project. The things to watch out for are *repetition, technique,* and *holes.*

Repetition

Never do anything twice without realizing it and questioning it. This is the one thought I want all young testers to get in their head. I see so many novices waste time on mundane tasks such as setting up test machines, configuring a test environment, installing the application under test in a lab, choosing a build to test, the list goes on and on until you find that so little of your time is actually spent testing software.

This is the mistake that many new testers make. They fail to see the repetitive nature of their day-to-day activity, and before they know it, they've gone hours without doing any actual testing. Pay attention to repetition, and note the amount of time it is taking away from your real job of testing the software. To get over the testing hump, you will have to be a tester, not a lab manager or test machine administrator.

Automation is the answer to repetition and a subject for later in the chapter.

Technique

Testers often analyze failures. When we analyze bugs, we are studying our developers' failure to write reliable code. We also analyze bugs we missed. After our application ships and customers begin reporting bugs, we face the prospect of dealing with our collective failure to find important bugs. Each field-reported bug indicates our broken processes and gaps in our testing knowledge.

But analyzing our successes is also important, and many new testers fail to take advantage of this low-hanging fruit. Every bug we find during testing is a success, an indication that our testing process is working. We need to fully grasp this excellence so that it gets repeated.

Sports teams do this. They watch tapes of games and analyze why each play worked and why each play didn't work. I vividly recall such an incident when a friend took pictures of my son playing soccer. One such picture captured his strike that ended up going past the opposing keeper for a goal. When I showed it to my son, I pointed out how his plant foot was perfectly positioned, and that his kicking foot was toe-down and placed so that the ball was struck on the sweet spot at his laces. He stared at the picture a long time, and since then he has rarely struck a ball incorrectly. He may have done it right by accident when he scored, but forever after his technique has been purposeful and near perfect.

Now back to the lesson for new testers. All of us will have our moment in the sun. We'll find that huge hole, that high-priority bug, and be celebrated for doing so. But take a moment to look at the bigger picture. What technique did we use to find that bug? Can we create a recipe for finding more just like it? Can we take to heart some real testing guidance and apply it over and over to make ourselves more effective? What symptoms did the software exhibit that clued us in to the presence of the bug? Can we now be more alert to those symptoms in the future? In other words, it's not just about this one bug and this one success. What does this bug teach us that will make us better testers in the future?

Just like my son's goal, even if the first bug is found by accident, it doesn't mean that the rest have to be so. It's important to understand the reasons we succeed, so that success gets repeated. For testers, these reasons will be a collection of testing techniques, advice, and tools that will increase our effectiveness on future projects.

Holes

Testers ultimately get pretty good at finding bugs, but to get over that testing hump we have to do it efficiently and effectively: high speed and low drag. In other words, we have to have a bug-finding technique that itself contains no bugs!

I like to think of it this way: Testers need to turn their bug-finding ability on themselves. We have to use the same bug-finding process to find bugs in our own testing processes and procedures. Is my testing process broken? Does it have bugs? Are there barriers that are preventing me from being more productive?

Always look for a better way. Purposefully identify those things that limit your ability, get in your way, slow you down, and so on. Just like bugs limit the ability of software to deliver on its requirements, what is limiting your ability to test? Using your testing powers to streamline your own testing processes will create a rapid ascent up the testing hump and increase the chances of coming out the other side as an expert.

The Summit

The summit of the testing hump is a good place to be; congratulations if you make it. But it is not the end game. It means that you've become a great individual tester, but the descent is where your insight and expertise help to make those around you good testers, too. It's one thing to summit a mountain, it's quite another to help others (who may not be as strong) do so.

Generally, folks who reach the testing summit become masters of tools. Commercial tools, open source and freeware tools, and (my personal favorite) homegrown tools are excellent ways to increase your productivity and amplify your effectiveness. But tools are only one way to accomplish this, and in many ways are limiting because too many people don't see beyond the capability of the tools. Instead, they become limited by what the tools can do for them and don't see or understand the bigger need. The real mastery required for the summit is *information.* Because many tools process information and make it easily available, testers put too much stock in their tools. But it is the information and how it is used that is the real key to success.

Mastering information means understanding what information is available, how it impacts testing, and ensuring that that impact is maximized. There are several types of information the test summiteer must pay attention to. The two I cover here are information from the application and information from prior testing.

Information from the application means information about requirements, architecture, code structure, source code, and even runtime information about what the application is doing while it is executing. The extent to which this type of information is considered when writing test cases and executing them weighs heavily on the ability of testers to make their testing matter. The more such information is used during testing, the more testing becomes like engineering and less like guesswork.

At Microsoft, our Games Test Organization (GTO), which owns testing of Xbox and PC game titles, takes the top prize when it comes to the use of information from an application. Games are incredibly rich and complex to test. Much of the testable content of a game is hidden (because discovery of the items that a gamer can interact with is part of the fun of playing the game), and if all GTO testers bothered doing was playing the game, they would be no more productive than their ultimate customers. To do better, they worked with the game developers to build information panels that exposed what is essentially cheating information to testers. Testers would know in advance where creatures would be spawned; they would know where objects were hidden; they would be able to see through walls and force certain behaviors from adversaries. Their "cheats" (aka testing tools) essentially make them gods within the game, controlling information as they see fit in order to test faster and test smarter. There is a lesson in this for all testers.

Information from testing means paying attention to what you are doing while testing and using what you learn to influence your testing going forward. Do you understand how your tests are tied to requirements and when a certain requirement has received enough testing? Do you use code coverage to influence future tests? Do you know which tests are impacted by code updates and bug fixes or do you just run them all? Understanding where your tests have been and adjusting your strategy as you test is a sure sign of testing maturity.

My former group within Visual Studio at Microsoft makes heavy use of code churn (code changes due to new features being added and bugs being fixed) and code coverage to influence our testing. We take great pains to expose code coverage and code churn to testers and help them understand which test cases contribute to coverage and help test churned/modified components. The end result is that when the code does churn, we know which tests are impacted and rerun those. We also understand how each new test case contributes to overall interface, feature, and code coverage. Our testers are thus guided to write more meaningful tests within the context of all prior testing performed by everyone on the team.

What information do you use to guide your testing? How do you ensure that the information is *available* so that you have ready access to it during testing? How do you make information *actionable* so that it influences your testing in positive ways? The answer to these questions will determine the speed of your descent down the expert side of the testing hump.

The Descent

By the time you've reached the summit of the testing hump, you've become a much more effective tester and are probably capable of performing at the level of any number of your peers put together. Whatever you do, don't try to outperform your whole team, no matter how good it might make you feel or how hard your boss is pushing you to do so. Once you're on the decent, it is no badge of honor to be the most prolific bug finder or the one who finds the best bugs. Instead, I recommend that you actually *reduce* the time you spend testing and make innovation your primary focus.

To innovate in test means to stand back and make insights, find bottlenecks, and improve how everyone else on the team manages to do their job. Your job becomes making others better. At Microsoft, we have an official role for this that we call Test Architect, but don't let the lack of a cool title stand in your way. No matter what they call you, if you are on the descent, the best thing you can do is to ensure that as many others as possible climb the other side of the hump.

APPENDIX B
A Selection of JW's Professorial "Blog"

"Those who can do, those who can't teach."

—*George Bernard Shaw*

Teach Me Something

As a long time teacher, I've come to appreciate the above quote from the Irish playwright and Nobel laureate. However, I would add that no matter what practical experience you may have, you never really know a subject until you have to teach it. There are so many nuances to engineering endeavors that we don't think about except at an intuitive level. Having to explain those nuances to someone else is a lot harder than it sounds.

I teach all the time, but my ten-year professorial career is the time in which I taught the most. Every day I was either teaching or preparing my course materials. It provided a lot of thinking time and in-class debate time to help me think through the whole job of testing.

I've included some of the more lively and obscure material in this chapter. Much of it is unpublished…the closest thing we had in the early 1990s to a blog. There is some insight here, but enough humor to make it palatable for what was then my primary constituency: the college student.

Software's Ten Commandments

Reprinted with permission from Software Quality Engineering. See this and more of James's work at www.stickyminds.com.

In 1996, I posted my version of the ten commandments of software testing on a website. I wrote these commandments in the middle of the night when I couldn't sleep. I was thinking about what things I could do to try to repro an elusive bug. As most testers will attest, sleep can be hard to come by in such a circumstance! Somehow in my slightly warped tester brain, these "things" took the form of commandments. It was a very spiritual moment.

I took the time to write the commandments down, and then promptly went into a very deep sleep that made me late for work the next day. I was determined not to make my sleepless night—and late arrival—completely without benefit and decided to post the commandments to my website. (You can still find them at www.howtobreaksoftware.com/.) I wondered if anyone would notice.

Well, I can now say for certain that, indeed, they noticed. It took a while, but I started getting mail about them. At first, the mail trickled in. Then, months later, it began pouring in, at the rate of two or three a month. It steadily increased until I would be surprised if a week would go by without getting at least one note about my commandments.

The mail was neither complimentary nor derogatory. In typical testing fashion, it was inquisitive. Could I please interpret one of the commandments? Would I settle a bet between two colleagues about commandment number four (except I thought "settle" meant "pay," and I told them "no")? And the most frequently asked question: Why are there only nine commandments?

Well, after hundreds of private e-conversations (some of them months long in duration) with individual testers around the globe, I have finally decided to come clean, publicly, and get these commandments "off my chest" once and for all. But it will take three of these columns to accomplish the task. This column explains the first two. The second will explain numbers three through six, then seven through nine (and the lack of the tenth) in the third column. I hope you enjoy them, as I have enjoyed them over the years.

First, I'll just list the commandments so that you can see them as original visitors to my old website saw them, listed but not explained:

1. Thou shalt pummel thine app with multitudes of input.
2. Thou shalt covet thy neighbor's apps.
3. Thou shalt seek thee out the wise oracle.
4. Thou shalt not worship nonreproducible failures.
5. Thou shalt honor thy model and automation.
6. Thou shalt hold thy developers' sins against them.
7. Thou shalt revel in app murder (celebrate the BSOD!).
8. Thou shalt keep holy the Sabbath (release).
9. Thou shalt covet thy developers' source code.[1]

And now, here are my interpretations of numbers one and two. I just hope I remember all the things I included in my earlier interpretations! Any of my old correspondents are welcome to chime in at the end of this column.

[1] There is a reason there are nine instead of ten—more about that later.

1. Thou Shalt Pummel Thine App with Multitudes of Input

One of the first things that any tester learns is that the input domain of almost any nontrivial software application is infinite. Not only are there lots of individual inputs, but inputs can be combined and sequenced in so many different combinations that it is impossible to apply them all. One of the second things testers learn is that the trick is to apply the right set of inputs so that infinity doesn't have to be faced head-on.

Well, of course I agree with this approach. My own writing and teaching is full of advice on how to select the right set of inputs. But I also counsel testers to buck up and face infinity anyway. The method of doing this: massive-scale random testing. It is a tool that should be in every tester's toolkit and few, if any, testing projects should be without it.

Massive-scale random testing must be automated. Although it isn't easy to do the first time, it does get progressively easier with each project and eventually becomes rote. It may not find a large number of bugs, but it is an excellent sanity check on the rest of your testing: If you are outperformed by random testing, you may have a problem on your hands. And I am always pleased with the high-quality (albeit few in number) bugs that random testing manages to find.

Another reason to apply massive-scale random testing is that setting up such tests requires a healthy knowledge about the input domain of the application under test. Testers must really get to know their inputs and the relationships that exist among the inputs. I almost always find bugs and get good testing ideas just from the act of planning massive-scale random testing.

2. Thou Shalt Covet Thy Neighbor's Apps

This commandment sounds a bit perverted, but I can assure you it has a "G" rating. The idea I am trying to get across here is not to test your application in isolation. Otherwise, you might run into the nightmare scenario of "application compatibility," or more specifically, lack thereof. Application compatibility, or "app compat" as it is widely abbreviated, means that one application does something to break another one. In case you are not sure, that is a bad thing.

One way to combat this problem is to keep a cache of apps (old ones, new ones, borrowed ones, blues ones—the more diverse the better) and make sure that you run your app at the same time each of these are running. Of course, we want to do this with operating systems as well. A user should not have to tell you that your application won't run with a specific service pack installed; that is something you should find out in your own testing.

So covet those apps and those service packs: The more the merrier!

3. Thou Shalt Seek Thee Out the Wise Oracle

We all know that there are at least two parts to testing. First we apply; then we check. When we apply inputs we are testing whether the software did what it was supposed to do with those inputs. Without the ability to verify that this is indeed fact, testing is much less effective.

Testers call this the "oracle problem" in reference to the wise oracle that knows all the answers. Of course, the answer we are interested in is "did the app do what it was supposed to do when I applied some test?" This requires our oracle to intimately understand what the application is supposed to do given any specific combination of inputs and environmental conditions. Automating the oracle is very hard, but a worthwhile pursuit, not only as a valuable testing tool but also as an intellectual pursuit. Forcing yourself to think like such an oracle can often be more productive than anything else that you might choose to do, whether or not you ultimately succeed in automating it.

4. Thou Shalt Not Worship Irreproducible Failures

We've all been here, haven't we? You see a bug, usually a good bug; then it won't reproduce. The better the bug, the worse you feel about it. I have seen many good testers waste hours and even days trying to reproduce a bug that they saw only once.

The effort to reproduce such a bug is often valiant but without the proper tools, the effort can be a waste of time. But the problem I see is that the time is wasted anyhow, without the tester even realizing it. I had a tester spend an entire day trying to remember the reproduction steps of a crashing bug, with no success. I would have preferred that the particular tester spend his time in better ways than that. I understand the frustration as well as any tester, but the pursuit of such a bug is often time not well spent.

The moral of this commandment is twofold. First, try your best to be ever alert and remember (or record) the sequences of actions you are taking against the software. Remember also the application's response. Second, consider using debugger-class tools that can track your actions and the state of the software. This takes much guesswork out of reproducing bugs and prevents otherwise good testers from breaking this commandment.

5. Thou Shalt Honor Thy Model and Automation

Commandment one was about the importance of random testing—emphasis on random. This commandment is about intelligent random testing—emphasis on intelligent. When intelligence meets automation, the result is called model-based testing. Get used to the term because it is the automation technology of the future.

Software models such as objects, black boxes, or structure diagrams help us to understand software. Testing models help us understand testing.

A testing model is a blend of intelligence about what an application does (the model) and how it does it (the automation). Good models can make your automation smart enough to respond to errors and cover code that is out of reach of dumb automation. Modeling is an exercise that at the very least will make you more prepared to test, even if you don't bother to automate it.

6. Thou Shalt Hold Thy Developers Sins Against Them

Development work is hard, very hard. Developers over the past few decades have had to solve the same problems over and over again, and in doing so, often make the same mistakes over and over again. We testers must remember those mistakes and design tests that ensure that lessons are being learned.

If one developer makes a mistake coding some module, then we should assume that other developers might make the same mistake on similar modules. If a particular developer is prone to coding infinite loops, then we need to make sure we test for such errors in every module that the developer writes. This is "learning from experience," and we are here to make sure that is what our developers do: understand their patterns of mistakes so those mistakes can be eradicated.

7. Thou Shalt Revel in App Murder (Celebrate the BSOD)

I often make an analogy between testers and physicians. Physicians, I say in the story, treat their patients gingerly. They say, "Does it hurt when I touch you here?" And then they promptly stop touching that spot when you say "Yes!" If testers were physicians, the story would be somewhat different.

Test-physicians would also inquire, "Does it hurt when I touch it here?" But when the pain is confirmed, a test-physician would then poke, prod, and probe, until the pain became unbearable. Why? Well, it isn't sadism; it's our job. No bad deed should go unpunished.

You see, every bug is a proud moment for a tester, but no bug should go without further investigation. So you found a bug that causes ill-formatted data to be displayed on the screen. Great, but can you go further and make that same bug corrupt data that the application is storing internally? If so, you have a better bug. And, can you then make that corrupt data be used by the application in some internal computation? If so, you have now turned a simple little formatting bug into a severity-one bug that causes data to be corrupted and the application to crash.

And, of course, the Holy Grail would be to crash not only your application, but also to cause the entire operating system to hang. Ah, the blue screen of death. I remember my first like it was yesterday, I anticipate my next every time I apply a test.

The moral of this commandment is that behind every good bug, there may be a better bug. Never stop exploring until you've discovered just how deep the bug goes and just how damaging it can be.

8. Thou Shalt Keep Holy the Sabbath (Release)

Oh so many times I hear testers whine about release dates. Testers most often want to extend release dates and, more often than not, their reasoning for wanting to do so is right on the mark. But their reasoning sometimes doesn't matter.

The fact is that there are more factors than just quality that go into determining when to release an application to users. Quality is important but market pressures, competition, strength of user demand, staffing and personnel issues, and many more nontesting issues must determine a suitable release date. As testers, we must simply get the most work done that we can in the amount of time allotted to us.

We should not complain about release dates. We should, instead, warn about consequences. That is the extent of our responsibility, and it should be the extent of our concern.

9. Thou Shalt Covet Thy Developer's Source Code

I am not much of a believer in white-box testing. I think that it is something developers should learn to do well so that we testers can concentrate on more important and complex behavioral tests. That said, however, don't look a gift horse in the mouth. If you have access to the source code, use it.

But, use it as a tester should, not as a developer would. My interest in source code is many fold and too involved to discuss all the issues here. But I think there is much to be learned from reading the source. Top of my list is looking for error-handling code and the dialog boxes that will indicate to us that the error code is executing. Error handlers are the hardest code to see or get to from the user interface. Understanding what error handlers have been written and what inputs it takes to trigger them is time well spent.

Indeed, there are many such clues we can glean from the source that give us insight into tests that need to be performed. We should not be shy about asking for and using the source code.

So that's the commandments. By the way, there is a reason there are nine instead of ten. We might assume that just because they are "commandments," there have to be ten of them. Since we know the assumption to be true (because that's the nature of an assumption), then we convince ourselves that there is no need to ever bother checking whether the assumption may become false.

Assumptions are a very bad thing for software testers. Assumptions can reduce productivity and undermine an otherwise good project. Assumptions can even undermine a career. Good testers can never assume anything. In fact, the reason we are called testers is that we test assumptions for a living. No assumption is true until we test and verify that it is true. No assumption is false until we test that it is false.

Any tester who assumes anything about anything should consider taking up development for a career. After all, what tester hasn't heard a developer say, "Well, we assumed the user would never do that!" Assumptions must always be tested. I once heard a test consultant give the advice: "Expect the unexpected." With this I disagree; instead, expect nothing; only then will you find what you seek.

Testing Error Code

Reprinted with permission from Software Quality Engineering. See this and more of James's work at www.stickyminds.com.

There are two types of code that developers write. First, there is the code that gets the job done—which we'll call this type of code functional code because it supplies the functionality that satisfies user requirements. Second, there is code that keeps the functional code from failing because of erroneous input (or some other unexpected environmental condition). We'll call this type of code error code because it handles errors. For many programmers, this is the code that they are forced to write out of necessity, not because it is particularly enjoyable.

Writing both types of code simultaneously is problematic because there are context switches that must be made inside the head of a software developer between the two types of code. These context shifts are problematic; they require the developer to stop thinking about one type of code and start thinking about the other.

Consider Johnny, a hardworking hypothetical developer, writing a new application. Johnny begins by writing the functional code, maybe even going so far as using something like UML to fully understand the various user scenarios that Johnny must code. Good, Johnny. Indeed, good programmers like Johnny can find a wealth of information out there to help them write good functional code. The books all address it, the tutorials address it, and there are many useful published examples to work from.

But, what happens when Johnny realizes the need for error code? Perhaps he is in the middle of writing or specifying some code object when he decides that, say, an input needs to be bounds-checked. What does Johnny do? One choice for Johnny is to stop writing the functional code and write the error code instead. This requires a context shift inside Johnny's developer-head. He must stop thinking about the user scenarios and the functional code that he is implementing, and start thinking about how to handle the error. Since handling errors can be complicated, this may take him some time.

Now, when Johnny returns to the task of writing the functional code, his mind has to recall what he was thinking about when he last put it down. This context shift is harder than the first, given the myriad design-decision details and minute technical details that go into writing any nontrivial program. You see the problem: Poor Johnny has had to endure two context switches to handle a single error. Imagine how many such context switches happen writing even a small application.

Another choice for Johnny would be to postpone writing the error code in order to avoid the context shift. Assuming Johnny remembers to eventually get around to writing the error code, he's probably going to have to spend some time recalling the nature of the error event he's trying to write a handler for. So now Johnny is writing the error code without the benefit of context. Writing error code is problematic no matter how you face it. And therefore, a ripe place for guys like me to look for bugs. So now let's look at the testing perspective; how do we approach testing error code?

Forcing error messages to occur is the best way to get error code to execute. Software should either appropriately respond to bad input, or it should successfully prevent the input from ever getting to the software in the first place. The only way to know for sure is to test the application with a battery of bad inputs. There are many factors to consider when testing error code. Perhaps the most important is to understand how the application responds to erroneous input. I try to identify three different types of error handlers:

- *Input filters* can be used to prevent bad input from ever getting to the software under test. In effect, bad inputs are filtered by, for example, a graphical user interface, and only legal inputs are allowed past the interface.
- *Input checking* can be performed to ensure that the software will not execute using bad input. The simplest case is that every time an input enters the system, the developer inserts an IF statement to ensure that the input is legal before it is processed; that is, IF the input is legal, THEN process it, ELSE display an error message. During this first attack, it is our goal to ensure that we see all such error messages.
- *Exception handlers* are a last resort and are used to clean up after the software has failed as a result of processing bad input. In other words, bad inputs are allowed into the system, used in processing, and the system is allowed to fail. The exception handler is a routine that is called when the software fails. It usually contains code that resets internal variables, closes files, and restores the ability of the software to interact with its users. In general, some error message is also displayed.

Testers must consider each input that the software under test accepts and focus on erroneous values. The idea here is to enter values that are too big, too small, too long, too short—which values that are out of the acceptable range or values of the wrong data type. The major defect one will find with this approach is missing error cases—input data that the developer did not know was erroneous or individual cases that were overlooked. Missing cases almost always cause the software to hang or crash. One should also be on the lookout for misplaced error messages. Sometimes the developer gets the error message right but assigns it to the wrong input values. Thus, the message seems like nonsense for the particular input values submitted.

Finally, of pure nuisance value are uninformative error messages. Although such messages cause no direct harm to the user, they are sloppy and will cast doubt in a user's mind on the credibility of the software producer. "Error 5—Unknown Data" might have seemed a good idea to some developer, but will cause frustration in the mind of the user who will have no idea what they did wrong. Whether one is testing an input field in a GUI panel or a parameter in an API call, one must consider properties of an input when conducting this attack. Some general properties to consider are

- **Input type:** Entering invalid types will often cause an error message. For example, if the input in question is an integer, then enter a real number or a character.
- **Input length:** For character (alphanumeric) inputs, entering a few too many characters will often elicit an error message.
- **Boundary values:** Every numeric data type has boundary values, and sometimes these values represent special cases. The integer zero for example is the boundary between positive and negative numbers.

Be prepared to find some spectacular bugs!

Will the Real Professional Testers Please Step Forward

Reprinted with permission from Software Quality Engineering. See this and more of James' work at www.stickyminds.com.

What is it that makes some companies havens for testing talent while other companies incite anger from their testing ranks? At every testing conference I attend, I hear the same laments:

- "Developers think they are better than us."
- "Development is always late in delivering the code and it's Test that gets blamed when the schedule slips. Everything is always our fault."
- "Upper management treats us like second-class employees."
- "How do we get the respect we deserve?"

And so on and so forth.

I've listened in on the conversations these folks have with the testing consultants in attendance. In general, the consultants are full of empathy, as well as suggestions about how to improve the situation. Most of the solutions I have overheard fall into two categories:

1. You need to improve communication between test, development, and upper management. This will allow a dialog that will lead to a better understanding and appreciation of testers.
2. The problem is that testers are not certified. Certification will legitimize testing as a field and help ensure adequate treatment.

Frankly, and with due respect to the test consulting community, the first solution sounds a lot like Dr. Phil giving marital advice, and the second sounds a lot like a labor union.

In my opinion, neither psychotherapy nor unionization will solve this problem. Respect is doled out in the technology sector only when it is deserved. That's a *good* thing. Too many times we hear people in other industries complain that it doesn't matter how talented you are, that merit has nothing to do with respect or advancement. Our goal is to get so good at what we do, that colleagues and management have no alternative but to respect us.

So I have been taking notes during the last year on a mission to understand this problem. I accomplished my mission by studying the organizations in which this problem does *not* occur, organizations where testers are respected by developers and management and are afforded pay and career paths equal to development.

The Common Denominators I Found Are (In No Particular Order)

Insistence Among Testers for Individual Excellence

The companies I studied have a large number of testers who take pride in their testing prowess. They are good, they know they are good, and they take great pride in demonstrating their excellence. I hear them speak about *their bugs* with as much pride as the developers talk about *their code*. They name their bugs and, if questioned, will recount their hunt, their technique, their insight, and every bit of minutiae that relates to isolating and reporting the problem they found. Personal pride in a job well done is not the exclusive domain of developers. To these testers I say, "Long live your stories and may your tests never lack targets!"

Primary Concern Focused on the Quality of the Product

Lest you read item number one above and thought those testers arrogant and self-absorbed, my subjects in this study had one singular focus: maximum contribution to product success. Whereas the developers can look with understandable pride at what they put *in* a product, testers can feel equal pride for what they keep *out* of the product. For this, testers deserve our respect. They deserve our thanks. And forward-looking companies are generally ready to give it. To those companies who refuse to generously dole out this respect, perhaps they would be willing to re-insert those bugs and do without the services performed by their best and brightest testers.

A Corporate Focus on Continuing Education for Testers

I often get invited to teach one-day testing seminars onsite. These courses are full of testers who are eager to learn. I start each class with one simple theorem: "Anyone who thinks they can learn testing in a single day is a fool who has no business testing software." I invite such people to leave my course and implore them to leave the discipline. By this rather harsh statement, I stand firm: Testing is not to be taken lightly.

Testing is a pursuit; testing begins, but it never ends. This is a fact of life: We can never be finished with our testing task. No matter how much code we cover, there is always more that remains uncovered. No matter how many input combinations we apply, there are so many more that we did not apply. No matter how much we think we excel at testing, there are more complexities and subtleties that elude our full understanding.

Testers must demand, and receive, the education they so desperately need. Companies that refuse continuing education benefits—conferences, onsite or remote courses, books, and (if you are lucky enough to find them) graduate college courses—should be banned from the practice of software development. Such companies are a hazard to software users everywhere. Testing is a challenging intellectual discipline. It not only requires training, but it also demands it. Companies that refuse to cover these expenses for testers are negligent.

The Hiring of Degreed Engineers for Test Positions

Testing is not a clerical task. It is an engineering discipline and is best carried out by trained engineers. Obviously, one cannot overgeneralize here. There are some people who have majored in the arts who make fine testers. And we always need domain experts to test applications that require specialized skill. (Imagine testing a flight simulator without a pilot or two on your team.) But, in general, a computer science degree (or related major) is necessary. There is background knowledge about algorithms, computational complexity, graph theory, and data structures that are requisite skills, building blocks for a deep and well-rounded testing education.

Now, if we could get more universities to actually teach testing, we'd all be even better off. But testers need to understand development, even if they don't practice it on a regular basis.

My Advice Can Be Summarized as Follows

Begin by hiring college graduates who have majored in something technical and related to computer science (electrical engineering, computer engineering, physics, math, and so forth). The education level of your testers should be equivalent to or better than that of your developers.

Insist on continuing-education benefits. Start by showing that the bugs that managed to slip into the released product could have been found with more advanced testing techniques, and make a strong bid for training concerning those techniques. You must make the argument, convincingly, that more training will equate to better software.

Nurture a testing culture in your company that allows you to learn from the bugs that you find and the bugs that your customers find. *Don't* apologize for the bugs that slip through. Make them a learning opportunity. Pick them apart and be sure every tester knows why that bug was overlooked. Bugs are corporate assets because they teach us about what we are doing wrong. Being proactive about correcting these mistakes will go a long way toward showing upper management that Test is a crucial aspect of product development that improves when it is taken seriously. You cannot expect upper management to take you seriously until you take yourselves and your discipline seriously. The more attention you pay to improving the performance of Test, the more respect you will gain.

Finally, I must note that the trend among software companies is moving in the right direction. More and more companies are taking Test seriously and recognizing its value. If you work for a company that treats testers as second-class employees, other opportunities are out there.

Your fate is in your own hands. Strive for individual excellence, recognize your importance to a project, celebrate the bugs that won't ship because of you and your team, and demand the continuing education you deserve. Respect your discipline and you will gain the respect that your discipline deserves.

Long live the professional tester!

Strike Three, Time for a New Batter

Reprinted with permission from Software Quality Engineering. See this and more of James's work at www.stickyminds.com.

In the late 1970s the software quality problem was all too apparent. Software was hard to write, hard to maintain, and often failed to meet its requirements. Even at this early stage in the history of software engineering, a move was afoot to correct this problem. Beginning with structured programming, researchers studied better ways to write code. The push for formal methods began. If you'd only do things more formally, the plea went, your code would be better! A few even went so far as to make "zero defects" their Holy Grail. The search was on. Unfortunately, the search still continues.

Following close on the heels of the formal methods advocates were the tool vendors. If you'd only use the right tools, they cried, your code would be better! Many tools have greatly simplified the task of developing software. Development organizations spend hundreds of thousands of dollars on tools. Software is still buggy.

The latest entry into the fray has been the process improvement people. If you'd only work more carefully, they beg, your code would be better! Now our managers are as busy as our developers. Developers not only have software to develop but also make-work reports to write. Software is still buggy.

This article discusses these three "silver bullets" and exposes their Achilles heels. I suggest that the answer to the problem must, by definition, be technical—not managerial—in nature. I end by launching the search for a fourth proposal.

Formal Methods

Formal methods are a great idea. Essentially, they equate programming a computer to solving a math problem. You can go about it using a mixture of creativity, intelligence, and lots of practice solving similar problems.

However, there are a couple of problems with formal methods that can't be overlooked.

First and foremost, software developers won't use them. This puzzles formal methods advocates to no end. However, it's fairly plain to the rest of us: No one can show developers just how to apply formal methods. The examples in books and papers are far too simple to scale the ideas to real development problems. Plus, once you get outside your comfort zone, the formal methods fall apart. You remember how you felt when you learned calculus after mastering algebra? Algebra problems were easy because you'd solved hundreds of them. But the methods you used didn't seem to apply to calculus problems. All the rules had changed. It turns out this same situation plagues software problems, too. They can be as different as algebra and calculus. Why should we be surprised that what works on one problem is useless on another? Formal methods don't scale in software because they don't scale in mathematics either.

Second, one can use formal methods and still write buggy code. Formal methods don't address anything but the algorithm. But we all know that an algorithm can be correct on paper but fail on a real computer. The problem is that real computers have space and time limitations, other applications, and very complex operating systems that must be dealt with by code that has nothing to do with the main algorithms of an application. Indeed, code to process inputs and handle errors is often much larger and more complex than the algorithm that actually gets the main work done. There are no formal methods for handling such code.

Formal methods are important, but they will only take you so far toward reliable software. Strike one.

Tools

Tools can make the software development task much less painful, but they cannot guarantee zero defects; in fact, they cannot even guarantee fewer bugs. Since the tools themselves can be buggy, they create one more unknown in a project. When a defect is found, is the product or the tool at fault?

Tools range from simple and indispensable text editors and compilers to more elaborate environments for analyses and design. Very few outrageous claims are made from the developers of editors and compilers—it's the design tool vendors that corner that market. What's more valuable to a project anyhow, a nicely drawn E-R diagram or a programmer who's expert in the target implementation language? Would you buy $100K worth of tools or hire a person who intimately understands the problem domain in which you are involved? Tools are great when used properly, but they can only offer you steep learning curves and limited functionality. Plus, they bring along a whole new set of bugs to worry about: their own.

You see, if tools really were a silver bullet, they wouldn't be buggy, would they? Strike two.

Process Improvement

The latest attempt at getting the software quality problem under control has been made by the process improvement people. Obviously, controlling and improving the software development process is in everyone's best interest. However, since software development is a technical problem and process improvement is a management problem, it simply cannot have a profound effect on quality. Good organizations can produce bad software. Bad organizations can produce good software.

Furthermore, process improvement initiatives are rarely met with enthusiasm from rank-and-file technical people. ISO certification is a pain. SEI assessment is demeaning. Both take away creativity and add management overhead. Heck, part of the joy of working in this field is not being micro-managed. Why would any developer in his or her right mind actually think this is a good idea?

Well, it is a good idea, but it won't help appreciably with the quality problem. I was once a part of a partnership in which a consulting company that specialized in formal methods was training an SEI level three—on their way to level five—organization. An example code fragment was used extensively throughout the training. Neither the formal methods advocates who wrote the buggy code, nor the mature process organization that studied the code, noticed that it possessed a fatal flaw. Not even during the course of proving the code fragment correct was the bug ever discovered. Why? Because the formal methods people were concerned about math, and the process people were concerned about documentation. No one was looking at the code! Fortunately, the test organization was paying attention and the bug was caught.

Management solutions cannot solve technical problems. Strike three.

The Fourth Proposal

What we need is for someone to come up with silver bullet number four. Except this one shouldn't be silver. In fact, I think it's important that proposal number four should be bland-colored, say brown, so that no one really notices it. It shouldn't be something so revolutionary (as a gold or platinum bullet might be) that it makes no sense and people avoid it. It should be so ordinary that developers can integrate it seamlessly into their normal pattern of design. It should be so straightforward that developers remark "this is simple, what's the big deal?" Not only should it be these things, it must be in order for it to be used and have some positive industry impact. Otherwise, it's just more ivory-tower nonsense that real practitioners don't appreciate.

It turns out that parts of such technology exist, are readily understandable by capable developers, and will not fundamentally change the manner in which software development occurs in an organization. If you are a great developer now, then you'll still be a great developer. (This is a fear of great developers that keeps them from being strong process advocates. They know they are not great at filling out forms.) If you are a mediocre developer, then perhaps you'll become better. Either way, it is likely that the code you write will be more understandable and have fewer bugs than it did before. In future installments of this bimonthly column series, I will survey many of the techniques that will one day contribute to the fourth, this time brown, bullet and show how developers and testers can adjust—but not change—their development process to improve quality and maintainability.

It's time for a new batter.

Software Testing as an Art, a Craft and a Discipline

The first book[2] on software testing set the tone for software testers and software testing careers. The title of that book *The Art of Software Testing* identified our discipline as a collection of artists applying their creativity to software quality. Practitioners of software testing and quality assurance have been sold short by such a label.

Testing is not an art.

Software testing is a far cry from those endeavors that most people accept as art: painting, sculpture, music, literature, drama, and dance. In my mind, this is an unsatisfying comparison given that my training as a tester has been more engineering than art.

Certainly, I'll agree that, like artists, software testers need to be creative, but art implies skill without training. Most virtuoso artists were born to the task, and those of us unlucky enough to have no artistic talent are unlikely to develop such skill despite a lifetime of practice.

I also understand that two authors attempted to copyright the title *The Craft of Software Testing*, acknowledging Myers's title and also implying a growth of the discipline from art to craft. This, too, sells testers far short of the difficulty of their calling. Indeed, the idea of software testing as a craft is equally unsettling as calling it an art. Craftsmen are carpenters, plumbers, masons, and landscape designers. Crafts are exemplified by a lack of a real knowledge base. Most craftsmen learn on the job, and mastery of their craft is a given as long as they have the drive to practice. Crafts are two parts dexterity and only one part skill. Indeed, carpenters have no need to understand the biology of trees, only to skillfully mold wood into beautiful and useful things.

Testing as arts or crafts doesn't begin to describe what we do; and I'll start a fight with anyone who attempts to call it arts and crafts!

I suggest the most fitting title for a book on software testing would be *The Discipline of Software Testing*. I would argue that *discipline* better defines what we do as testers and provides us with a useful model on which to pattern our training and our careers. Indeed, this is the best reason to call it a

---

[2] Although several collections of testing papers were published as books before Myers's *The Art of Software Testing* in 1979, his was the first book to be written from scratch as a software testing text.

discipline: By studying other disciplines, we gain more insight into testing than using the analogies of arts or crafts.

A discipline is a branch of knowledge or learning. Mastery of a discipline is achieved through training, not practice. Training is different than practice. Practice requires doing the same thing over and over again, the key being repetition. One can practice throwing a ball for example and even though "practice makes perfect," simply throwing a ball will not make you a major league pitcher; becoming that good requires training.

Training is much more than just practice. Training means understanding every nuance of your discipline. A pitcher *trains* by building his muscles so that maximum force can be released when throwing a ball. A pitcher *trains* by studying the dynamics of the mound, where to land his foot for maximum effect on any given pitch and how to make use of his much stronger leg muscles to propel the ball faster. A pitcher *trains* by learning how to effectively use body language to intimidate batters and runners. A pitcher *trains* by learning to juggle, to dance, and to do yoga. A pitcher who trains to be at the top of his game does many things that have nothing to do with throwing a ball and everything to do with making himself a better ball thrower. This is why Hollywood's "karate kid" waxed cars and balanced on fence posts; he wasn't practicing to fight, he was training to be a better fighter.

Treating software testing as a discipline is a more useful analogy than treating it as an art or a craft. We are not artists whose brains are wired at birth to excel in quality assurance. We are not craftsmen who perfect their skill with on-the-job practice. If we are, then it is likely that full mastery of the discipline of software testing will elude us. We may become good, indeed quite good, but still fall short of achieving black belt—dare I say Jedi?—status. Mastery of software testing requires discipline and training.

A software testing training regime should promote understanding of fundamentals. I suggest three specific areas of pursuit to guide anyone's training:

- First and foremost, master software testers should understand software. What can software do? What external resources does it use to do it? What are its major behaviors? How does it interact with its environment? The answers to these questions have nothing to do with practice and everything to do with training. One could practice for years and not gain such understanding.

  Software works in a complex consisting of four major categories of software *users* (i.e., entities within an application's environment that are capable of sending the application input or consuming its output). These are (1) the operating system, (2) the file system, (3) libraries/APIs (e.g., the network is reach through a library), and (4) humans who interact through a UI. It is interesting to note that of the four major categories of users, only one is visible to the human tester's eye: the user interface. The interfaces to the operating system, the file system, and other libraries happen without scrutiny. Without understanding these interfaces, testers are taking into account only a very small percentage of the total inputs to their software. By paying attention only to the visible user interface, we are limiting what bugs we can find and what behaviors we can force.

Take as an example the scenario of a full hard drive. How do we test this situation? Inputs through the user interface will never force the code to handle the case of a full hard drive. This scenario can only be tested by controlling the file system interface. Specifically we need to force the files system to indicate to the application that the disk is full. Controlling the UI is only one part of the solution.

Understanding the environment in which your application works is a nontrivial endeavor that all the practice in the world will not help you accomplish. Understanding the interfaces that your application possesses and establishing the ability to test them requires discipline and training. This is not a task for artists and craftspeople.

- Second, master software testers should understand software faults. How do developers create faults? Are some coding practices or programming languages especially prone to certain types of faults? Are certain faults more likely for certain types of software behavior? How do specific faults manifest themselves as failures?

  There are many different types of faults that testers must study, and this forum is too limited to describe them all. However, consider default values for data variables as an example. For every variable used in a program, the variable must be first declared and then given an initial value. If either of these steps is skipped, a fault exists for testers to look for. Failure to declare a variable (as is the case with languages that allow for implicit variable declaration) can cause a single value to be stored in multiple variables. Failure to initialize a variable means that when a variable is used, its value is unpredictable. In either case, the software will fail eventually. The trick for the tester is to be able to force the application to fail and then be able to recognize that it has failed.

- Third, master software testers should understand software failure. How and why does software fail? Are there symptoms of software failure that give us clues to the health of an application? Are some features systemically problematic? How does one drive certain features to failure?

And there is more, *always* more to learn. Discipline is a lifelong pursuit. If you trick yourself into thinking you have all the answers, mastery will elude you. But training builds knowledge, so the pursuit itself is worthwhile whether or not you ever reach the summit.

Restoring Respect to the Software Industry

Fifty plus years of software development has resulted in one overwhelming truth: Our industry develops crappy applications. We've made insecurity and unreliability the norm.

It's true and as an industry, we can no longer deny it. You can look at studies such as that performed at the National Institute of Standards and Technology (NIST) in 2002 that implicate defect removal as a major cost of software deployment. (The study is available at www.mel.nist.gov/msid/sima/sw_testing_rpt.pdf.) Or you could simply take a look at pop tech culture and observe that our buggy software is creating new dictionary entries: Spam, phishing, and pharming are only a sampling. Are bad apps so prevalent that we have resorted to assigning amusing monikers to our failure to protect our users? Is this a situation that any self-respecting software professional can be proud of?

The answers are clearly yes to the first and a resounding *no!* to the second. Investigating why this is and what we might do about it is one of the most worthwhile tasks that our industry can undertake. In fact, it may be the very thing that saves us from creating the next generation of security holes and quality problems to plague our users.

This article begins this investigation in the hopes that it will be joined by an enthusiastic army of quality-minded software developers.

The Well-Intentioned but Off-Target Past

Past attempts at writing secure and reliable code have been decidedly front-loaded. By this, I mean that the focus of software development practices has been on specification, architecture, and development: The early parts of the software development life cycle. The intuition being that we need to focus on *preventing* defects because "quality cannot be tested in."

This concept was so intuitively pleasing that many software construction paradigms picked up on it beginning as early as the 1970s: structured analysis/structured design, clean room, OOA/OOD/OOP, and aspect-oriented programming are some examples.

Software defects continued and so did the process communities' ill-fated attempts to squash them: design by contract, design patterns, RUP, and yes, oh yes, there were more.

Finally, we woke up and realized that such front-loaded processes simply don't work. The idea that we can specify requirements and plan tests in advance when reality was changing too fast to predict hit our industry square in the face.

And we answered with more methodologies: Extreme (spell it whatever way you wish) programming and agile development took center stage. Progress? Hmm. Well, the jury is still out, but I am not holding out much hope. You see the problem with all of these methodologies is that they teach us *the right way to do things.*

Now granted, many industries have figured out the right way to do things. Artists study Picasso, Rembrandt, and the many other masters of their craft. Musicians have no lack of masters to study: Beethoven, Handel, Mozart, and Bach are only a few. Architects can study the pyramids, the Taj Mahal, and Frank Lloyd Wright for that matter. All these professions have existed for long enough that there are many, many examples of people getting it right so that those wishing to follow in their footsteps and master the craft have examples to study.

But it is our sad misfortune (and grand opportunity) to be in the software game so early that no such examples of perfection or inspiration exist. If they did, we'd be studying these "classic" programs so that the new generation of programmers could learn the discipline from those that went before them.

Moving On to Better Ideas

So is it even possible to construct a software development methodology without prior knowledge of how to do software right? I say no and the evidence I present is that software is getting no better. Indeed, I would argue that the complexity of the systems we build is far outpacing the small advances that any of the current menu of development methodologies offer our industry.

Throw them all away and face the fact that we have no idea how to build a high-quality software system of any reasonable size.

When pop tech culture stops naming our bugs and the other headaches we create for our users, that may be an indication that we are progressing. But until then, we need a better plan.

We cannot study success in an environment where only failure exists. So I propose, instead, that we study failure and build our development processes rear-loaded.

Let me explain what I mean by that: There is no more clear indication of what we are doing wrong than the bugs we write, fail to detect, and then ship in our products. But all of the past methodologies treat bugs as something to avoid, something to hush up.

This is unfortunate and I propose we stop treating bugs as a bad thing. I say we should embrace our bugs as the only sure way to guide them to extinction. There is no better way to improve than by studying the very thing that makes our industry the laughing stock of engineering disciplines.

We should be studying our bugs.

A Process for Analyzing Security Holes and Quality Problems

I propose starting with bugs and working backward toward a process that just might work. Here's how I think we should proceed:

Step 1: Collect all the bugs that we ship to our customers (paying special attention to security vulnerabilities). Instead of treating them like snakes that might jump out and bite us, consider them corporate assets. After all, they are the surest indication of our broken processes, misdirected thinking, and mistakes that we have made. If we can't learn from what we are doing wrong, shame on us. If we refuse to admit that we are doing wrong, then we have a bigger problem.

Step 2: Analyze each of these bugs so that we (1) stop writing them, (2) get better at finding them, and (3) understand how to recognize when they occur.

Step 3: Develop a culture in our organization in which every developer, tester, and technician understands every bug that we've ever written.

Step 4: Document the lessons learned. This becomes the basis for a body of knowledge about the bugs we write and the basis for a new set of methodologies that are aimed squarely at preventing our most egregious mistakes.

We can do this by questioning our bugs. I think the following three questions are a good start and will teach us a great deal about what we are doing wrong. For each bug we ship, we should ask ourselves:

1. What fault caused this bug in the first place?

   The answer to this question will teach developers to better understand the mistakes they are making as they write code. When every developer understands their own mistakes and the mistakes of their colleagues, a body of knowledge will form inside our development groups that will reduce mistakes, help guide reviews and unit tests, and reduce the attack surface for testers.

   The result will be better software entering test.

2. What were the failure symptoms that would alert us to the presence of this bug?

   Remember that I am proposing to study *bugs that shipped*, so the assumption is that somehow the bug slipped by or was found and not fixed purposefully. In the former case, testers will create a body of knowledge and tools about how to better isolate buggy behaviors from correct behaviors, and in the latter the entire team will learn to agree on what an important bug really is.

   The result will be better software shipping to our customers.

3. What testing technique would have found this bug?

   For those bugs that were totally missed in test, we need to understand what test would have found the failure and helped us diagnose the fault. Now we are adding to the testing body of knowledge with tests that actually work to find important bugs.

   The result will be more effective tests and a shorter test cycle.

What I am proposing here is that because we cannot possibly understand how to do software right, let's understand how we're doing it wrong and simply stop doing it that way. The resulting body of knowledge will not tell us what to do to develop software; it will tell us what *not* to do.

Perhaps we can follow this rear-loaded process using our existing front-loaded methodologies and meet somewhere in the middle.

Now that's what I call progress toward a discipline we can all be proud of.

Let the celebration of bugs begin!

APPENDIX C
An Annotated Transcript of JW's Microsoft Blog

"If you can't say anything nice, don't say nothing at all."

—*Disney's Thumper (quoting his father)*

Into the Blogoshere

As a former professor, I wasn't thrilled when the blogging revolution occurred. To one used to carefully researched academic papers that required anonymous peer review, technical editing, and editorial approval, blogging seemed an unprofessional and chaotic approach to publishing. Any idiot with an opinion, educated or not, could publish anything he or she wanted.

But the twenty-first century finally caught up with me, and I did a number of guest posts for various Microsoft blogs. When my boss first asked me to start blogging regularly, it was obvious why. We have a product to sell, and he thought my blog would drive a lot of interest.

That was his plan, and part of it worked out well. My blog has drawn a lot of traffic and sits in a place of respect among Microsoft developers (although nowhere near the top of the pile). But I didn't use it to sell anything, I used it like the rest of the idiots in the blogosphere, to spout off about my favorite subject: software quality. I wanted to use it to drive the conversation to a higher level rather than to sell tools, and whether I have succeeded is not for me alone to decide.

I've gotten a lot of input and comments about my blogging. Some are posted on the blog itself at http://blogs.msdn.com/james_whittaker, but most were emailed to me or occurred in hallway conversations here and at conferences and didn't get documented. Some are additive to the subject I was blogging about, and some pointed out just how misguided I was. And a few were complaints that I was portraying my employer in a less-than-glowing light (one such from a corporate VP, no less). I've tried to capture the essence of those comments in this annotated transcript that appears here in the order I wrote them.

Finally, given that I have left Microsoft, the blog on MSDN is likely to disappear, and this will be the only place where they are preserved. (Any contemporary context required to help you understand these postings is provided in italic.)

July 2008

Two years before this blog started, I joined Microsoft as a security architect in our core operating system division. Security is not something that is easily talked about, and my colleague Michael Howard had the security space covered so well that I didn't bother. It was a constant source of annoyance that people were asking me where they could find my blog. Now, it is the consummate irony that I am going around telling people where to find it, even when they don't ask.

Before We Begin

Okay, here it is. I submit.

I've been bugged about blogging for years. "Where's JW's blog?" "Why doesn't JW blog?"...and so forth and et cetera. Well, the blog is here and why I haven't been blogging up to now is no longer relevant so I won't bore you with it. Instead, here's the blog and I'll do my best to ensure that it's worth the wait.

For those of you familiar with my writing, I plan to update some of my more dated work (history of testing, testing's ten commandments, and so forth) and preview some of the information that I will be publishing in paper and book form in the future. Specifically, I now (finally) have enough notes to revise my tutorial on manual exploratory testing: *How to Break Software* and will be embarking on that effort soon. This blog is where I'll solicit feedback and report on my progress.

For now, here's an update on what's happening, testing-wise, for me at Microsoft:

- I am the Architect for *Visual Studio Team System — Test Edition*. That's right, Microsoft is upping the ante in the test tools business and I find myself at the center of it. What can you expect? We'll be shipping more than just modern replacements for tired old testing tools. We'll be shipping tools to help testers to *test*: automated assistance for the manual tester; bug reporting that brings developers and testers together instead of driving them apart; and tools that make testers a far more central player in the software development process. *I can't wait!*
- I am the Chair of the *Quality and Testing Experts Community* at Microsoft. This is an internal community of the most senior testing and quality thought leaders in the company. We kicked off the community with record-breaking attendance (the most of any of Microsoft's technical network communities) at our inaugural event this past spring where some of our longest-tenured testers shared a retrospective of the history

of testing at Microsoft followed by my own predictions for the future of the discipline. It was a lively discussion and underscored the passion for testing that exists at this company. In this quarter's meeting we're doing communal deep dives into the testing-related work that is coming out of Microsoft Research. MSR, the division responsible for Virtual Earth and the Worldwide Telescope also builds test tools! I can't wait to ship some of this stuff!

- I am representing my division (DevDiv) on a joint project with Windows called a *Quality Quest*. Our quest is concerned with quality, specifically, what we need to do to ensure that our next generation of platforms and services are so reliable that users take quality for granted. Sounds like I took the blue pill, doesn't it? Well, you won't find us dancing around acting like our software is perfect. Anyone who has ever heard me speak (either before or after I joined Microsoft) has seen me break our apps with abandon. In this Quest, we'll leave no stone unturned to get to the bottom of why our systems fail and what processes or technology can serve to correct the situation.

So here it is: the start of a blog that I hope will allow me to share my testing enthusiasm with a wide variety of folks who both agree and disagree with my strategy and tactics. Perhaps, just perhaps, enough of us will join the dialog to help add to the collective voice of those who just want software to work.

PEST (Pub Exploration and Software Testing)

Anyone who has read Chapter 6 of *How to Break Software* knows my fondness of mixing testing with pubs. Many of the training and challenge events I designed for my students actually took place in a pub. Somehow the pub atmosphere tore down walls and inhibitions and helped focus the conversation on testing. There were simply none of the usual office distractions to hold people back, and pubs just give me a Zen feeling that few other places can match. Perhaps this effect can be achieved in other settings but I haven't bothered trying those places. Indeed, the only other place I've ever tried is a soccer pitch, but that blog post can wait. (Let me know if you're interested.)

How wonderful it was to experience a group in England who have formalized it: PEST is Pub Exploration of Software Testing…that's right, a group of visionary. (Would they be anything else in my mind?) England-based testers meet monthly (or thereabouts) in a pub to talk testing and challenge each other's knowledge and understanding of the subject of exploratory testing. The end result is clearer-headed (at least after the hangover the next day) thinking about testing, techniques, automation, and many other subjects that they imbibe.

I had the pleasure of joining them July 17 at a pub just outside Bristol. Apparently in a nod to my work, the focus of this PEST was bug finding. They set up a total of four breaking stations: (1) a computer with the PEST website (still under development), (2) a vending machine (released product), (3) a child's video game (released product), and (4) a machine running an app intentionally seeded with bugs. As attendees filed in (~40 in all), they were given one of 10 different beer mats and people with matching mats were teamed up for exploratory testing sessions. I helped adjudicate one of the stations and rang an old style hotel bell with every verified bug. The same happened at the other stations. Each team tested all four products for identical periods of time in a round-robin fashion, and at the end of the night, prizes were given for the team with the most bugs, the most severe bug, and the best test case.

The only problem is that as a designated passenger (and all the duties that entails on behalf of the designated driver), I was having too much fun to take notes and don't have the official score sheet. Can anyone who attended please report the results for us? However, I remember well the quote of the night came from Steve Green of Labscape: "It's quite strange actually, testing with other people."

Steve (who clearly excelled in exploratory testing to the point that I'd hire him without further interview), please clarify for us whether the help was welcome? As a lone Jedi of the Testing Force…weigh in on the whole paired (or in this case, teamed) vs. solo testing debate!

PEST is a fantastic idea. I'm glad I had a ride home after it though.

Measuring Testers

This post stands as one of the most viewed and commented upon posts I have written. It resonated with a lot of testers inside and outside the company. Mostly the comments were positive, but many testers hated the idea of "being measured at all and in any way whatsoever." But that's what performance reviews are! Sorry, but measuring people is a way of life in the business world; why shouldn't we enter into a discussion on how to go about measuring in a meaningful way? And fundamentally, our bug-finding ability is nothing unless we wield it to reduce the number of bugs that get written. That's the real point of the post anyway, it's not about measuring…it's about improvement.

Yeah, I know…scary subject. But as it is review time here at the empire, this is a subject that has been front and center for both testers and the managers they report to, so I've been asked about it a lot. I always give the same advice to test managers, but I've done so with much trepidation. However, I suddenly feel better about my answer because I'm in good company.

Before I give it away, let me tell you why I am feeling better about my answer. I came across a quote today while looking at the slides that Jim Larus is using for his keynote tomorrow at ISSTA (the International Symposium on Software Testing and Analysis). The quote captures exactly my advice to managers here at Microsoft who ask me how to rate their SDETs. Moreover, the quote comes from Tony Hoare who is a professional hero of mine and a friend of my mentor Harlan Mills (and a Knight, a Turing Award winner and Kyoto Prize winner). If Tony had said the opposite, I would have a whole lot of apologizing to do to the many test managers I've given this advice to. Whenever we disagree, you see, I am always wrong.

So here's my advice: don't count bugs, their severity, test cases, lines of automation, number of regressed suites, or anything concrete. It won't give you the right answer except through coincidence or dumb luck. Throw away your bug finding leader boards (or at least don't use them to assign bonuses), and don't ask the other testers in the group to rate each other. They have skin in this game, too.

Instead, measure how much better a tester has made the developers on your team. This is the true job of a tester, we don't ensure better software, we enable developers to build better software. It isn't about finding bugs because the improvement caused is temporal. The true measure of a great tester is that they find bugs, analyze them thoroughly, report them skillfully, and end up creating a development team that understands the gaps in their skill and knowledge. The end result will be developer improvement, and that will reduce the number of bugs and increase their productivity in ways that far exceeds simple bug removal.

This is a key point. It's software developers that build software, and if we're just finding bugs and assisting their removal, no real lasting value is created. If we take our job seriously enough, we'll ensure the way we go about it creates real and lasting improvement. Making developers better, helping them understand failures and the factors that cause them will mean fewer bugs to find in the future. Testers are quality gurus and that means teaching those responsible for anti-quality what they are doing wrong and where they could improve.

Here's Tony's exact words:

"The real value of tests is not that they detect bugs in the code,
but that they detect inadequacies in the methods, concentration
and skill of those who design and produce the code."
— Tony Hoare 1996

Now replace the word "tests" with "testers" and you end up with a recipe for your career. I imagine I'll be examining this subject more in future posts. Follow the link above to get Jim Larus' take on this as well as a guided tour through some of MSRs test technology, some of which is wide of Tony's mark and some a bit closer.

By the way, note my use of the term "empire" to describe Microsoft. I got a few scathing complaints about this. Funny enough, none of the complaints came from Microsoft employees. Can it be that we actually take the term "empire" as a compliment?

Prevention Versus Cure (Part 1)

I wrote these next five blog posts over a two-day period while sitting at the offices of Stewart Noakes's company TCL in Exeter, England. I had a visa issue that prevented me from taking a scheduled flight to India and was stuck in a sunny and warm Exeter and hung out with Stewart, drank a lot of ale, and talked about testing almost nonstop. This series on Prevention Versus Cure was a reader favorite, not far behind the Future series. Many readers said they were funny. I credit Stewart and delicious English ale for that.

Developer testing, which I call prevention because the more bugs devs find the fewer I have to deal with, is often compared to tester testing, which I call detection. Detection is much like a cure, the patient has gotten sick and we need to diagnose and treat it before it sneezes all over our users. Users get cranky when they get app snot all over them, and it is advisable to avoid that situation to the extent possible.

Developer testing consists of things like writing better specs, performing code reviews, running static analysis tools, writing unit tests (running them is a good idea too), compilation, and such. Clearly developer testing is superior to detection for the following reasons:

1. An ounce of prevention is worth a pound of cure. For every bug kept out of the ecosystem, we decrease testing costs and those (censored) testers are costing us a (censored) fortune. (editor note to author: the readers may very well detect your cynicism at this point, suggest tone-down. Author note to editor: I'm a tester and I can only contain my cynicism for a finite period; that period has expired.)
2. Developers are closer to the bug and therefore can find it earlier in the lifecycle. The less time a bug lives, the cheaper it is to remove. Testers come into the game so late, and that is another reason they cost so much.

Tester testing consists of mainly two activities: automated testing and manual testing. I'll compare those two in a future post. For now, I just want to talk about prevention versus cure. Are we better to keep software from getting sick or should we focus on disease control and treatment?

Again the answer is obvious: Fire the testers. They come to the patient too late after the disease has run rampant and the cure is costly. What the heck are we thinking hiring these people in the first place?

To be continued.

Users and Johns

Lee Copeland hates this post, and I like Lee. But I think my added insight of the John is funny. In the immortal words of Larry the cable guy, "That's funny; I don't care who you are."

Does anyone out there know who was the origin of the insight that the software industry and the illegal drug trade both call their customers users? Brian Marick was the person I stole it from but as far as I know he doesn't claim it.

Anyway, it's an interesting insight. There are so many sweet terms we could use for those creatures who so consistently pay our salary and mortgages. My favorite is client. It has such a nice professional, mysterious ring to it. But perhaps we are in good company with the drug dealers. We get the user addicted to our functionality to the point that they overlook its downside and they come gagging for another fix (uh, version, don't forget to plug the rush-hole!).

I suppose we should be pleased that it stopped with "user." I, for one, would quit this industry if we start calling them "johns." Being associated with the drug dealers is one thing, but pimps? That's where I draw the line.

Ode to the Manual Tester

This is the post that really cemented my love affair with manual testing. I complained loudly around the halls at Microsoft that Vista suffered because its testing was overautomated. A few good manual testers would have gone a long way. The manual tester provides a brain-in-the-loop that no automation can match. Humans can't test faster, but they can test smarter. If you've read this entire book without understanding the depth of my passion for manual testing, you haven't really read this book.

Anyone who has ever seen me present knows my fondness for bug demos. I have made the point for years that there is a lot to learn from the mistakes we make, and studying past bugs represents one of the most powerful ways to learn about preventing and detecting new ones. But this post won't belabor that point. Instead, I want to open a discussion about the various ways in which we treat bugs. And I will end up with a point that many people won't like: that manual detection beats automation. But let's not get ahead of ourselves, because that point will be made with more than one caveat.

Bugs are a necessary byproduct of human endeavor. We make mistakes and software isn't the only human-produced product that is imperfect. So in many ways we are stuck with bugs, but that doesn't mean that **prevention** techniques aren't important. We can and should try our best not to introduce impurities into the software ecosystem. Failing that our next line of defense is **detection** and removal. Clearly detection is inferior to prevention (the whole ounce versus pound debate), but since we humans are stuck with it, we should try to detect as many bugs as possible and as soon as possible.

The first chance of detection is had by developers since they are there at the very moment of creation. (The same can be said of architects and designers so switch those roles in this argument as you will, it does not change the outcome.) In general, the tools of the trade here are first manual **inspection** of the written code followed by automated **static analysis**. I have no doubt that developers find and destroy many bugs as they write, review, and refine their code. Another round of bugs is likely found in the process of compilation, linking, and debugging.

The number, type, and relative importance of the bugs found and fixed during these developer rituals remains unknown but in my opinion, these are the easiest and lowest hanging fruit in the bug forest. They are the bugs that surface solely on the basis of the code alone. The really complex bugs that require system context, environment context, usage history, and so forth are mostly out of bounds. Simply put, developers can't find most of these kinds of bugs.

Enough bugs escape the net to necessitate the next round of bug finding. Round two is still mainly in the hands of developers (often with tester backup): **unit testing** and **build verification**/smoke testing. The key differentiator here is that the software is executing as opposed to just sitting there to be read. This opens the door to a whole new category of bugs as execution context is brought to bear on the problem.

After years of performing, observing, and studying unit test activities, I have to say I am unimpressed. Is there anyone out there that is really good at this? Developers, who are creators at heart, approach it unenthusiastically, and testers generally consider it not to be their job. Lacking clear ownership the reality is that if the code runs from end to end on whatever input scenarios come to mind first, it gets checked into the build. Again, lacking serious study we don't know the relative importance of the bugs found during this second phase of detection, but given the fact that so many slip through to the next phase, it can't be working as well as it could. My own opinion is that with such little time actually spent doing unit testing, no real software state gets built up, nor do realistic user scenarios actually get run. Our expectations should be low.

Testers own the third shot at detection. At Microsoft where I now work and the dozens of companies I consulted for prior, it's test automation that reigns supreme. I have to wonder if years ago some phenom SDET at Microsoft created an automation platform, found a boat load of bugs with it, got some huge promotion because of it, and as a result word got out that automation is the way to improve your career. Too bad. Although I salute the many fine automators at this company, we have to face facts that despite all our automation heroics, bugs...and I mean important, customer-found bugs...are slipping through. Bugs that, in my opinion, can't or won't be found with automation.

Automation suffers from many of the context problems that I mentioned earlier (environment, state build up, and such.) but its actual Achilles' heel is its inability to catch most failures. Unless a crash occurs, an exception is thrown or an assert is triggered, automation won't notice the failure. Granted: automation is important and it finds a lot of bugs that need to be found, but we have to realize that ten thousand test cases a day isn't as good as it sounds if you don't notice if any of them fail.

The only way to catch many of the bugs that make their way to our customers' desktop is by creating an environment that looks like our customers' environment, running the software to build up data and state and being there to notice when the software actually fails. Automation can play a role in this, but in 2008, it's manual testing that is our best weapon. Frankly, I don't see the balance of power shifting away from the manual tester in the near term. If I am right and manual testing is our best chance to find the most important bugs that put our customers at risk, we should be spending a lot more time thinking about it and perfecting it.

I'd like to hear your opinion. What say you to the prospects for manual testing?

Prevention Versus Cure (Part 2)

I got this comment from a test manager at Intel after I posted this one: "After having a team concentrate almost exclusively on automation and bragging about our 1,500 automated tests, our application crashes the first time fingers hit the keyboard. Manual testing reigns when you want to find bugs customers will see."

I like this guy.

Ok, re-hire the testers.

Perhaps you've noticed but the whole prevention thing isn't working so well. Failures in software are running rampant. Before I talk about where we should invest our resources to reverse this trend, I want to talk about why prevention fails.

I see a number of problems, not the least of which is that good requirements and specifications seldom get written and when they do they often fall out-of-date as the focus shifts to writing and debugging code. We're working on that problem in Visual Studio Team System but let's not get ahead of ourselves. The question in front of us now is why prevention fails. It turns out, I have an opinion about this:

The developer-makes-the-worst-tester problem. The idea that a developer can find bugs in their own code is suspect. If they are good at finding bugs, then shouldn't they have known not to write the bugs in the first place? This is why most organizations that care about good software hire a second set of eyes to test it. There's simply nothing like a fresh perspective to detect defects. And there is no replacement for the tester attitude of *how can I break this* to complement the developer attitude of *how can I build this.*

The software-at-rest problem. Any technique such as code reviews or static analysis that don't require the software to actually run, necessarily analyzes the software *at rest.* In general this means techniques based on analyzing the source code, byte code, or the contents of the compiled binary files. Unfortunately, many bugs don't surface until the software is running in a real operational environment. Unless you run the software and provide it with real input, many bugs will simply remain hidden.

The no-data problem. Software needs input *and* data to execute its myriad code paths. Which code paths actually get executed depends on the inputs applied, the software's internal state (the values of the data structures and variables), and external influences like databases and data files. It's often the accumulation of data over time that causes software to fail. This simple fact limits the scope of developer testing which tends to be short in duration…too short to catch these data accumulation errors.

Perhaps tools and techniques will one day emerge that allow developers to write code without introducing bugs. Certainly it is the case that for narrow classes of bugs like buffer overflows that developer techniques can and have driven to near extinction. If this trend continues, the need for a great deal of testing will be negated. But we are a very long way, decades in my mind, from realizing that dream. Until then, we need a second set of eyes, running the software in an environment similar to real usage and using data that is as rich as real user data.

Who provides this second set of eyes? Software testers provide this service, using techniques to detect bugs and then skillfully reporting them so that they get fixed. This is a dynamic process of executing the software in varying environments, with realistic data and with as much input variation as can be managed in the short cycles in which testing occurs.

In part 3 of this blog series I will turn my attention to tester testing and talk about whether we should be doing this with automation or with manual testing.

Hail Europe!

I've been accused often of being a Europhile, and I have to admit that it's true. I admire Europe's culture, history, and generally find its people likable. (Even if they don't always feel the same way about me...I've been told on more than one occasion that my speaking style is a little too forward for more conservative Europeans...I'd believe it except that they keep inviting me back). From a testing point of view, I have to say that, apologies to America and Asia, Europe takes testing to a level of respectability that we have not yet reached.

I had the extreme privilege to speak to a crowd of test practitioners based in the UK last week. The event was hosted by Transition Consulting (TCL) and boasted some of the UK's top consumers of testing services. A list of those companies is posted here, but you'll have to scroll down a bit because Stewart Noakes has been an active blogger recently.

One comment that some of my American readers might not like: European test audiences tend to be a lot more aware and a lot more involved in this discipline of testing. Everyone seemed familiar with my writing and the writing of people like Beizer, Kaner, and Bach. I was especially surprised at the discussion of the history of the Kaner and Beizer school's of thought in the early '90s and the general knowledge of both industry and academic testing conferences and publications. There seems to be more eagerness to delve into the field and its history here than I generally see in my own country. These folks are really well read!

Proponents of certification might point to that as a reason since certification of testers seems far more popular in Europe. Does certification help spark people's passion for testing? Test training in general seems more popular in Europe.

I think it might have something to do with the American bias toward test automation, particularly Microsoft's. Most in our test community are SDETs and approach testing from a very developer-oriented perspective. They may be less inclined to think of themselves as testers and less inclined to involve themselves in its culture and history. That's a shame. (Obviously there are many counterexamples at Microsoft but I think this is generally true among the population of tens of thousands of us.)

I am probably going to get in a lot of trouble for this post. But now that I've mentioned certification, I have a hankering to blog about that now. I can almost guarantee that what I have to say about certification would draw some fire.

The Poetry of Testing

Okay. I admit it. I was in the pub a little too long to be blogging at this point. But I stand behind everything in this post! This is also one of the first indications of my second Euro-inspired passion: My favorite sport is soccer. Blame it on my kids; I never liked the sport either until they started playing it. Now it's an addiction, and since the Champions League is a lunchtime event here in Seattle, you can find me and all my foreign friends at the local pub for every single game.

God Save the Queen! (A curious statement…from my American point of view. But given what history has recorded of certain of England's kings I'll grant the gender bias. Anyway, Save Her all the same as she presides over a country of such glorious breweries!)

If you haven't guessed it already, I'm visiting England. I'm also in a pub. (You probably guessed that, too.) And I just met with a half dozen or so local testers who convinced me (with the offer of free pints) to meet for a book signing. I almost never turn down a signing and I never turn down free beer, especially at the current exchange rate.

Upon parting, they urged me to turn our conversation into a blog post. Here it is. I hope it doesn't embarrass me in the morning.

A single signature seeker was a developer. When I asked him why he bought my book, he answered that he wanted to make sure his testers weren't successful with the "tricks" I preached in it. He intended to frustrate them by writing code that wouldn't fail that way.

I smiled and told him that if this was a soccer, excuse me…football, game I would rip my shirt off and celebrate my goal. He looked at me funny. I think the testers got it. I bet you do, too.

He went on to describe why developing code was better than testing it. He talked about the challenge of wrestling with the compiler and deftly parrying the attempts of the IDE and the operating system to thwart him on his mission. It was a battle to him, a conquest. He was a Knight, fighting for User and Binary.

It was a great story, and I didn't get permission to identify him so I won't, but his passion was fantastic, and the world is a better place because he's in software development.

But if developers are the fighters, I think of myself and my fellow testers as the bards. Testing, to me, is poetry. As I test software I have visions of inputs mingling with data, some are stored internally; some are used temporarily and discarded. I hear music playing as inputs move through the app and find their way to a data structure or get used in some computation. It helps me to think about the inputs in this way; it helps me understand what the application is doing with the input I give it, and that in turn helps me to think of ways to break it. Every potential sour note represents some possible way the developer may have screwed up. Imagine your app processing input. Listen to the poetry it recites; it will tell you when it's going to fail.

I find this especially true of testing web apps. I envision in my mind the formation of SQL queries that my inputs cause the application to make. I form impressions in my mind of the HTML traffic that is transmitted from client to server and the response back again. *What is the application doing? Where is the data going and with what purpose?* These are deep, existential questions worthy of the bard in all testers. And they find bugs. The more I can picture the internal processes going on in the application, the better I am able to understand how the developer might have made a mistake.

The music of the pounce is what makes it all worthwhile. That moment in which it becomes obvious that the software can do nothing but *fail*. It's euphoria; the equivalent to scoring a winning goal. But, please, keep your shirt on. That's a cautionable offense in football, and we don't want developers to be brandishing yellow cards at us.

Prevention Versus Cure (Part 3)

After this post, I got loads of email from Microsoft testers who "came out of the closet" as manual testing sympathizers. Automation has taken precedence over manual testing at Microsoft much the same as development presides over testing. There's just something in the genetics of the field that makes us admire coders. But the amount of manual testing that gets done is amazing to me. People don't talk about it because it doesn't help their review. But people do it because it helps their software.

Now that the testers are once again gainfully employed, what shall we do with them? Do we point them toward writing test automation or ask them to do manual testing?

First, let's tackle the pros and cons of test automation. Automated testing carries both stigma and respect.

The stigma comes from the fact that tests are code and writing tests means that the tester is necessarily also a developer. Can a developer really be a good tester? Many can, many cannot, but the fact that bugs in test automation are a regular occurrence means that they will spend significant time writing code, debugging it, and rewriting it. One must wonder how much time they are spending thinking about testing the software as opposed to writing the test automation. It's not hard to imagine a bias toward the latter.

The respect comes from the fact that automation is cool. One can write a single program that will execute an unlimited number of tests and find bugs. Automated tests can be run and then rerun when the application code has been churned or whenever a regression test is required. Wonderful! Outstanding! How we must worship this automation! If testers are judged based on the number of tests they run, automation will win every time. If they are based on the quality of tests they run, it's a different matter altogether.

The kicker is that we've been automating for years, decades even, and we still produce software that readily falls down when it gets on the desktop of a real user. Why? Because automation suffers from many of the same problems that other forms of developer testing suffers from: it's run in a laboratory environment, not a real user environment, and we seldom risk automation working with real customer databases because automation is generally not very reliable (it is software after all). Imagine automation that adds and deletes records of a database—what customer in their right mind would allow that automation anywhere near their database? And there is one Achilles heel of automated testing that no one has ever solved: the oracle problem.

The oracle problem is a nice name for one of the biggest challenges in testing: How do we know that the software did what it was supposed to do when we ran a given test case? Did it produce the right output? Did it do so without unwanted side effects? How can we be sure? Is there an oracle we can consult that will tell us—given a user environment, data configuration and input sequence—that the software performed exactly as it was designed to do? Given the reality of imperfect (or nonexistent) specs, this just is not a reality for modern software testers.

Without an oracle, test automation can only find the most egregious of failures: crashes, hangs (maybe), and exceptions. And the fact that automation is itself software often means that the crash is in the test case and not in the software! Subtle and/or complex failures are missed in their entirety.

So where does that leave the tester? If a tester cannot rely on developer bug prevention or automation, where should she place her hope? The only answer can be in manual testing. That will be the topic of part four of this series.

Back to Testing

As I said earlier I started my Microsoft career in security. I took a lot of flack from my testing readers when I "abandoned" testing for security back in 1999. But I couldn't help myself. After the nonevent of Y2K, I was looking for the next big bug when David Ladd (who blogs at http://blogs.msdn.com/sdl) introduced me to security. I was so uneducated on security that it was a veritable intellectual playground, and I found my testing skills to be incredibly useful. Anyone who could find security bugs could make serious impact. I wrote my second and third books in the How to Break *series during this time, invented a new way to find viruses, and got gobs of funding from a very paranoid U.S. government. But security turned out to be…well read on and you'll find out.*

Since starting this blog a couple weeks ago, I've received more comments via email than have been posted on the blog. Many more.

It reminds me of when I was a professor and ended every class with "Anyone have a question?" Silence almost always followed that query only to have students line up after class *with questions*. There is something about one-on-one interactions that just seems pleasing to people. I tried to take the time to remember the questions, so I could answer them later for the entire class when I thought those answers would be generally helpful.

Well, this is the blogging business, not the teaching business and I wonder how much of any of it is helpful; however, the question that has come most frequently to my inbox is "What made you leave security to come back to testing?" Perhaps the answer has some claim to general interest.

That answer: ignorance.

In fact, ignorance was what sent me the other direction back in 2000 when my friend and colleague David Ladd (who blogs here) tweaked my interest. Ignorance is core to progress in science, Matt Ridley explained it best: "Most scientists are bored by what they have already discovered, it is ignorance that drives them on." When David laid out the wonder of security testing (and in that sense I never really left testing) to me and I was hooked. This is an important problem in a field I know nearly nothing about. Eight years, two patents, two security books, more than a dozen papers, and two startups later I have to admit I became a bit bored.

In some ways security is getting easier. Many of the problems with security are of our own creation. Buffer overflows, for example, never had to happen. They were a result of poor implementation of programming languages. Viruses didn't either for other reasons. Microsoft and many other companies are changing the game. Better compilers, hardened operating systems, and managed code have made many security problems simply vanish. Virtualization and cloud computing will continue this trend. Ignorance is being replaced with knowledge and nowhere is that more noticeable than in security.

When I heard Visual Studio was looking for an architect for the test business, I found my juices stirring…the siren call of unbounded ignorance.

Working in security made me realize just how hard testing really is. Testing is not a problem created by humans; it's the nature of the beast. It's part of the very fabric of the computer and the network in their infinite possibilities. In fact, someone wondered in another private exchange if I found much had changed in my eight years "away." "No" was my answer "and I did not expect to." Security has changed so fundamentally in eight short years that had the situation been reversed and it was security I took a sabbatical from, my skills would likely be suspect. Instead I find myself working on much the same testing problems as I had before.

This is not an indictment of any testing researcher, practitioner, or testing in general: It is a nod to the complexity of the problem. There is a lot of ignorance to keep all of us busy trying to find the right knowledge with which to replace it. But we cannot let the seeming lack of progress deter us from working on one of the loveliest scientific problems of our time.

Thanks for asking.

August 2008

I am still in England at this time; the next is my last post before going back to Washington. So whatever conclusions you draw about the effect of English ale on my writing must end after this next one.

Prevention Versus Cure (Part 4)

Manual testing is human-present testing. A human tester using their brain, their fingers, and their wit to create the scenarios that will cause software either to fail or to fulfill its mission. Manual testing often occurs after all the other types of developer and automated techniques have already had their shot at removing bugs. In that sense, manual testers are at somewhat of an unlevel playing field. The easy bugs are gone; the pond has already been fished.

However, manual testing regularly finds bugs and, worse, users (who by definition perform manual testing) find them, too. Clearly there is some power in manual testing that cannot be overlooked. We have an obligation to study this discipline in much more detail...there's gold in them-thar fingers.

One reason human-present testing succeeds is that it allows the best chance to create realistic user scenarios, using real user data in real user environments and still allow for the possibility of recognizing both obvious and subtle bugs. It's the power of having an intelligent human in the testing loop.

Perhaps it will be the case that developer-oriented techniques will evolve to the point that a tester is unnecessary. Indeed, this would be a desirable future for software producers and software users alike, but for the foreseeable future, tester-based detection is our best hope at finding the bugs that matter. There is simply too much variation, too many scenarios, and too many possible failures for automation to track it all. It requires a brain-in-the-loop. This is the case for this decade, the next decade, and at perhaps a few more after that. We may look to a future in which software just works, but if we achieve that vision, it will be the hard work of the manual testers of this planet that made it all possible.

There are two main types of manual testing.

Scripted manual testing

Many manual testers are guided by scripts, written in advance, that guide input selection and dictate how the software's results are to be checked for correctness. Sometimes scripts are specific: Enter this value, press this button, check for that result and so forth. Such scripts are often documented in Microsoft Excel tables and require maintenance as features get updated through either new development or bug fixes. The scripts serve a secondary purpose of documenting the actual testing that was performed.

It is often the case that scripted manual testing is too rigid for some applications or test processes and testers take a less formal approach. Instead of documenting every input, a script may be written as a general scenario that gives some flexibility to the tester while they are running the test. At Microsoft, the folks that manually test Xbox games often do this, so an input would be "interact with the mirror" without specifying exactly the type of interaction they must perform.

Exploratory testing

When the scripts are removed entirely, the process is called *exploratory testing*. A tester may interact with the application in whatever way they want and use the information the application provides to react, change course, and generally explore the application's functionality without restraint. It may seem ad hoc to some, but in the hands of a skilled and experienced exploratory tester, this technique can be powerful. Advocates would argue that exploratory testing allows the full power of the human brain to be brought to bear on finding bugs and verifying functionality without preconceived restrictions.

Testers using exploratory methods are also not without a documentation trail. Test results, test cases, and test documentation is simply generated as tests are being performed instead of before. Screen capture and keystroke recording tools are ideal for this purpose.

Exploratory testing is especially suited to modern web application development using agile methods. Development cycles are short, leaving little time for formal script writing and maintenance. Features often evolve quickly so that minimizing dependent artifacts (like test cases) is a desirable attribute. The number of proponents of exploratory testing is large enough that its case no longer needs to be argued so I'll leave it at that.

At Microsoft, we define several types of exploratory testing. That's the topic I'll explore in part five.

If Microsoft Is So Good at Testing, Why Does Your Software Still Suck?

I had no idea what kind of traffic a blog could generate until I wrote this. This is the first blog post I wrote that made the MSDN home page, and man did it generate the hits. My inbox was on fire, and mostly the comments were positive. But I remain convinced that this is the post that got certain execs watching me. Seriously, Microsoft has produced software that we are less than proud of…so has every other *software company on the planet. Software is hard to write, harder to test, and hard to get even near to perfect. We desperately need to talk about the pains and be honest about the result so that we can improve what we are doing. The most gratifying part of this post was the mail I got from our competitors. They praised my honesty and admitted their own culpability. This is software, and we are all in this together.*

What a question! I only wish I could convey the way that question is normally asked. The tone of voice is either partially apologetic (because many people remember that I was a major ask-er of that same question long before I became an ask-ee), or it's condescending to the point that I find myself smiling as I fantasize about the ask-er's computer blue-screening right before that crucial save. (Ok, so I took an extra hit of the Kool-Aid today. It was lime and I like lime.)

After 27 months on the inside I have a few insights. The first few are, I readily concede, downright defensive. But as I've come to experience firsthand, true nonetheless. The last one though is really at the heart of the matter: That, talent notwithstanding, testers at Microsoft do have some work to do.

I'm not going down the obvious path: that testing isn't responsible for quality and to direct the question to a developer/designer/architect instead. (I *hate* the phrase "you can't test quality in"; it's a deflection of blame and as a tester, I take quality directly as my responsibility.)

But I am getting ahead of myself. I'll take up that baton at the end of this post. Let's begin with the defensive points:

1. **Microsoft builds applications that are among the world's most complex.** No one is going to argue that Windows, SQL Server, Exchange, and so forth aren't complex, and the fact that they are in such widespread use means that our biggest competitors are often our own prior versions. We end up doing what we call "brown field" development (as opposed to "green field" or version 1 development) in that we are building on top of existing functionality. That means that testers have to deal with existing features, formats, [and] protocols along with all the new functionality and integration scenarios that make it very difficult to build a big picture test plan that is actually doable. Testing real end-to-end scenarios must share the stage with integration and compatibility tests. Legacy sucks and functionality is only part of it…as testers, we all know what is *really* making that field brown! Be careful where you step. Dealing with yesterday's bugs keeps part of our attention away from today's bugs.

   (Aside: Have you heard that old CS creationist joke: "Why did it take god only seven days to create the universe?" The answer: "No installed base." There's nothing to screw up, no existing users to piss off, or prior functionality and crappy design decisions to tiptoe around. God got lucky, us…not so much.)

2. **Our user-to-tester ratio sucks, leaving us hopelessly outnumbered.** How many testers does it take to run the same number of test cases that the user base of, say, Microsoft Word can run in the first hour after it is released? The answer: far more than we have or could hire even if we could find enough qualified applicants. There are enough users to virtually ensure that every feature gets used in every way imaginable within the first hour (day, week, fortnight, month, pick any timescale you want and it's still scary) after release. This is a lot of stress to put our testers under. It's one thing to know you are testing software that is important. It's quite another to know that your failure to do so well will be mercilessly exposed *soon* after release. Testing our software is hard; only the brave need apply.

3. **On a related point, our installed base makes us a target.** Our bugs affect so many people that they are newsworthy. There are a lot of people watching for us to fail. If David Beckham wears plaid with stripes to fetch his morning paper, it's scandalous; if I wore my underpants on the outside of my jeans for a week few people would even notice. (In

their defense though, my fashion sense is obtuse enough that they could be readily forgiven for overlooking it.) Becks is a successful man, but when it comes to the "bad with the good" I'm betting he's liking the good a whole lot more. You're in good company, David.

But none of that matters. We'll take our installed base and our market position any day. No trades offered. But still, we always ready to improve. I think testers should step up and do a better job of testing quality in. That's my fourth point.

4. **Our testers don't play a strong enough role in the design of our apps.** We have this "problem" at Microsoft that we have a whole lot of wicked smart people. We have these creatures called technical fellows and distinguished engineers who have really big brains and use them to dream really big dreams. Then they take these big dreams of theirs and convince general managers and VPs (in addition to being smart they are also articulate and passionate) that they should build this thing they dreamt about. Then another group of wicked smart people called program managers start designing the hell out of these dreams and developers start developing the hell out of them and a few dozen geniuses later this thing has a life of its own *and then someone asks "how are we going to test this thing"* and of course it's A LITTLE LATE TO BE ASKING THAT QUESTION NOW ISN'T IT?

Smart people who dream big inspire me. Smart people who don't understand testing and dream big scare the hell out of me. We need to do a better job of getting the word out. There's another group of wicked smart people at Microsoft, and we're getting involved a wee bit late in the process. We've got things to say and contributions to make, not to mention posteriors to save. There's a part of our job we aren't doing as well as we should: pushing testing forward into the design and development process and educating the rest of the company on what quality means and how it is attained.

We *can* test quality in; we just have to start testing a lot sooner. That means that everyone from TF/DE through the entire pipeline needs to have test as part of their job. We have to show them how to do that. We have to educate these smart people about what quality means and take what we know about testing and apply it not only to just binaries/assemblies, but to designs, user stories, specs and every other artifact we generate. How can it be the case that what we know about quality *doesn't* apply to these early stage artifacts? It does apply. We need to lead the way in applying it.

I think that ask-ers of the good-tester/crappy-software question would be surprised to learn exactly how we are doing this right now. Fortunately, you'll get a chance because Tara Roth, one of the directors of Test for Office is speaking at STAR West in November. Office has led the way in pushing testing forward and she's enjoyed a spot as a leader of that effort. I think you'll enjoy hearing what she has to say.

By the way, Tara kicked butt at STAR.

Prevention Versus Cure (Part 5)

This is the last part of the Prevention versus Cure series and shows some of my early thinking on how to divide exploratory testing into smaller more consumable parts. But if you have read this book, you'll see that my thinking evolved a great deal. I decided against the freestyle-strategy-feedback model in favor of the in-the-small and in-the-large model that I used in this book. Now you can compare which one you like better.

Okay, we're getting to the end of this thread and probably the part that most of you have asked about: exploratory testing, particularly how it is practiced at Microsoft.

At Microsoft, we define four types of exploratory testing. This isn't meant as a taxonomy, it's simply for convenience, but it underscores that exploratory testers don't just test; they plan, they analyze, they think and use any and all documentation and information at their disposal to make their testing as effective as possible.

Freestyle Exploratory Testing

Freestyle exploratory testing is ad hoc exploration of an application's features in any order using any inputs without regard to what features have and have not been covered. Freestyle testing employs no rules or patterns; just do it. It's unfortunate that many people think that *all* exploratory testing is freestyle, but that undersells the technique by a long shot as we'll see in the following variations.

One might choose a freestyle test as a quick smoke test to see if any major crashes or bugs can be easily found or to gain some familiarity with an application before moving on to more sophisticated techniques. Clearly, not a lot of preparation goes into freestyle exploratory testing, nor should it. In fact, it's far more "exploratory" than it is "testing" so expectations should be set accordingly.

There isn't much experience or information needed to do freestyle exploratory testing. However, combined with the exploratory techniques below, it can become a very powerful tool.

Scenario-Based Exploratory Testing

Traditional scenario-based testing involves a starting point of user stories or documented end-to-end scenarios that we expect our ultimate end user to perform. These scenarios can come from user research, data from prior versions of the application, and so forth, and are used as scripts to test the software. The added element of exploratory testing to traditional scenario testing widens the scope of the script to inject variation, investigation, and alternative user paths.

An exploratory tester who uses a scenario as a guide will often pursue interesting alternative inputs or pursue some potential side effect that is not included in the script. However, the ultimate goal is to complete the scenario so these testing detours always end up back on the main user path documented in the script.

Strategy-Based Exploratory Testing

If one combines the experience, skill, and Jedi-like testing perception of the experienced and accomplished software tester with freestyle testing, one ends up with this class of exploratory testing. It's freestyle exploration but guided by known bug-finding techniques. Strategy-based exploratory testing takes all those written techniques (like boundary value analysis or combinatorial testing) and unwritten instinct (like the fact that exception handlers tend to be buggy) and uses this information to guide the hand of the tester.

These strategies are the key to being successful; the better the repertoire of testing knowledge, the more effective the testing. The strategies are based on accumulated knowledge about where bugs hide, how to combine inputs and data, and which code paths commonly break. Strategic testing combines the experience of veteran testers with the free-range habits of the exploratory tester.

Feedback-Based Exploratory Testing

This category of testing starts out freestyle but as soon as test history is built up, the tester uses that feedback to guide future exploration. "Coverage" is the canonical example. A tester consults coverage metrics (code coverage, UI coverage, feature coverage, input coverage, or some combination thereof), and selects new tests that improve that coverage metric. Coverage is only one such place where feedback is drawn. We also look at code churn and bug density, among others.

I think of this as "last time testing": the last time I visited this state of the application I applied *that* input, so next time I will choose another. Or the last time I saw this UI control I exercised property A; this time I will exercise property B.

Tools are very valuable for feedback-based testing so that history can be stored, searched, and acted upon in real time.

The Future of Testing (Part 1)

Microsoft has this really cool home of the future built on campus that shows how technology and software will change the way families live and communicate. If you've ever been to the "carousel of progress" at Disney World, you have the right picture, except that Microsoft's is by far more modern. (Disney's was an old exhibit and a picture of the future from a 1960's point of view.) We've also made a series of videos about the future of retail, health care, productivity, manufacturing, and the like, and one day I stumbled across these videos. As beautifully done as they are, they represent a very compelling future where computers, RFIDs, and software are everywhere. As a tester, this scared me, and I couldn't help but think that with quality as bad as it is with today's software, how will we ever manage to test tomorrow's apps?

Thus began my future quest, and I talked about this with dozens of people around the company and started doing presentations to get input from hundreds more. The result was a keynote presentation at Euro STAR and this blog series. Again, I updated this vision in this book, but this will help you see how the idea progressed.

Outsourcing. It's a familiar term and the way a lot of testing gets done here in 2008. However, it wasn't always so and it's not liable to be that way in the future either. In this post I will talk about how I think testing will get done in the future and how outsourcing might fundamentally change as a business model for software testing.

In the beginning, very little testing was outsourced. Testing was performed by insourcers, people employed within the same organization that wrote the software. Developers and testers (often the same people performing both tasks) worked side by side to get the software written, tested and out the door.

The vendors' role in the insourcing days was to provide tools that supported this self service testing. But the vendors' role soon changed as demand for more than just tools surfaced. Instead of just providing tools to insourcers, vendors emerged that provided testing itself. We call this outsourcing, and it is still the basic model for the way many development shops approach testing: hire it out.

So the first two generations of testing look like this:

Generation	**Role of Vendors**
(1st) Insourcing	Provide tools
(2nd) Outsourcing	Provide testing (which subsumes the tools)

The next logical step in the evolution of testing is for vendors to provide *testers* and this is exactly the era we've entered with *crowdsourcing*. Yesterday's announcement by Utest marks the beginning of this era, and it is going to be very interesting to see it unfold. Will crowdsourcers outperform outsourcers and win this market for the future? Clearly market economics and the crowds' ability to execute will determine that, but my personal view is that the odds are stacked in favor of the crowd. This is not really an either-or situation but the evolution of the field. The older model will, over time, make way for the newer model. This will be a case Darwinian natural selection played out in the matter of only a few short years. The fittest will survive with the timeframe determined by economics and quality of execution.

That gives us the third generation:

(3rd) Crowdsourcing	Provide testers (which subsumes the testing and tools)

And what about the future? Is there an aggressive gene buried deep in the DNA of our discipline that will evolve crowdsourcing into something even better? I think so, though it is many years and a few technological leaps away. I'll coin a new term for now just to put a name on this concept: *testsourcing*.

(4th) Testsourcing	Provide test artifacts (which subsumes the testers, testing and tools)

Testsourcing cannot be explained however without one key technological leap that has yet to occur. This technological leap is virtualization will be described in part two of this series.

The Future of Testing (Part 2)

For testsourcing to take hold of the future of testing, two key technological barriers must be broken: the reusability of test artifacts and the accessibility of user environments. Let me explain:

Reusability: The reusability of software development artifacts, thanks to the popularization of OO and its derivative technologies in the 1990s, is a given. Much of the software we develop today is comprised of preexisting libraries cobbled together into a cohesive whole. Unfortunately, testing is not there yet. The idea that I can write a test case and simply pass it off to another tester for reuse is rare in practice. Test cases are too dependent on my test platform: They are specific to a single application under test; they depend on some tool that other testers don't have; they require an automation harness, library, network config (and so forth) that cannot be easily replicated by a would-be re-user.

Environment: The sheer number of customer environments needed to perform comprehensive testing is daunting. Suppose I write an application intended to be run on a wide variety of mobile phones. Where do I get all these phones to test my application on them? How do I configure all these phones so they are representative of my intended customers' phones? And the same thing goes for any other type of application. If I write a web app, how do I account for all the different OS, browsers, browser settings, plug-ins, Registry configurations, security settings, machine-specific settings, and potentially conflicting application types?

The answer that is emerging for both of these needs is *virtualization*, which is steadily becoming cheaper, faster, and more powerful and is being applied to application domains that run the gamut from lab management to IT infrastructure deployment.

Virtualization has great potential to empower the "crowd" for crowdsourcing. Specialized test suites, test harnesses, test tools can be one-clicked into virtual machines that can be used by anyone, anywhere. Just as software developers of today can reuse the code of their colleagues and forebears, so too will the testers in the crowd be able to reuse test suites and test tools. And just as that reuse has increased the range of applications that a given developer can reliably build, it will increase the types of applications that a tester can test. Virtualization enables the immediate reusability of complicated and sophisticated testing harnesses.

Conveniently, virtualization does the same favor for testers with respect to user environments. A user can simply one-click their entire computer into a virtual machine and make it available to testers via the cloud. If we can store all the videos in the world for instant viewing by anyone, anywhere, then why can't we do the same with virtual user environments?

Virtualization technology is already there (in the case of PCs) or nearly there (in the case of mobile or other specialized environments). We simply need to apply it to the testing problem.

The end result will be the general availability of a wide variety of reusable, automated test harnesses, and user environments that can be employed by any tester anywhere. This serves to empower the crowd for crowdsourcing, putting them on more than even footing with the outsourcers from a technology standpoint, and since they far outnumber the outsourcers (at least in theory if not yet in practice), the advantage is clearly in favor of this new paradigm.

Market forces will also favor a crowdsourcing model powered by virtualization. User environments will have a cash value as crowd testers will covet them to gain a competitive advantage. Users will be incentivized to click that button to virtualize and share their environment. (Yes, there are privacy implications to this model, but they are solvable.) And since problematic environments will be even more valuable than those that work well, there will be an upside for users who experience intermittent driver and application errors: The test VMs they create will be more valuable…there's gold in those lemons! Likewise, testers will be incentivized to share out testing assets and make them as reusable as possible. Market forces favor a future with reusable test artifacts and virtualization makes it possible.

So what does this virtualization-powered future mean to the individual tester? Well, fast forward 20-30 years in which time millions (?) of user environments will have been captured, cloned, stored, and made available. I can envision open libraries of such environments that testers can browse for free or proprietary libraries available by subscription only. Test cases and test suites will enjoy the same treatment and will be licensed for fees commensurate with their value and applicability.

Perhaps, there will come a time when there are very few human testers at all, only a few niche, and specialized products (or products of extreme complexity like operating systems) will actually require them. For the large majority of development, a single test designer can be hired to pick and choose from the massive number of available test virtual environments and execute them in parallel: millions of person-years of testing wrapped up in a matter of hours because all the automation and end-user configurations are available and ready to use. This is the world of testsourcing.

It's the end of testing as we currently know it, but it is the beginning of a whole new set of interesting challenges and problems for the test community. And it's a viable future that doesn't require more than virtualization technology that either already exists or is on the near term horizon. It also implies a higher-order effort by testers as we move into a design role (in the case of actually performing testing) or a development role (in the case of building and maintaining reusable test artifacts). No more late cycle heroics; testers are first class citizens in this virtualized future.

September 2008

In addition to the Future series, I snuck in a few one-offs. This next one on certification generated a lot of attention. Apparently, certification is making the consultants who do training a lot of money, and my skepticism toward the value of certification was not appreciated. This post generated the first real hate mail as a result of this blog. I was accused of sabotaging the certification movement by implying that Microsoft thought it was nonsense. I did much more though than simply imply it... Most people at Microsoft really do think its nonsense!

On Certification

How do you feel about tester certification? I've heard all the arguments for and against and looked at the different certifications and their requirements. Frankly, I have not been impressed. My employer doesn't seem impressed either. I have yet to meet a single tester at Microsoft who is certified. Most don't even know there is such a thing. They've all learned testing the old fashioned way: by reading all the books and papers they can get their hands on, apprenticing themselves to people at the company that are better at it than they are, and critiquing the gurus and would-be gurus who spout off in person and in print.

Simple logic tells me this: Microsoft has some of the best testers I have ever met. (I mean, seriously, the empire knows their testing and they know their testers. I've studied testing and have been credited with more test innovation than perhaps I deserve, but I know this field, and rarely a day goes by that I don't meet a tester who is a far shot better than I am. I'd love to name some of them here, but invariably I'd leave some out and they'd be pissed. Pissed testers are not easy to deal with so that's why I haven't bothered naming them.) So *in my experience* there is an inverse relationship between certification and testing talent. The same is true of testers at other companies I admire that I meet at conferences and meetings. The really good testers I know and meet just aren't certified. There is the occasional counterexample, but the generalization holds. (Whether the reverse is true, I have little data with which to form an opinion.)

Let me repeat, this is my experience and experience does not equate to fact. However, the reason I am blogging about this is because I met three office managers/administrators recently who are certified. These three are not testers, but they work around software testers, and they hosted a certification course and thought it would be helpful to sit in and understand what the people around them did day in and day out. They sat the courses, took the exam, and got their certification.

Hmm.

Okay, I'll grant they are smart, curious, and hard working. But there is more to testing than that triad. They readily admit they know little about computing, even less about software. From the time I spent with them, I didn't get the impression that they would have made good testers. Their skill lies elsewhere. I doubt they would pass any class I ever taught at Florida Tech, and I imagine they'd find the empire's training a bit too much for them to digest as well. Yet they aced the certification exam without breaking a sweat.

What am I missing? Isn't the point of a certification to *certify* that you can do something? Certify is a really strong word that I am uncomfortable using so lightly. When I hire a certified plumber, I expect said plumber to plumb beyond my uncertified ability. When I hire a certified electrician, I expect that electrician to trivialize the problems that vexed me as an amateur. If I hired a certified tester, I would expect them to test with a similar magnitude of competence and skill. I wonder if an office manager of a plumbing company could so easily get certified to plumb.

Well I checked into it. Plumbers (at least in Seattle) are indeed certified, but they don't get that certification by taking a course and an exam (although they do both). They serve time apprenticing to a master plumber. You better believe that by the time they get that seal of approval, they can plumb till the cows come home.

I realize testing isn't plumbing but the word *certification* gives me pause. It's a strong word. Is there something more to tester certification that I am missing? Is it simply that you understand the base nomenclature of software or that you can converse with other testers and appear as one of the crowd? Or that you simply sat through a course with enough of an open mind that some of it sunk in? What value does this actually bring to the discipline? Are we any better off because we have these certifications? Are we risking certifying people who really can't test and thereby water down the entire discipline?

I don't think these certifications are really certifications at all. It's just training. Calling it a certification is over selling it by a long shot. In my mind a certification means you have a seal of approval *to do something beyond what an amateur/tinkerer can accomplish.* Otherwise, what has the certification accomplished?

I am proud of being a tester, and if I seem arrogant to be that way then *so be it*. What I do and what my compatriots do is beyond a single course that an office manager, no matter how smart, can just pick up.

However, if I am wrong about certification, I'd like to be enlightened. For the life of me, I don't see the upside.

The Future of Testing (Part 3)

This is my favorite prediction and THUD is a tool we are actively constructing.

So we are now at my third prediction that deals with information and how testers will use information to improve their testing in the future.

Prediction 1: Testsourcing

Prediction 2: Virtualization

Prediction 3: Information

What information do you use to help you test your software? Specs? User manuals? Prior (or competing) versions? Source code? Protocol analyzers? Process monitors? Does the information help? Is it straightforward to use?

Information is at the core of everything we do as software testers. The better our information about what the software is supposed to be doing and how it is doing it, the better our testing can actually be. I find it unacceptable that testers get so little information and none of it is specifically designed to make it easier to do our jobs. I am happy to say that this is changing…rapidly…and that in the near term we will certainly be gifted with the right information at the right time.

I take my inspiration for testing information from video games. In video games, we have the surfacing and use of information darn near perfected. The more information about the game, the players, the opposition, the environment, the better you play and the higher score you achieve. In video games this information is displayed in something called a HUD, or heads up display. All a players' abilities, weapons, health info are displayed and clickable for immediate use. Likewise, your location in the world is displayed in a small minimap and information about opponents is readily available. (My son used to play Pokémon in which he had access to a Pokédex which kept information about all the various species of Pokémon he might encounter in the game…I'd like a Bug-é-dex that did the same for bugs I might encounter.)

But most of the testing world is mired in black box testing without such a rich information infrastructure. Where's is our minimap that tells us which screen we are testing and how that screen is connected with the rest of the system? Why can't I hover over a GUI control and see source code or even a list of properties the controls implements (and that I can test)? If I am testing an API, why can't I see the list of parameter combinations that I and all my fellow testers have already tried? I need all of this quickly and in a concise and readily consumable format that assists my testing rather than shuffling through some SharePoint site or database full of disconnected project artifacts.

My colleague at Microsoft, Joe Allan Muharsky, calls the collection of information that I want so badly a THUD — the Tester's Heads Up Display — putting the information a tester needs to find bugs and verify functionality in a readily consumable format for software testers. Think of a THUD as a skin that wraps around the application under test and surfaces information and tools that are useful in context of the application. Few THUDs are in use today or even contain the right information. In the future, no tester would think of testing without one, just like no gamer could imagine traversing an unpredictable and dangerous world without their HUD.

If this sounds a little like cheating, then so be it. Gamers who add cheats to their HUD have an even bigger advantage over gamers who don't. And as in-house testers who have access to the source, the protocols, the back-end, front-end and middleware we, can indeed "cheat." We can have a massive bug-finding advantage over ordinary black box testers and users.

This is exactly the situation we want: to be in a position to find our own bugs faster and more efficiently than anyone else. This is cheating I approve of wholeheartedly but we're not currently taking advantage of the information required for the cheats.

In the future, we will. That future will be fundamentally different than the information-starved present in which we are current working.

The Future of Testing (Part 4)

There is some magic in this prediction that in retrospect, the world has not yet perfected. But as these are predictions of the future, that seems appropriate. Many people talk about moving testing forward, but they mean simply getting testers involved earlier. From where I sit, we've been getting testers involved in spec reviews and the like for decades. That's moving testers forward, not moving ***testing*** *forward. What we really need to do is to get testable stuff earlier so that we can apply our trade earlier in the process.*

Moving Testing Forward

There is a gap that exists in testing that is eating away at quality, productivity, and the general manageability of the entire development life cycle. It is the gap between when a bug is created and when that same bug is detected. The larger the gap, the more time a bug stays in the system. Clearly that's bad, but pointing out that the longer bugs stay in the system, the more expensive they are to remove is what we've done in the past.

What we're going to do in the future is *close the gap.*

But closing the gap means a fundamental change in the way we do testing. In 2008 a developer can introduce a bug, quite by accident mind you — our development environments do little to discourage that, and *few concerted attempts are made to find the bug until the binary is built.* We insert bugs and then simply allow them free reign until far too late in the process where we depend on late cycle bug finding heroics to bail us out.

As software testers we provide a valuable set of bug finding and analysis techniques; what we have to do in the future is apply these techniques earlier in the process, far sooner than we do now. There are two main things I foresee that will help us accomplish this. One is simply not waiting for the binary and applying our tests on early development artifacts. The second is building the binary earlier so we can test it earlier.

Let's take these in order beginning with "testing on early development artifacts." During late-cycle heroics we apply any number of bug finding strategies on the binary *through its published interfaces.* We take the compiled binary or collection of assemblies, byte code and such hook them to our test harnesses, and pummel them with inputs and data until we ferret out enough bugs to have some confidence that quality is good enough. (Perhaps I'll cover measurement and release criteria in a future blog entry.) But why wait until the binary is ready? Why can't we apply these test techniques on architecture artifacts?...On requirements and user stories?...On specifications and designs? Can it be possible that all the technology, techniques, and testing wisdom collected over the past half century applies only to an artifact that *executes?* Why aren't architectures testable in the same way? Why can't we apply what we know to designs and storyboards? Well the answer is that there is no good reason we don't. I actually think that many progressive groups at Microsoft do apply testing techniques early, and that in the future we'll figure out how to do this collectively. Testing will begin, not when something *becomes testable* as is the case now, but instead testing will begin the moment *there exists something that needs testing*. It's a subtle but important distinction.

"Building the binary earlier" is the second part of this but doing so represents a technological hurdle that needs jumping. In 2008 we write software component by component and we can't build the whole without each of the parts being ready. This means that testing must wait until all the components achieve some level of completion. Bugs are allowed to sit for days and weeks before testing can be brought to bear on their discovery. Can we substitute partially completed components with virtual ones? Or with stubs that mimic external behavior? Can we build general purpose chameleon components that change their behavior to match the system into which they are (temporarily) inserted? I predict we will…because we must. Virtual and chameleon components will allow testers to apply their detection craft soon after a bug is created. Bugs will have little chance to survive beyond their first breath.

Testing is too important to wait until the end of the development cycle to start it. Yes, iterative development and agile create testable code earlier (albeit smaller, incomplete functionality), but we still have far too many bugs appearing after release. Clearly what we are doing is not enough. The future must bring the power of testing to bear on early development artifacts and allow us to scaffold together a workable, testable environment long before the code is entirely build-able.

The Future of Testing (Part 5)

Visualization is one area in which we are making a lot of progress in the test tools world. This is an area only a few short years away. Software testing will become much more like playing a video game within two to five years.

Visualization.

What does software look like? Wouldn't it be helpful if we had a visualization of software that we could use while the software was being constructed or tested? With a single glance we could see that parts of it remain unfinished. Dependencies, interfaces, and data would be easy to see and, one would hope, easier to test. At the very least we could watch the software grow and evolve as it was being built and watch it consume input and interact with its environment as it was being tested.

Other engineering disciplines have such visuals. Consider the folks who make automobiles. Everyone involved in the assembly process can see the car. They can see that it has yet to have bumpers or a steering wheel installed. They can watch it progress down the mechanized line from an empty shell to a fully functional product ready to be driven to a dealer. How much longer until it is complete? Well, its forty feet from the end of the line!

The fact that everyone involved in making the car has this shared vision of the product is extremely helpful. They speak in terms they can all understand because every part, every connection, every interface is where it is supposed to be when it is supposed to be there.

Unfortunately, that is not our world. Questions or the sort asked above "How long until it is complete?" or "What tasks remain undone?" vex us. This is a problem that 21st century testers will solve.

Architects and developers are already solving it. Visual Studio is replete with diagrams and visualizations from sequence charts to dependency graphs. Testers are solving it, too. Visualization solutions exist within the empire's walls for seeing code changes in an Xbox title (objects whose code has churned glow green when rendered and then revert to normal after they have been tested) to identifying untested complexity within the Windows code base, (Heat maps of code coverage versus code complexity can be viewed in three dimensional space leading testers right to the problem areas.) The visualizations are stunning, beautiful, and allow testers to determine what needs testing simply by glancing at the visual.

We need more of this but we need to approach the problem carefully. We can't simply accept the diagrams provided to us by the UML and modeling crowds. Those visuals are meant to solve other problems that may or may not overlap with the problems we face. Many of the existing visuals were created to serve architects or developers whose needs are different. We need to think this through as testers. We need visuals that map requirements to code, tests to interfaces, code churn to the GUI, and code coverage to controls. Wouldn't it be nice to launch the app under test and be able to see controls glow with an intensity that reflects the amount of coverage or the number of tests that have touched them? Wouldn't it be nice to be able to see a graphic animating network utilization or real time database communication? Why shouldn't we be able to see the network traffic and the SQL queries as they happen? There is much that is going on unseen beneath the covers of our application, and it's time we surfaced it and leveraged it to improve code quality.

This is an imminently solvable problem and one that many smart people are working on. This is software testing in living color.

October 2008

During the month of October I continued my series on the future of testing and my blog numbers really started to pick up, which brought some front-page exposure on MSDN and that caused even more traffic. I also began to get a lot more requests for my Future of Testing talk around the company, so I found myself talking about this subject more and debating it with a lot of smart Microsofties. This really helped expose some weaknesses and solidify the strengths of the vision. I began to gravitate toward the "information" prediction as the primary one of the eight predictions.

But in this next part, I talk about culture. I've never revealed to anyone who the technical fellow/distinguished engineer actually is in the following story. I very much doubt I ever will, but I am still meeting with him regularly about software testing.

The Future of Testing (Part 6)

Testing Culture

A couple of months ago I attended a lecture given by one of the Empire's cache of technical fellows (maybe he was a distinguished engineer, I am not sure as they look so much alike). Like all our TFs the guy was wicked smart, and as he presented a design for some new product he and his team were building, I had an epiphany.

Evidently epiphanies cause me to display facial expressions akin to one who is passing a kidney stone. The TF noticed (so did the gal sitting next to me, but I don't want to talk about that) and approached me after the talk. Here's how that conversation went:

"James," (he knew my name!) "you seem to have some issue with my design or with the product. I'd love to get your feedback."

"No, I have no problem with either your product or with your design. My problem is with *you*."

"Excuse me?"

"People like you scare me," I told him. "You spend all your time dreaming about features and enabling scenarios and designing interfaces and protocols. You are in a position of importance and people listen to you and build the stuff you dream about. And you do all this *without knowing squat about testing.*"

And this was the moment he sought to do the right thing…reach out to test. He invited me review the design [and] get involved. It's exactly what you'd expect him to do.

But it is exactly the wrong response.

Having a tester involved in design is better than not having test represented at all. But not much better. Testers will be looking for testability issues. Developers will be looking for implementation issues. Who will be looking at both? Who will be able to decide on the right trade-off? Neither. Getting testers involved in design is only incremental improvement; getting designers (and every other role) involved in test is the future.

Seriously, how is it that the people who build software understand so little about testing? And why have we not tried to fix this before? Are we, as testers, so vested in our current role that we are jealously guarding the keys to our intellectual kingdom? Is testing so arcane and obscure that developers can't find the answers they seek? Have developers grown so accustomed to handing off this "less interesting" aspect of the process to us that they now take it for granted?

Adding testers to the mix hasn't worked. Getting them involved earlier hasn't worked. We have products that have a 1:1 ratio of developers to testers and yet those products are not seen as highly reliable. We also have products that have far "worse" ratio that are clearly better products. I think in the future we will come to see that the separation of roles isn't working. The separation of roles might even guarantee that testing comes late to the dance and fails to fully leverage its intellectual potential on the product.

The current testing culture and separation of roles is broken and the way to fix it is by merging roles. Quality needs to be everyone's job. Think of it in Tolkiensian terms: *one role to rule them all!*

Imagine a world where testing knowledge is contained in each and every contributor's head. The architects know testing, the designers know testing, the developers know testing, and they apply that knowledge constantly and consistently in everything they do. This doesn't wipe out the separate testing role; there is something to be said for some amount of test independence; it enables better testing. If each decision made throughout product development asks the right testing questions, then the final system test can reach a level of thoroughness we can only dream about now. If everyone on the project understood testing, imagine what a few dedicated testers could accomplish!

Getting to this testing utopia is going to require a massive cultural change. Testing must reach into academia and the other places where programming is taught. As developers progress in their careers, this education must continue and become more advanced and powerful. We need to get to the point that all project stakeholders understand testing *and can't help but to apply its principles in everything they do.* Tools will one day support this as well. One day we will be to the point that untestable software just never gets written, not because some strong tester made it happen, but because everyone on the project made it happen.

Testing is too important to be the "bit at the end" of the process. It is early in the process where design decisions impact testing, and it is there that the solutions lay. It's also too important to leave it in the hands of a single role dedicated to quality assurance. Instead we need a fundamental cultural shift that makes quality everyone's job and embeds its principles in everything we do.

The Future of Testing (Part 7)

I blew this one. I should have called it "Testing as Design" because that is much more what I meant. The day-to-day activities of testing will move to a higher level with all the core assets such as test environments and reusable test cases available to pick and choose from. But here it is in its original and slightly flawed form.

Testers as Designers

Modern testers play largely a role of late cycle heroics that often goes unappreciated come review and bonus time. When we find the big bug it is because we were supposed to…that's the expectation. When we miss the big bug, people ask questions. It's often a case of ignored-if-you-do and damned-if-you-don't.

This is going to change and it is going to change soon because it must. My friend Roger Sherman (Microsoft's first companywide director of Test) describes this change as the testing caterpillar becoming a butterfly. According to Roger: Testing's butterfly is design.

I couldn't agree more. As testing and test techniques move earlier in the process, testers will do work more similar to software design than software verification. We will place more emphasis on designing quality strategy for all software artifacts and not just the binary. We will spend more time recognizing the need for testing rather than actually executing test cases. We will oversee and measure automation rather than building and debugging it. We will spend more time reviewing the status of pre-existing tests than building new ones. We will become designers and our work will be performed at a higher level of abstraction and earlier in the life cycle.

At Microsoft this role is often that of the test architect and I think most testing jobs are moving in this direction. If you've read the first six posts on this Future of Testing thread, then you'll appreciate the changes that are making this design centric role possible in the first place.

Now this sounds like a nice future but there is a decidedly black lining to this silver cloud. The blackness comes from the types of bugs and the types of testing we are currently good at in 2008. It is no great stretch to say that we are better at finding structural bugs (crashes, hangs, and bugs having to do with the software and its plumbing rather than its functionality) than we are at finding business logic bugs. But the future I've painted in this series has any number of technological solutions to structural bugs. That will leave the software tester to deal with business logic bugs, and that is a category of issues that I do not think our entire industry deals with in any organized or intentional fashion.

Finding business logic bugs means that we have to understand the business logic itself. Understanding business logic means far more interaction with customers and competitors; it means steeping ourselves in whatever industry our software operates; it means not only working earlier in the software life cycle but also involving ourselves with prototypes, requirements, usability, and so forth like we have never done before.

There's hard work early in the software life cycle that testers aren't experienced in doing. Performing well up front will mean facing these challenges and being willing to learn new ways of thinking about customers and thinking about quality.

Things are decidedly different at the front end of the assembly line, and it's a place more and more testers will find themselves as the future makes way for the present.

The Future of Testing (Part 8)

I got a call from our privacy folks after this one. Microsoft takes great pains to protect customer information and to behave in a manner that doesn't create identity-theft problems and the like. Still, I think that we need to migrate testing into the field through our software. It's self-testing and self-diagnostic software. Yes there are some privacy implications, but surely we can work through those.

Testing Beyond Release

This is the final part of my series on the future of testing. I hope you've enjoyed it. For this post I've saved what might be one of the more controversial of my predictions: Namely that in the future we will ship test code with our products and be able to exercise that code remotely. I can see the hackers' grins and hear the privacy advocates' indignation already, but I'll respond to those concerns in a minute.

I was in the Windows org when Vista shipped, and I recall demonstrating it to my then 8-year-old son at home one evening. He plays (and works if you'll believe that) on computers a great deal, and he really liked the Aero interface, the cool sidebar gadgets, and the speed at which his favorite games (which at that time were Line Rider and Zoo Tycoon) ran really impressed him. I recall thinking "too bad he's not an industry blogger," but I digress.

At the end of the demo, he hit me with the question every tester dreads: "Daddy, which part did you do?"

I stopped speaking, which is rare for me, and stammered something unintelligible. How do you tell an 8 year old that you worked for months (I had just started at Microsoft and only got in on Vista toward the end of its cycle) on something and didn't actually create any of it? I tried my canned answers to this dreaded question (exclamation points required...they help me convince myself that what I am saying has some truth to it):

"I worked on making it better!"

"The fact that it works as well as it does...well that's me!"

"If it weren't for us testers, this thing would be a menace to society!"

I am especially fond of that last one. However, all of them ring hollow. How is it that I can work on a product for so long and not be able to point to more than the *absence of some of the bugs* as my contribution?

I think that's where this idea came from: that test code should ship with the binary and it should survive release and continue doing its job without the testers being present. This isn't a lame attempt to give me and my compatriots something to point to for bragging rights, but to provide ongoing testing and diagnostics. Let's face it; we're not done testing when the product releases, so why should we stop?

We already do some of this. The Watson technology (the famous "send/don't send" error reporting for Windows apps) that ships in-process allows us to capture faults when they occur in the field. The next logical step is to be able to do something about them.

Watson captures a fault and snaps an image of relevant debug info. Then some poor sap at the other end of the pipe gets to wade through all that data and figure out a way to fix it via Windows update. This was revolutionary in 2004, still is actually. In 2–5 years it will be old school.

What if that poor sap could run additional tests and take advantage of the testing infrastructure that existed before the software was released? What if that poor sap could deploy a fix and run a regression suite in the actual environment in which the failure occurred? What if that poor sap could deploy a production fix and *tell the application to regress itself*?

He'd no longer be a poor sap, that's for sure.

To accomplish this it will be necessary for an application to remember its prior testing and carry along that memory wherever it goes. And that means that the *ability to test itself* will be a fundamental feature of software of the future. Our job will be to figure out how to take our testing magic and embed it into the application itself. Our reward will be the pleasure of seeing that sparkle in our kids' eyes when they see that the coolest feature of all is the one we designed!

Oh, and to the hackers and privacy folks: never fear! Hugh Thompson and I warned about including test code in shipping binaries (see Attack 10 in *How to Break Software Security*) long ago. Since we know how to break it, we'll be in a great position to get it right.

Speaking of Google

Why is it that every time I use Google in the title of one of my posts, traffic seems to spike? This post was only a dumb announcement but was read more than many others! But given that I am now a Google employee, perhaps it was a premonition.

Actually, it is more like speaking **at** Google as I am headed to GTAC tomorrow to give the newest version of my Future of Testing talk. Hope to see you there.

I've received tons of feedback on my blog posts about the future. So much so that I spent most of this weekend integrating (or stealing, I suppose you could say, depending on your perspective) your insights, corrections, and additions. Thanks to all of you who have discussed these things with me and shared your wisdom.

If you happen to miss GTAC, I'll be giving a similar but darker version at EuroSTAR entitled *The End of Testing As We Know It* in The Hague on November 11. Yes I was drinking and listening to REM when I made the presentation.

Both GTAC and EuroSTAR were big successes. I think my EuroSTAR talk benefited a great deal from the trial run and both sparked a lot of discussion. I made some fantastic contacts at Google to boot. Odd how so many of them used to work for Microsoft.

Manual Versus Automated Testing Again

I can't believe how much mail I got over the whole manual versus automation question, and it's fairly easy to see why. My Ph.D. dissertation was on model-based testing, and for years I taught and researched test automation. Now my obsession with manual testing is in full gear. It's not an either-or proposition, but I do believe that manual testing has an extreme advantage of having a human testers brain fully engaged during the entire process whereas automation foregoes that benefit the moment it starts to run.

In my Future series I was accused of supporting both sides of the manual versus automated debate and flip-flopping like an American politician who can't decide whether to kiss the babies or their moms. Clearly this is not an either-or proposition. But I wanted to supply some clarity in how I think about this.

This is a debate about when to choose one over the other and which scenarios one can expect manual testing to outperform automated testing and vice versa. I think the simplistic view is that automation is better at regression testing and API testing whereas manual testing is better for acceptance testing and GUI testing. I don't subscribe to this view at all and think it diverts us from the real issues.

I think the reality of the problem has nothing to do with APIs or GUIs, regression or functional. We have to start thinking about our code in terms of business logic code or infrastructure code. Because that is the same divide that separates manual and automated testing.

Business logic code is the code that produces the results that stakeholders/users buy the product for. It's the code that gets the job done. Infrastructure code is the code that makes the business logic work in its intended environment. Infrastructure code makes the business logic multi-user, secure, localized, and so forth. It's the platform goo that makes the business logic into a real application.

Obviously, both types of code need to be tested. Intuitively, manual testing should be better at testing business logic because the business logic rules are easier for a human to learn than they are to teach to a piece of automation. I think intuition is bang-on correct in this situation.

Manual testers excel at becoming domain experts, and they can store very complex business logic in the most powerful testing tool around: their brains. Because manual testing is slow, testers have the time to watch for and analyze subtle business logic errors. Low speed but also low drag.

Automation, on the other hand, excels at low-level details. Automation can detect crashes, hangs, incorrect return values, error codes, tripped exceptions, memory usage, and so forth. It's high speed but also high drag. Tuning automation to test business logic is very difficult and risky. In my humble opinion I think that Vista got bit by this exact issue: depending so much on automation where a few more good manual testers would have been worth their weight in gold.

So whether you have an API or a GUI, regress or testing fresh, the type of testing you choose depends on what type of bug you want to find. There may be special cases, but the majority of the time manual testing beats automated testing in finding business logic bugs, and automated testing beats manual testing in finding infrastructure bugs.

November 2008

This was the month I spoke at EuroSTAR. After my keynote, I was told that another speaker at the conference was quoting me: "James Whittaker sees no need for testers in the future." So, I felt compelled to set the record straight.

I gave a keynote at EuroSTAR on the future of software testing where I began by painting a picture of the **promise of software** as an indispensible tool that will play a critical role in solving some of humankind's most vexing problems. Software, I argued, provides the magic necessary to help scientists find solutions for climate change, alternative energy, and global economic stability. Without software how will medical researchers find cures for complex diseases and fulfill the promise of the human genome project? I made the point that software could very well be the tool that shifts the balance of these hard problems in our favor. But what, I asked by means of a litany of software failures, will **save us from software**?

Somehow as I painted my predictions of a future of software testing that promises a departure from late cycle heroics and low quality apps, some people got the impression that I predicted "no more testers." How one can latch onto a 20-second sound bite while tuning out the remainder of a 45-minute keynote is beyond me. The U.S. elections are over, taking sound bites out of context is no longer in season.

This blog is replete with my biases toward manual testing and my admiration for the manual tester. If you read it and if you managed to listen for more than a couple of minutes during my keynote, you'd have to conclude that I believe that the role of the tester is going to undergo fundamental change. I believe that testers will be more like test designers and that the traditional drudgery of low level details like test case implementation, execution, and validation will be a thing of the past. Testers will work at a higher level and be far more impactful on quality.

I quite imagine that the vast majority of testers who actually listened to my full message will rejoice at such a future. I invite the others to take a second read.

Software Tester Wanted

I cannot believe people actually questioned whether I was joking with this post. Clearly, this description of a tester want ad was a little too close to the mark. I was accused of disrespecting my employer and my discipline with this one. Frankly, I think both the post and the reaction to it are just plain funny.

Software tester wanted. Position requires comparing an insanely complicated, poorly documented product to a nonexistent or woefully incomplete specification. Help from original developers will be minimal and given grudgingly. Product will be used in environments that vary widely with multiple users, multiple platforms, multiple languages, and other such impossibilities yet unknown but just as important. We're not quite sure what it means, but security and privacy are paramount and post release failures are unacceptable and could cause us to go out of business.

Keeping Testers in Test

This is a sore point for a lot of testers at Microsoft: that many of the best testers move to development and program management. There is a perception that it increases promotion velocity, and it seems that perception is even stronger in other places.

I did a webinar for UTest.com today and got some great questions. One question seemed to really resonate: How do you keep good testers from moving to development.

I hear this question a lot. Many engineers see Test as a training ground for development. A testing job is just a foot in the door for a quick move to development. Sigh.

Let's be honest, this is not a bad thing. I think that the more developers we have trained as testers is categorically good. They'll write fewer bugs, communicate with test better and generally appreciate the work their test teams do on their behalf. I think the real sadness comes from the fact that Test as a discipline loses so many talented people.

I am not convinced that the folks who leave are really doing so because of the developers' greener pastures. After all, there is a lot of code to write as a tester and it's often a freer coding atmosphere. I think people leave because too many test managers are stuck in the past and living just to ship. Everywhere I see testers move to development I see teams that lack a real innovative spirit and the converse is most certainly true. The happiest, most content testers are in groups that covet innovators and provide opportunity to invent, investigate, and discover.

Want your testers to stay. Give them the opportunity to innovate. If all you see is test cases and ship schedules, all your testers will see is the door. Can't say I blame them either.

December 2008

I wasn't very busy in December blog-wise. So if you aren't going to write much, then use the titles that draw the readers: Google. Believe it or not, this one also made the front page of MSDN! Talk about a formula that works.

Google Versus Microsoft and the Dev:Test Ratio Debate

Every since I gave a talk at Google's GTAC event here in Seattle this past October, I've had the chance to interact with a number of Google testers comparing and contrasting our two companies' approach to testing. It's been a good exchange.

Now it seems that, Google focuses on testing with an intensity that is in the same general ballpark as ours. We both take the discipline and the people who do it seriously. But I think that there are some insights into the differences that are worth pondering.

Specifically, the disparity between our respective developer-to-tester ratios is worth a deeper look. At Microsoft the d:t ratio varies somewhat from near 1:1 in some groups to double or triple that in others. At Google just the opposite seems to be the case with a single tester responsible for a larger number of bug-writing devs. (Clearly we have that in common!)

So which is better? You tell me, but here are my thoughts (without admission of any guilt on Microsoft's part or accusations against Google):

1. 1:1 is good. It shows the importance we place on the test profession and frees developers to think about development tasks and getting the in-the-small programming right. It maximizes the number of people on a project actively thinking about quality. It speeds feature development because much of the last minute perfecting of a program can be done by testers. And it emphasizes tester independence, minimizing the bias that keeps developers from effectively testing their own code.
2. 1:1 is bad. It's an excuse for developers to drop all thoughts of quality because that is someone else's job. Devs can just build the mainline functionality and leave the error checking and boring parts to the testers.

It's interesting to note that Microsoft testers tend to be very savvy developers and are often just as capable of fixing bugs as they are of finding bugs. But when they do so, do devs really learn from their mistakes when they have someone else cleaning up after them? Are testers, when talented and plentiful, an excuse for devs to be lazy? That's the other side of this debate:

1 Many:1 is good. When testers are scarce, it forces developers to take a more active role in quality and increases the testability and initial quality of the code they write. We can have fewer testers because our need is less.

2. Many:1 is bad. It stretches testers too thin. Developers are creators by nature and you need a certain number of people to take the negative viewpoint or you're going to miss things. Testing is simply too complicated for such a small number of testers. Developers approach testing with the wrong, creationist attitude and are doomed to be ineffective.

So where's the sweet spot? Clearly there are application-specific influences in that big server apps require more specialized and numerous testers. But is there some general way to get the mix of testers, developers, unit testing, automated testing, and manual testing right? I think it is important that we start paying attention to how much work there really is in quality assurance and what roles are most impactful and where. Test managers should be trying to find that sweet spot.

January 2009

The year 2008 ended with a now-famous bug from our Zune product. It was the talk of the testing circles at Microsoft. We debated the bug, how it got there, and why it was missed. This post was my take.

The Zune Issue

As you can imagine there is a pretty lively debate going on over the Zune date math issue here in the hallways and on our internal mailing lists. There are plenty of places one can find analyses of the bug itself, like here, but I am more interested in the testing implications.

One take: This is a small bug, a simple comparator that was "greater than" but should have been "greater than or equal to." It is a classic off-by-one bug, easily found by code review and easily fixed then forgotten. Moreover, it wasn't a very important bug because its lifespan was only one day every leap year, and it only affected the oldest of our product line. In fact, it wasn't even our bug; it was in reused code. Testing for such proverbial needles is an endless proposition, blame it on the devs and ask them not to do it again. (Don't get your knickers in a twist, surely you can detect the sarcasm.)

Another take: This is a big bug, *in the startup script* for the device and thereby affected *every* user. Moreover, its effect is nothing short of bricking the device, even if only for a day (as it turns out, music is actually a big deal on that specific day). This is a pri-1, sev-1, run-down-the-halls-screaming-about-it kind of bug.

As a tester can I take any view but the latter? But the bug happened. Now we need to ask *what can we learn from this bug?*

Clearly, the code review that occurred on this particular snippet is suspect. Every code review I have ever been part of, a check on every single loop termination condition is a top priority, particularly on code that runs at startup. This is important because loop termination bugs are not easily found in testing. They require a "coming together" of inputs, state, and environment conditions that are not likely to be pulled out of a hat by a tester or cobbled together using unthinking automation.

This brings me to my first point. We testers don't do a good job of checking on the quality of code reviews and unit testing where this bug could have been more easily found. If I were still a professor I would give someone a Ph.D. for figuring out how to normalize code review results, unit test cases, and system test cases (manual and automated). If we could aggregate these results, we could actually focus system testing away from the parts of the system already covered by upstream "testing." Testers would, for once, be taking credit for work done by devs, as long as we can trust it.

The reason that system testing has so much trouble dealing with this bug is that the tester would have to recognize that the clock was an input (seems obvious to many, but I don't think it is a given), devise a way to modify the clock (manually or as part of their automation), and then create the conditions of the last day of a year that contained 366 days. I don't think that's a natural scenario to gravitate toward even if you are specifically testing date math. I can imagine a tester thinking about February 29, March 1, and the old and new daylight savings days in both Fall and Spring. But what would make you think to distinguish Dec 31, 2008 as any different from Dec 31, 2007? Y2K seems an obvious year to choose and so would 2017, 2035, 2999, and a bunch of others, but 2008?

This brings me to my second point. During the discussions about this bug on various internal forums, no less than a dozen people had ideas about testing for date related problems that no one else involved in the discussions had thought of. I was struck by a hallway debate between two colleagues who were discussing how they would have found the bug and what other test cases needed to be run for date math issues. Two wicked smart testers that clearly understood the problem date math posed but had almost orthogonal approaches to testing it!

The problem with arcane testing knowledge (security, y2k, localization all come to mind) is that we share our knowledge by discussing it and explaining to a tester *how to do something*. "You need to test leap year boundaries" is not an ineffective way of communicating. But it is exactly how we *are* communicating. What we should be doing is share our knowledge by passing test libraries back and forth. I wish the conversation had been: "You need to test leap year boundaries and here's my library of test cases that do it." Or "Counting days is a dangerous way to implement date math, when you find your devs using that technique, run these specific test cases to ensure they did it right."

The testing knowledge it took to completely cover the domain of this specific date math issue was larger than the set of folks discussing it. The discussion, while educational and stimulating, isn't particularly transportable to the test lab. Test cases (or models/abstractions thereof) *are* transportable, and they are a better way to encapsulate testing knowledge. If we communicated in terms of test cases, we could actually accumulate knowledge and spread it to all corners of the company (we have a lot of apps and devices that do date math) much faster than sitting around explaining the vagaries of counting time. Someone who didn't understand the algorithms to count time could still test it using the test assets of someone else who did understand it.

Test cases, reusable and reloadable, are the basis for accumulated knowledge in software testing. Testing knowledge is simply far too distributed across various experts' heads for any other sharing mechanism to work.

Exploratory Testing Explained

As I got closer to finishing this book, I ramped up my exploratory testing rhetoric and began looking for skeptics who would help me find flaws and improve it. One thing you can say about Microsoft is that we have our share of skeptics. This post came as a result of debating and learning from such skeptics. Even though it is pretty vanilla flavored, it has been a reader favorite.

I just finished talking (actually the conversation was more like a debate) to a colleague, exploratory testing critic, and a charter member of the plan-first-or-don't-bother-testing-at-all society.

I am happy to say, he conceded the usefulness (he would not grant superiority) of exploratory testing. Perhaps I have finally found a useful explanation of the efficacy of exploration. Here's what I said:

"Software testing is complicated by an overload of variation possibilities from inputs and code paths to state, stored data and the operational environment. Indeed, whether one chooses to address this variation in advance of any testing by writing test plans or by an exploratory approach that allows planning and testing to be interleaved, it is an impossible task. No matter how you ultimately do testing, it's simply too complex to do it completely.

However, exploratory techniques have the key advantage that they encourage a tester to plan as they test and to use information gathered during testing to affect the actual way testing is performed. This is a key advantage over plan-first methods. Imagine trying to predict the winner of the Super Bowl or Premier League before the season begins...this is difficult to do before you see how the teams are playing, how they are handling the competition, and whether key players can avoid injury. The information that comes in as the season unfolds holds the key to predicting the outcome with any amount of accuracy. The same is true of software testing and exploratory testing embraces this by attempting to plan, test, and replan in small ongoing increments guided by full knowledge of all past and current information about how the software is performing and the clues it yields in the testing results.

Testing is complex, but effective use of exploratory techniques can help tame that complexity and contribute to the production of high quality software."

Test Case Reuse

I got an email from Capers Jones on this one urging me to consider reuse of other artifacts like specs and design, and so on. I like getting email from famous people. But dude (may I call you dude, Mr. Jones?), I am a tester. Someone else needs to think about reuse in those spaces.

I've given my "future of testing" talk four times (!) this week and by far the part that generates the most questions is when I prophesize about test case reuse. Given that I answered it differently all four times (sigh), I want to use this space to clarify my own thinking and to add some specifics.

Here's the scenario: One tester writes a set of test cases and automates them so that she can run them over and over again. They are good test cases, so you decide to run them as well. However, when you do run them, you find they won't work on your machine. Your tester friend used automation APIs that you don't have installed on your computer and scripting libraries that you don't have either. The problem with porting test cases is that they are too specific to their environment.

In the future we will solve this problem with a concept I call environment-carrying tests (nod to Brent Jensen). Test cases of the future will be written in such a way that they will encapsulate their environment needs within the test case using virtualization. Test cases will be written within virtual capsules that embed all the necessary environmental dependencies so that the test case can run on whatever machine you need it to run on.

The scope of technological advances we need for this to happen are fairly modest. However, the Achilles heel of reuse has never been technological so much as economic. The real work required to reuse software artifacts has always been on the consumer of the reused artifact and not on its producer. What we need is an incentive for testers to write reusable test cases. So, what if we create a "Testipedia" that stored test cases and paid the contributing tester, or their organization, for contributions? What is a test case worth? A dollar? Ten dollars? More? Clearly they have value, and a database full of them would have enough value that a business could be created to host the database and resell test cases on an as-needed basis. The more worthy a test case, the higher its value and testers would be incentivized to contribute.

Reusable test cases will have enough intrinsic value that a market for test case converters would likely emerge so that entire libraries of tests could be provided as a service or licensed as a product.

But this is only part of the solution. Having test cases that can be run in any environment is helpful, but we still need test cases that apply to the application we want to test. As it turns out, I have an opinion on this and I'll blog about it next.

More About Test Case Reuse

We mostly write test cases that are specifically tied to a single application. This shouldn't come as any big surprise given that we've never expected test cases to have any value outside our immediate team. But if we want to complete the picture of reusable test cases that I painted in my last post, we need to write test cases that can be applied to any number of different apps.

Instead of writing a test case for an application, we could move down a level and write them for features instead. There are any number of web applications, for example, that implement a shopping cart, so test cases written for such a feature should be applicable to all such apps. The same can be said of many common features like connecting to a network, making SQL queries to a database, username and password authentication, and so forth. Feature-level test cases are far more reusable and transferable than application-specific test cases.

The more focused we make the scope of the test cases we write, the more general they become. Features are more focused than applications, functions and objects are more focused than features, controls and data types are more focused than functions, and so forth. At a low enough level, we have what I like to call "atomic" test cases. A *test atom* is a test case that exists at the lowest possible level of abstraction. Perhaps you'd write a set of test cases that simply submits alphanumeric input into a text box control.

It does one thing only and doesn't try to be anything more. You may then replicate this test atom and modify it for different purposes. For example, if the alphanumeric string in question is intended to be a username; then a new test atom that encoded the structure of valid usernames would be refined from an existing atom. Over time thousands (and hopefully orders of magnitude more) of such test atoms would be collected.

Test atoms can be combined into *test molecules*. Two alphanumeric string atoms might be combined into a test molecule that tests a username and password dialog box. I can see cases where many independent test authors would build such molecules and then over time the best such molecule would win out and yet the alternatives would still be available. With the proper incentives, test case authors would build any number of molecules that could then be leased or purchased for reuse by application vendors that implement similar functionality.

At some point, enough test atoms and molecules would exist that the need to write new, custom tests would be minimal. I think that Wikipedia, a site with user supplied, policed, and maintained content, would be what the industry would need to store all these tests. Perhaps such a community Testipedia can be constructed or companies can build their own internal Testipedias for sensitive applications. But a library of environment-carrying (see my last post) test atoms and molecules would have incredible value.

A valuable extension of this idea is to write atoms and molecules in such a way that they will understand whether they apply to an application. Imagine highlighting and then dragging a series of ten thousands tests onto an application and having the tests themselves figure out whether they apply to the application and then running themselves over and over within different environments and configurations.

Ah, but now I am just dreaming.

I'm Back

I got email from a number of former students (it's so nice that they continue to follow my work even now when I can no longer grade them) who remember my post-vacation intensity. Time to think is very important for those of us in a position to make work for other people with those thoughts!

When you're on vacation do you think about work? Not thoughts of dread, worry, or angst but reflection, planning, and problem solving. I just did. Last Sunday I awoke in Seattle to freezing temps and a dusting of snow. By midday I was building a sandcastle on Ka'anapali Beach, Maui, in 79 degree sunshine. If that's not getting away from it all, I don't know what is.

Yet my mind wasn't really away. In fact, I thought about work all the time. Given that software was everywhere I looked, it's not hard to see why. My entire trip was booked online, even the taxi to the airport. Not a single person besides myself took part in the process. Just me...and a load of software.

The taxi cab itself contained software, as did the airplane. The baggage carousel, the espresso machine, the car rental counter (no person there, just a self serve terminal), and even the surveillance camera that watched my son juggle his soccer ball while I packed our bags in the trunk. All alone, except for the software. Even the frozen concoction machine had software that helped it maintain the right temperature. (It broke, incidentally, making me thankful that I am a beer drinker.)

Is it possible for anyone in this field to really get away from it all? (Don't get me started on the motion sensors that control the air conditioning in the hotel room. I'm all for turning them off when they are not in use, but apparently sitting still and being cool was not one of their end-to-end scenarios.)

The truth of the matter is that getting away from it all just isn't necessary for me. I like seeing software in action and I enjoy brooding over problems of testing it. Vacations free my mind from the daily grind and leave my mind to question things that back home I might overlook. Does this make me work obsessed or just indicate that I really like what I do?

Vacations have always been like this for me. When I was a professor, two students who led my research lab, Ibrahim El-Far and Scott Chase, actually avoided me when I returned from a trip, afraid of the work my new insights would bring. They never quite managed to successfully do so.

Which brings me back to the motion sensor in my room. The problem isn't so much a poor tester, rather poor testing guidance. The sensor does exactly what it is designed to do and testing it based on those requirements got me in the sit-and-sweat loop. The problem is that no one thought to give it a field try…what I call "day in the life" testing. Had the tester thought to take the sensor through a 24-hour cycle of usage they would have identified that problematic ten-hour period (yes, ten, it's a vacation after all) when motion is low and the desire to be cool is high. But what tool gives such guidance? Modern tools help testers in many ways, but helping them think of good test scenarios isn't one of them. They help us organize, automate, regress, and so forth, but do they really help us to test?

That's the tool I want. Tomorrow, when I return, I am going to direct someone to build it for me. Ibrahim and Scott, you are off the hook this time.

Of Moles and Tainted Peanuts

There was a full page ad for Jif peanut butter in my morning paper that caught my attention. (For those non-U.S. readers, our nation is experiencing a salmonella bacteria outbreak that has been traced back to contaminated peanuts.) The ad touted Jif's rigorous testing processes and reassured readers that testing for salmonella was a long-time habit for the Jif company, and we should feel confident in consuming their products.

Now clearly peanut butter is not software. I very much doubt that the processes for making peanut butter have changed much over the past few decades. I also imagine that one batch of peanut butter is about the same as the last batch. I concede that we have a harder problem.

But the term "long-time habit" really caught me. Because I haven't seen too many long-term habits established in the testing industry. We plan tests, write test cases, find bugs, report bugs, use tools, run diagnostics, and then we get a new build and start the process all over again. But how much do we learn in the process? How much do we retain from one build to the next? Are we getting better each time we test? Are we getting better purposefully or are we just getting more experienced? In many ways, the only real repository of historical wisdom (those long-term habits of Jif) is embodied in our tools.

My friend Alan Page likens testing to playing whack-a-mole. You know the one: Chuck a quarter in and plastic moles pop up through a random sequence of holes and you whack them on the head with a mallet. Whack one, another appears, and even previously whacked moles can pop up again requiring additional mallet treatment. It's a never ending process, just add quarters.

Sounds familiar? Testing is whack-a-mole with developers applying the quarters liberally. Now, defect prevention notwithstanding, we can take a lesson from Jif. They understand that certain risks are endemic to their business, and they've designed standard procedures for mitigating those risks. They've learned how to detect salmonella, and they have wired those tests into their process.

Have we paid enough attention to our history that we can codify such routine test procedures and require their consistent application?

Clearly software is not peanut butter. Every piece of software is different; Office's salmonella is likely irrelevant to Windows and vice versa. But that is no excuse to play whack-a-mole with bugs. We have to get better. Perhaps we can't codify a salmonella testing procedure into a cookbook recipe, but we can start being more proactive with the whole business of learning from our mistakes.

I propose that testers take a break from finding bugs and just take some time to generalize. When the bug pops its head from some coded hole, resist the temptation to whack it. Instead, study it. How did you find it? What was it that made you investigate that particular part of the app? How did you notice the hole and what was happening in the app that caused the bug to pop out? Is the test case that found the bug generalizable to find more bugs similar to the one you are ready to whack? Is there some advice you could pass along to other testers that would help them identify such holes?

In other words, spend part of your time testing the current product you are trying to ship. Spend the rest of the time making sure you learn to test the next product better. There is a way to do this, a metaphor we use here at Microsoft to help.

I'll discuss the metaphor and how we apply it to form long-time habits, peanut butter style, in my next post.

And that's where I end this annotated posting and the exact place where this book begins. The metaphor I speak of is the tourist metaphor, which is presented in the pages of this book, primarily Chapter 4, "Exploratory Testing in the Large."

Index

A

B

C

D

F

G

H

I

J

K–L

M

N–O

P

Q–R

S

T

U

V

W–Z